Dystopias of Infamy

Campos Ibéricos:
BUCKNELL STUDIES IN IBERIAN LITERATURES AND CULTURES

Series Editors
Isabel Cuñado, Bucknell University
Jason McCloskey, Bucknell University

Campos Ibéricos is a series of monographs and edited volumes that focuses on
the literary and cultural traditions of Spain in all of its rich historical, social,
and linguistic diversity. The series provides a space for interdisciplinary and
theoretical scholarship exploring the intersections of literature, culture, the
arts, and media from medieval to contemporary Iberia. Studies on all authors,
texts, and cultural phenomena are welcome and works on understudied writers
and genres are specially sought.

Recent Titles in the Series
Dystopias of Infamy: Insult and Collective Identity in Early Modern Spain
Javier Irigoyen-García
Founders of the Future: The Science and Industry of Spanish Modernization
Óscar Iván Useche
Shipwreck in the Early Modern Hispanic World
Carrie L. Ruiz and Elena Rodríguez-Guridi, eds.
Calila: The Later Novels of Carmen Martín Gaite
Joan L. Brown
Indiscreet Fantasies: Iberian Queer Cinema
Andrés Lema-Hincapié and Conxita Domènech, eds.
Between Market and Myth: The Spanish Artist Novel in the Post-Transition, 1992–2014
Katie J. Vater

For more information about the series, please visit www.bucknelluniversity
press.org.

Dystopias of Infamy

Insult and Collective Identity in
Early Modern Spain

JAVIER IRIGOYEN-GARCÍA

LEWISBURG, PENNSYLVANIA

Library of Congress Cataloging-in-Publication Data

Names: Irigoyen-García, Javier, 1975– author.
Title: Dystopias of infamy : insult and collective identity in early modern
    Spain / Javier Irigoyen-García.
Description: Lewisburg, Pennsylvania : Bucknell University Press, [2022] |
    Series: Campos ibéricos: Bucknell studies in Iberian literatures and
    cultures | Includes bibliographical references and index.
Identifiers: LCCN 2021046261 | ISBN 9781684484003 (paperback ; alk. paper) |
    ISBN 9781684484010 (hardback ; alk. paper) | ISBN 9781684484027 (epub) |
    ISBN 9781684484034 (mobi) | ISBN 9781684484041 (pdf)
Subjects: LCSH: Spanish literature—Classical period, 1500–1700—History
    and criticism. | Invective in literature. | Group identity in literature. |
    Cervantes Saavedra, Miguel de, 1547–1616—Criticism and interpretation. |
    LCGFT: Literary criticism.
Classification: LCC PQ6066 .I75 2022 | DDC 860.9/003—dc23/eng/20220106
LC record available at https://lccn.loc.gov/2021046261

A British Cataloging-in-Publication record for this book is available from the British Library.

References to internet websites (URLs) were accurate at the time of writing. Neither the
author nor Bucknell University Press is responsible for URLs that may have expired or
changed since the manuscript was prepared.

♾ The paper used in this publication meets the requirements of the American National
Standard for Information Sciences—Permanence of Paper for Printed Library Materials,
ANSI Z39.48-1992.

www.bucknelluniversitypress.org

Distributed worldwide by Rutgers University Press

Manufactured in the United States of America

Al hombre que me cantaba el mundo al revés

Contents

Contents

Dystopias of Infamy

Introduction

"NAMES FULL OF VITUPERATIONS"

In Fernando de Rojas's *Tragicomedia de Calisto y Melibea* (c. 1502) when Pármeno criticizes the go-between Celestina by calling her "puta vieja alcoholada" (alcoholic old whore), his master Calisto scolds him for using such language to refer to the intermediary of his declarations of love for Melibea. Pármeno, however, defends himself by arguing that, in this specific context, the apparent insult is no such thing, because Celestina feels proud of being named in such terms:

> ¿Y tú piensas que es vituperio en las orejas désta el nombre que yo la llamé? No lo creas, que ansí se glorifica en lo oýr, como tú quando dizen: "Diestro cavallero es Calisto." Y demás desto es nombrada y por tal título conoscida. Si entre cient mugeres va y alguno dize "¡Puta vieja!," sin ningún empacho luego buelve la cabeça y responde con alegre cara.[1]

> [Do you think that the name that I just used for her is an insult in her ears? Don't think so, because she is glorified to hear it, in the same way that you feel glorified when people say, "Calisto is a good gentleman." She is named and known for such a title. If, among one hundred women, one shouts "Old Whore!" she turns unashamedly and answers with a good face.][2]

Pármeno goes on to describe in hyperbolic terms how even animals use such words to label Celestina; he ends up suggesting that inanimate objects do the same: "Qué quieres más, sino que, si una piedra topa con otra, luego suena 'Puta vieja'" [What else do you want, but to know that, if a stone hits another, it sounds "Old Whore"].[3]

By recontextualizing his insult and suggesting that Celestina herself identifies with the name "puta vieja," Pármeno reframes an initial act of verbal aggression as a carnivalesque and celebratory compliment. Yet, as Lourdes Albuixech points out, Celestina's alleged joyful assumption of this insult as imagined by

Pármeno does not conform to her personality within the fiction.[4] Celestina, despite her marginal place in society, is not alien to the system of honor and reputation of her own time, and she is extremely wary every time someone addresses an insult to her. Yet pointing out that Pármeno is crafting a manipulated, inaccurate portrait of Celestina is only the first step in trying to explain why he projects on her the image of an individual who identifies with her insult. Pármeno's rumination about Celestina's identification with the insult is not only a strategy to deflect his master's outrage for his use of such harsh language but also a manifestation of a recurrent cultural fantasy in early modern Spanish society. This fantasy has larger implications for the formation of collective identity, because it expresses the anxiety of how the role of infamy as a tool of social control is prone to failure. Such cultural fantasies about the fallibility of infamy are the subject of the present book.

Defining Insults

The insult "puta vieja" addressed to Celestina is only one of the many infamous categories that one could catalog in early modern Spanish society: cuckold, Moor, marrano, prostitute, sodomite, dog, sorcerer, blasphemer, slave, penitent, eggplant eater, Lutheran, thief, Galician, bigamous, villain, fag, shepherd, one-handed, go-between, heretic, to name only in a chaotic order some of the insults that will be mentioned throughout these pages. The list of such infamous categories in early modern Spain (in almost any culture, I should add) grows quickly as soon as one takes up the task of writing them down: compiling such a list reveals itself to be an endless project, which is rife with issues not only of exhaustivity but also of inclusivity and heterogeneity. Moreover, the fact that all these terms are usually found in the same category of insults does not mean that they work in the same way: any comprehensive study of insults is complicated by the fact that each one structures social meaning in very different ways. For instance, the social pairing of certain categories at the legal and discursive level is not necessarily the same in the early modern period and the present. A good example of the historicity of such categorization systems is the opposition between "cuckold" and "sodomite." Given that the term "sodomite" includes mostly what would today comprise the category "homosexuality" (although they are not at all equivalent), many readers would find comparisons between cuckolds and sodomites inappropriate in modern terms. It is inapt primarily because there is a general awareness of the long history of institutionalized persecution of homosexuality, whereas there is no popular memory of the legal persecution of cuckoldry—even though cuckoldry is still a prominent target of social scorn or at least a permissible subject for jokes. Yet in the early modern period the categories "cuckold" and "sodomite" were conceptually linked in ways that they are not in the present.[5]

Even though studies about homosexuality, as an isolated topic, in the early modern period are amply justified, most begin with a necessary methodological caution clarifying that the term "sodomite" comprises many other sexual and social practices that are not considered today under the homosexuality rubric.[6] This methodological caution is necessary not only to avoid projecting anachronistic categorizations but also because there is a fundamental difference in how each insult is supposed to relate to the formation of social identity. The historiographical debate centers on whether a homosexual identity existed in the past or whether the historical record only frames it as an individual sexual preference (one that was most usually persecuted), which did not define the social identity of that individual nor assigned this person to a specific collective identity.[7] This book barely touches on early modern homosexuality, not so much because it takes the side of those scholars who believe that there is no homosexual identity in the early modern period, but because homosexuality is not conceived of in the social imaginary as a form of collective identity—at least not in the corpus analyzed here.

In this sense, it is also illustrative to compare cuckolds with other stigmatized categories. Although cuckolds were not conceived to form any kind of community through the insults they received because they were interpellated as individuals and not as a collective (as analyzed in chapter 2), it was often thought, in contrast, that the insults that Old Christians threw against the descendants of Jews and Muslims actually reinforced their feeling of community (as analyzed in chapters 3 and 4). This means that, in the cultural imagination, not every insult is supposed to work in the same way: some are conceived of as addressing only individuals, whereas others are considered as being directed to individuals as representatives of their communities.

Although, we may agree, more or less, on what an insult is, insults are indeed a complex linguistic phenomenon subject to analysis from different disciplines, each with its own methodological cautions. From the point of view of pragmatic linguistics, it is necessary to distinguish between insults' referential level and performative use, which can be conative, when they address the target with an offensive intention, or merely expressive, when four-letter words are used merely to convey a mental state.[8] There is certainly a wealth of scholarship on legislation and legal trials regarding slander and insults, especially in the medieval period.[9] Yet, despite the laws against verbal abuse, insults were ubiquitous, being present in almost every sphere of social life in early modern Spain.

Literary studies have also dealt with insults in the early modern period but mostly from the perspective of production; they have analyzed the rhetorical and stylistic strategies of satire, a literary form that was especially rich in inventive games of words.[10] Satire was particularly rich in the works of certain authors and periods, such as medieval *cancionero* poetry, Celestina comedy, and eminently satirical writers such as Francisco de Quevedo.[11] Because of the complex ethnoreligious landscape of the Iberian Peninsula at the beginning of the early modern period, one field that has received special attention is the stereotyped slurs against ethnoreligious minorities, be they Moriscos, *conversos* of Jewish origin, Gypsies, or Blacks. The obsession with blood purity produced numerous libels against nobles, accusing them of mixing with conversos, and clichéd jokes about lineages comprise the entire social spectrum.[12]

Although we usually understand insult as a verbal aggression, there are also nonlexical forms of injury. Methods and marks of infamy are multiple and evolve through time. During the Middle Age, sumptuary laws required Jews and Muslims to make their religious identity visible in their clothing, while also preventing commoners from using adornments and luxury textiles that were considered a sign of status.[13] Whether they were implemented or not, sumptuary laws promoted the logic of making social difference visible. The increase in the number of conversos to Christianity between the fifteenth and sixteenth centuries triggered the creation of several blood purity statutes that transformed and bureaucratized the logic of marking ethnoreligious groups, mandating the recording of blood lineages. The most visible, nonlexical mark of infamy—the most extreme form of "wearable insult," as one of my anonymous readers put it–was undoubtedly the *sambenito*, the garment that the Inquisition forced those punished in the *auto de fe* to wear (as chapter 4 analyzes in detail). To these forms of institutionalized infamy we should add myriad offensive ceremonies and rituals of exclusion at the local level, such as the festivals that celebrated the Christian conquest and ridiculed former Muslim inhabitants or that defamed conversos in the community.[14] Other prominent markers of infamy were the "relaciones de excomulgados" (lists of the excommunicated), which displayed in local churches the names of those individuals whose behavior was considered inappropriate within their own community.[15] Thus insults and marks of infamy lurked everywhere as an omnipresent form of policing society, yet their very ubiquity produced a recurring anxiety about their effectiveness.

INSULTS, SUBJECTIVATION, AND CULTURAL IMAGINATION

Despite my insistence on the ubiquity of infamy, this book does not intend to inscribe early modern Spain within a paradigm of an alleged Mediterranean identity characterized by honor and shame. Honor has been traditionally privileged as an inherent Mediterranean feature by several influential anthropological studies.[16] Yet this paradigm has been questioned as reductionist and essentialist, because the importance of honor as a social structuring principle is common to other societies in early modern Europe.[17] The study of honor in early modern Spain has been a privileged locus for critical debates, especially in literary studies.[18] These debates tend to make a distinction between the Spanish terms "honor" and "honra," the former one meaning the interior sense of honor, whereas the second term considers social reputation. Yet, as Marta Madero points out, the divide between subjective honor and social reputation is hardly tenable, because it is impossible to conceive of a sense of honor that is not dependent on an external gaze.[19] The poststructuralist emphasis on the performative, social nature of identity has collapsed this traditional distinction between an interior and exterior form of honor. Furthermore, many scholars have shown that the apparent omnipresence of honor in political and literary discourses does not entirely match actual legal practice and social reality.[20]

The most common view is that, both at the individual and the collective levels, the social need to refute insult and infamy is assimilated by their recipients as models of identity. Even if the importance of honor (either as a social discourse or as a social practice) is hardly deniable, historians have written mostly about responding with violence to any attack to personal honor, as if there existed no other kind of responses to insults—thus disregarding as marginal the existence of individuals who may just ignore or even appropriate insults as a source of identity. Such a focus is largely conditioned by the available sources, because violent or juridical responses to insults are probably the only reactions that left traces in the archives. In addition, the insistence on portraying a society obsessed with honor in the early modern period somehow establishes a continuity with past discourses of honor and idealizes our own perception of how social identity works, by assuming that rejecting insults is the only acceptable option to cement social existence then and now.

The traditional perspective is that insults are repressive instances of discrimination and social control that seek to impose a social impact that is harmful to the insulted person or community.[21] When broaching the possible productive value of insult for the community that sets it in motion, scholarship tends to emphasize at best how bonds of solidarity are reinforced through opposition to a designated scapegoat.[22] Certainly, insults are a powerful tool to cement a feeling of community and redesign the parameters of belonging by disparagingly excluding some of their members. Yet the power of insults is not limited to the destruction or humiliation of the intended target nor to community formation: it is also a twofold rhetorical tool that generates a specter in the imaginary. This book analyzes precisely that residual life of insults in the collective imaginary, the intuition that their effectiveness is uncertain, and the fantasies about how, once in circulation, insults can affect the relationship between the perpetrator and the target, redesigning the boundaries of the community to which they both believe they belong.

A different trend in scholarship, without denying the repressive nature of insults, has shifted focus to look at how they could have a productive value regarding subjective formation for their targets. Louis Althusser proposes that ideology reproduces itself by turning individuals into subjects through interpellation and hailing.[23] In *The Psychic Life of Power*, Judith Butler redeploys

Althusser's concept to show that insults are the most visible form of interpellation and that, even if individuals are not able to evade interpellation's power to
constitute themselves as subjects, the effects of such subjectivation are always
unpredictable and prone to failure.[24] One of those possible failures is that the
subject can create a "stubborn attachment" with the injurious name, no longer
perceiving it as an insult but rather as an affirmation of identity.[25] The injurious
name, while seeking to degrade the subject, contains a potentially narcissistic
element that the subject can appropriate as constitutive of itself, thus granting
its social existence. As Butler states,

> Called by an injurious name, I come into social being, and because I have a
> certain inevitable attachment to my existence, because a certain narcissism
> takes hold of any term that confers existence, I am led to embrace the terms
> that injure me because they constitute me socially. . . . As a further paradox,
> then, only by occupying—being occupied by—that injurious term can I resist
> and oppose it, recasting the power that constitutes me as the power I oppose.[26]

The possibility of appropriating insults as a way to build a collective identity has
been widely recognized in the field of LGBTQ studies, which has analyzed how
originally derogatory terms such as "queer" or "gay" have been appropriated by
the communities targeted by such words.[27] These theoretical approaches mostly
refer to actual insults circulating in society, but we must take into account that
the "psychic life" of insults goes beyond their actual utterance. Because insults
help anchor the subject in a social space, they are still functional even when they
are merely predicted or imagined.[28]

Although Butler's concept of stubborn attachment is this book's main theoretical frame, these pages barely consider the perspective of the recipient of
insults in social reality. Analyzing how real individuals and collectives assumed,
contested, or appropriated insults in early modern Spain would certainly constitute a fascinating project, and indeed this book hints at a few such cases. Yet,
studying this phenomenon in this period in a comprehensive way is plagued by
a series of methodological issues. The passage from *Celestina* that opens this
introduction perfectly illustrates the methodological reasons for not taking the
perspective of the subject as this book's primary focus. The first objection is, quite
obviously, that *Celestina* is a literary text and not the real testimony of a person
tainted by the injurious name. Even if we put aside literary texts and similar documents, it would be hard to identify appropriate sources. Useful as inquisitorial
trials can be to trace testimonies of defamed people who assumed injurious
terms, they most usually convey voices mediated through the filters of inquisitors and notaries or even through the expectations that accused people may have
about what they needed to confess. The study of civil suits would be equally misleading for this purpose, because by their very nature, they overwhelmingly
show the normative response to an insult when they litigate against it—naturally,

nobody who bore insults with resignation or even pride would litigate against those affronts. The passage of *Celestina* is also revealing about the methodological problems of studying the perspective of the recipient with the extant documents available to us: although Pármeno pretends to express the perspective of the subject, what his comment actually conveys is how hegemonic society imagines that certain subjects may respond to insults. And this is true of most of the texts and documents analyzed in this book.

What can be analyzed in these documents is their imaginary reflection of the group generating the insult as it projects a fantasy on the hypothetical response from the insulted subject. Although literary, inquisitorial, and moralist texts barely allow for the study of how collective identity could be articulated around the injurious word, they bear witness to how their authors imagined the effect that insults and other infamous signs could have, what kind of individual subjectivation or collective identification they could entice, and what kinds of communities (utopian or apocalyptic) could be potentially articulated around insults. Therefore, when I adopt the theoretical frame developed by scholars such as Butler and Eribon, I do not apply it to study actual resilient subjectivation in early modern Spain but rather to illustrate how the theoretical issues they raise were already glimpsed by the early modern authors analyzed here when considering the function of infamy in their own society. In the same way that Butler's and Eribon's conceptualizations of infamy are interventions in ideological debates at the time of their writing, the authors studied here use their own conceptualizations of infamy to articulate a determined political agenda, sometimes more and sometimes less explicitly. Thus, by focusing on the perspective of the perpetrator, it is possible to perceive a persistent anxiety about the proper proportion of infamy to use as a tool of social control. Such anxiety about how an excessive application of discrediting language can be counterproductive to its own goal of social control generates a residual fantasy about the target identifying with the insult. The premise underlying the documents analyzed in this book is that there is a turning point in which certain forms of infamy stop being discriminatory and become the reverse of what they were intended to be: previous categories of exclusion are turned into an instance of collective identification.

The passage from *Celestina* is also illustrative in its uniqueness. Pármeno's male fantasy about Celestina, illustrated by addressing the insult "puta vieja" at her, is an exceptional case in my corpus, because it is the only instance analyzed here in which a female character is imagined as appropriating the insult targeted at her.[29] In all the other cases analyzed in this book, the cultural imagination is about male characters appropriating insults either as individuals or as a collective; I was not able to find similar instances of communities of women doing so. One possible interpretation for that disparity is that, because stubborn subjective formations such as these assume a certain degree of agency and even defiance, it was unthinkable for early modern Spanish society to imagine women appropriating infamous categories and, even more importantly, to imagine a moment in which such appropriation at the collective level could lead to any kind of potential change in women's social condition—all of which is precisely because more active, forceful expressions of will are characteristics usually denied to women. There is certainly a wealth of works, written by both men and women, in which strong female characters take a leading role[30]; however, when they do so, they are always imagined as identifying with conventional codes of honor and reputation, never as embracing infamous categories.[31] The other possible interpretation for the lack of female characters who appropriate insults in my book is that it failed to find such evidence. There are certainly gaps in my corpus, both in the one analyzed here and in the larger corpus that was part of this research project but was not included here. The hypothetical imagination about women threatening to subvert the social order by embracing insult may exist, and I may have simply been unable to find it. I would hope this book serves to inspire other scholars to fill that gap and correct the interpretation that women were not thought of to identify with insults in the early modern Spanish imaginary, which my book implicitly seems to support, much to my own chagrin.

Most studies analyzing the perspective of the individual or collective target of injurious words focus on their psychological or ideological effects, whereas those works analyzing production focus on the formal rhetorical aspect, be it literary or linguistic. What is generally overlooked in the studies about insults is the effect that they may have on the perpetrator. I must emphasize that my book is not intended as a justification of verbal aggression, despite my continuing attempts to explore the perspective of the perpetrator. Playing the devil's advocate is a necessary intellectual exercise to shed some light on the logic of certain cultural practices and the formative value of insult (for both the perpetrator and the real or imagined recipient), on the bonds that affronters establish both with their target and with the society in which the insult is uttered, and on the fantasies that the perpetrating society generates about the efficacy of insults and marks of infamy. Such fantasies indirectly acknowledge that insults not only have a prominent role in articulating collective identity but also potentially shape social change by expanding the limits of thinkable alternate communities.

INSULTS AND DYSTOPIA

The imagination of alternate communities in the early modern period has been studied mostly from the perspective of utopia and millenarianism.[32] Important as these utopian movements were, the focus of this book is on dystopian imaginings when they are related to the social dynamics of insult. I therefore rely on more recent approaches to how early modern subjects "thought about, planned for, and manipulated futures full of uncertainty and risk," as Matthew O'Hara frames it in his study of future-making in Colonial Mexico.[33] The fantasies of alternative social formations around insults, at least the ones selected for this book, can hardly be conceived of as desirable restructurings of the social order; rather they are scenarios of chaos and apocalyptic imagination. The possible futures analyzed here are mostly potential nightmares to be avoided, not opportunities to promote social change—yet the prospective avoidance of dystopian horizons is most often conceived of as a rhetorical strategy to propose changes in certain dynamics of social exclusion.

I follow here M. Keith Booker's definition of dystopia as "a critique of existing social conditions or political systems, either through the critical examination of the utopian premises upon which those conditions and systems are based or through the imaginative extension of those conditions into different contexts that more clearly reveal their flaws and contradictions."[34] I am aware that dystopia is a term usually applied to the analysis of science fiction and that some readers may find it an anachronistic category when applied to early modern texts. Certainly, the term "dystopia" was unknown to the authors analyzed here—but they were also unaware of the opposite term "utopia," which, despite the success of Thomas More's 1516 *Utopia*, had not yet created its own genre. A more important objection is that there was not a discursive genre (literary or otherwise) that could be recognized as dystopic. What I analyze in this book is far from an established genre with formal conventions; instead, it provides glimpses of dystopian situations in which theorization about infamy as a tool of social control leads to the imagination of a reversed social order in a looming, uncertain future. Properly speaking, what the texts analyzed here offer is a range of dystopian horizons, rather than fully developed imaginary worlds. Yet for the purposes of this book, dystopia seems the convenient term, because most of the literary fantasies of alternative social order analyzed here are based on the transposition of infamy into the future, as these authors predict the turning point in which the acceleration in repression may lead to the phantasmatic imposition of the repressed object as the hegemonic locus of collective identity.

As I claimed earlier, insults anchor subjects in a social space; yet they also anchor them in a timeline, plotting this kind of speech act in a temporal frame of plausible causes and probable expectations. We can illustrate this with a negative example in which such a recognizable time frame is conspicuously absent. At the end of chapter 68 of the second part of *Don Quixote*, the errant knight and his squire are kidnapped by some men on horseback who throw at them a strange tirade of insults:

—¡Caminad, trogloditas!
—¡Callad, bárbaros!
—¡Pagad, antropófagos!
—¡No os quejéis, scitas . . . , Polifemos matadores, leones carniceros! (II:68, 1101)

["Get a move on, you troglodytes!"

"Keep quiet, you barbarians!"

'We'll make you pay, you cannibals!'

"Don't complain, you Goths . . . , you murderous Polyphemuses, you blood-
thirsty lions!"] (Trans. Rutherford 948)[35]

Don Quixote, naturally surprised, wonders, "Qué serían aquellos nombres llenos
de vituperios que les ponían" (II:68, 1102) [What might be the meaning of all
those insults being directed at them] (Trans. Rutherford 948). Don Quixote's surprise is not due to his ignorance of the meaning of these learned words, which
he undoubtedly knows from his readings, but from the context in which they
are uttered. Even if Don Quixote is familiar with the referential meaning of terms
such as "troglodytes," "anthropophagus," "Scythians," and "Polyphemuses,"
what is unusual is the pragmatic denotative value attributed to them by their kid-
nappers. As Joaquín García-Medall points out, these learned words have a
comic effect because they lack the routinization of most common terms used as
insults.[36]

Rutherford's translation of this passage, although appropriate for his intended
readership, does not entirely convey the strange phraseology used by the narrator when referring to those insults as "nombres llenos de vituperios," which could
be translated literally as "names full of vituperations." The way the narrator
phrases it, focusing on Don Quixote's perspective, sounds as if insults were not
names in themselves but ghostly signifiers haunting meaning, ready to inhabit
any name. That is, he refers to insults as if they were outside the lexical order
and as if they existed as sheer, performative interpellation with no real content.
Although Don Quixote and Sancho know they are being insulted, they cannot
relate this strange form of slandering to any particular frame of reference,
because they are obviously not troglodytes, nor anthropophagus (cannibals),
nor "scitas" (an old people usually found in classical sources), nor Polyphemuses
(cyclops). Thus, the narrator is semantically correct when he says that Don Quixote hears "names full of vituperations"; yet they are not vituperations properly
speaking, because those terms are devoid of any recognizable social reference
and do not appeal to any particular trait that one can either assume or reject.
Insults that happen in a social void are recognized as the absolute state of interpellation, because they are perceived as naked insults, without any references
still attached to their particular manifestations. Both Sancho and Don Quixote
(as well as the reader) do not know the motivation for their being kidnapped and
insulted. Therefore, they cannot place these insults in a timeline, which emphasizes their disorientation.

In contrast to this literary example, any conception of insult assumes a sto-
ryline in which there is past (the motivation for the insult, real or imagined), a
present of the speech act, and some sort of reaction. It is in this potential reac-

tion where the concept of dystopia comes into play. That potential reaction—the goal that the speaker intends to achieve and the fear that the target can be missed and therefore the insult turns into something different than intended—is the basis for the fantasies analyzed in this book: it represents a ghostly potential future in which insulters fear triggering the very reaction they seek to avoid with their speech act.

CERVANTINE FANTASIES ABOUT INSULTS

The quoted passage in the second part of *Don Quixote* is just one of the many instances in Cervantes's work in which we can find an exploration of how insults work. Many of these instances have been analyzed in isolation as episodic passages; yet, when woven together within the proposed theoretical frame, they allow a glimpse of a fragmentary yet recurrent exploration of the complex mechanics of insults that reflects larger intellectual debates about the capacity of infamy to inform collective identity. Anthony Close minutely contextualizes Cervantes within the evolution of humor and satire at the turn of the sixteenth to the seventeenth century, positing that his theory of humor is based on a rejection of the satirical and injurious tradition.[37] In general, it is probably true that Cervantes's particular trait, which makes his works more palatable to modern tastes, is his relatively compassionate approach to the target of humor— at least when compared to eminent satirists such as Quevedo. I would add, as I argue throughout this book, that what makes Cervantes modern is not only some sort of moderation toward humor (which would make him a rather mild, insubstantial writer) but also his sophisticated literary reflection (conscious or otherwise) that thoroughly dissects and exposes the complex and sometimes paradoxical mechanisms of infamy and subjectivation, as well as their place in the cultural imaginary. To structure the content of this book in a meaningful way, each chapter wraps (in some cases more loosely than others) around Miguel de Cervantes's works. The book begins with the exploration of individual subjectivation vis-à-vis insults and then moves to a more general understanding of collective identity formations.

Chapter 1 deals with how the act of insulting reinscribes the affronter in a specific social place. Early modern moralist formulations of slandering frame it as an act that damages the reputation of both the target and the producer, sometimes linking it to blasphemy. Yet actual social practice shows that producing insults not only does not undermine affronters' social standing but also helps anchor them in their community. This chapter also analyzes early modern lexicography to reveal the existence of competing views of what categories should be stigmatized in society: some authors put the emphasis on ethnoreligious genealogy, whereas others stress class difference as the central generator of the insulting landscape.

Chapter 2 deals with narratives of self-deprecation and of individuals appropriating infamous categories, the most well-known being the anonymous *Lazarillo de Tormes*, the tale of a consenting cuckold who simultaneously negates
and asserts his infamous social status as a form of social existence. As I argue,
the figure of the cuckold becomes a successful literary trope because it allows
an exploration of the potential failure of subjectivation while avoiding the risk
of invoking alternative collective formations.

Chapter 3 moves from the individual to the collective to analyze how an ill-
conceived management of infamy as a tool for social control can trigger dystopias of social change. The first part tackles how proposals to reform the statutes
of blood purity, most notably Agustín Salucio's work of 1599, imagine that stig-
matizing too many people can paradoxically produce an inverted social structure in which repressed categories can become the model for society. The second
part of this chapter studies how such dystopias of social change are portrayed
in Cervantes's short play *El retablo de las maravillas* (1616), in which two tricksters make the inhabitants of a Castilian town believe that they are all
descendants of Jews. The open ending of the play suggests that the unchecked
exploitation of social fear about blood purity may lead to the embrace of the
repressed identity.

Chapter 4 deals with political and literary fantasies about the circulation and
potential appropriation of the sambenito as a form of social distinction. It is a
garment worn by those who were punished by the Inquisition in the autos de fe;
afterward it was hung on the walls of local churches to maintain the memory of
the families tainted by heretical ancestors. Focusing again on one episode of Cervantes's *Don Quixote*, this chapter broaches intellectual debates about the effectiveness of marks of infamy in early modern Spain, which crystallize in the
cultural fantasy that the sambenito may end up losing its punitive value. Tales
of individuals bragging about their sambenitos circulated abundantly, especially
regarding the Moriscos, who became the object of increased inquisitorial persecution by the end of the sixteenth century. Regardless of whether these stories
reflected actual Morisco identification with the sambenito or whether they were
a form of Islamophobic propaganda, they were used to discuss reforms of
the policies of social exclusion and to create fantasies of alternative political
communities.

Chapter 5 is articulated around another episode from Cervantes's *Don Quixote*, in which two towns compete in braying, a seemingly irrelevant anecdote that
is developed to the extreme of absurdity to expose the essential role that some
insults may have in structuring collective identity, even when they have been
theoretically stigmatized by the very same society that sets them in motion. This
analysis proposes therefore the possibility of a hybrid model of subject formation, based on the simultaneous rejection and appropriation of the insult. The
epilogue moves to the present to suggest that the model of hybrid subjection for-

mation analyzed in chapter 5 can be found in recent instrumentalizations of
the past, as coined in the historiographical concept of the black legend of Spain,
which has often been deployed to create a defensive form of national identity.

Dystopias of Infamy relies on archival materials and religious and political
texts to provide a comprehensive study of how early modern theorizations
acknowledged the value of insults to articulate collective identity and regulate
policies of exclusion. This project did not begin as a study of Cervantes and is
not intended primarily as such. Despite my lack of reverence for this author, I
soon found that organizing each chapter around a close analysis of some selected
works from this well-known writer would help structure the book in a meaningful way. The reason to select Cervantes's oeuvre as a thread for this project is
because it is full of parodies of the regulatory fantasies about infamy that circulated in early modern society. Precisely because he was not the primary object
of study when I started this project, I must acknowledge that Cervantes, although
not the only author to do so, is probably the one who most persistently exposes
cultural anxieties about the limits of infamy as a social practice and hints at how
repressive laws carry with them the seeds of both individual and collective resistance to the process of subjectivation.

CHAPTER 1

Communities of Affronters

Confieso que conozco que no es deshonra llamar hijo de puta a nadie cuando cae debajo del entendimiento de alabarle.

[I confess that I recognize that it isn't dishonourable for somebody to be called a bastard, when it comes under the heading of meaning to praise him.] (Trans. Rutherford 568)

—Miguel de Cervantes, Don Quijote (II:13, 672)

At some point during the second part of Cervantes's *Don Quixote*, published in 1615, the two protagonists discover not only that their earlier adventures are already circulating in print but also that there is a spurious account of their continuing story. *El ingenioso hidalgo don Quijote de la Mancha* (1614), published under the name of Alonso Fernández de Avellaneda quite probably while Cervantes was still writing his own second part, is usually designated by literary scholarship as the apocryphal *Don Quixote*, a description that emphasizes its derivative nature. Such an accusation of literary appropriation, along with Cervantes's suggestion in his own second part of *Don Quixote* that Fernández de Avellaneda was not the real name of the author, has conditioned most scholars not to analyze the text in itself but mostly as supporting evidence to establish their proposals of authorship identification.[1]

What interests me here is that, when thinking that Fernández de Avellaneda has been unfair by depicting him as a vulgar rustic, Cervantes' Sancho claims that he is a good Catholic and "enemigo mortal, como lo soy, de los judíos" (II:8, 633) [mortal enemy, as I am, of all Jews] (Trans. Rutherford 534). Juan Diego Vila points out that, although insults and mockeries of all sorts are abundant in *Don Quixote*, slurs about Jews and *conversos* are conspicuously absent; he also suggests that Sancho's anti-Semitic statement must be contextualized within a period in which the only way to constitute oneself as a legitimate subject was by occupying the place of the producer of insults and that failure to adopt such a position would entail assuming by inertia the position of the object of scorn.[2] We can combine both observations, which Vila makes separately throughout his

article, to state that what is revealing is that Sancho identifies himself as a slanderer of Jews, but that such identification is a mere enunciation that does not
materialize in the text, because we never hear any anti-Semitic comments from
him. Therefore, Sancho identifies with an injurious anti-Semitic tradition that
he does not practice: If we can put it this way, he defines himself as a nonpracticing slanderer of Jews.

The issue of how Sancho positions himself in relation to insults becomes more
complex when we consider the larger context of the interrelationship between
Cervantes's *Don Quixote* and Fernández de Avellaneda's continuation, in which
Sancho is portrayed as a blatant anti-Semite. Even though Cervantes's Sancho
does not say it explicitly, his anti-Semitic comment in *Don Quixote* may well be
a response to Fernández de Avellaneda's characterization of Sancho; in a rather
serendipitous way, he is emphasizing how the construction of a character is centered around the issue that delivering insults may grant a certain social status.

Cervantes's stylistic superiority over Fernández de Avellaneda has influenced
the interpretation of their respective ideological positions, generating a series of
premises that have been imposed on the latter's text without a careful reading.
This biased approach toward the works by Cervantes and Fernández de Avellaneda is especially revealing when analyzing their references to Jews (which are
conspicuously absent in Cervantes, as Vila notes) and the expulsion of the Moriscos (1609–1614), to which both explicitly refer. Whereas most scholarship tends
to perceive a relatively tolerant vision in Cervantes and to emphasize his complex representation of the Moriscos,[3] the few scholars who have analyzed the
representation of ethnoreligious difference in Fernández de Avellaneda's text
consider it a defender of the expulsion because of the blatant xenophobic language used by their main characters.[4]

Although it is always problematic to identify the author's opinion with that
of his characters, it is especially so in the case of Fernández de Avellaneda,
because it is obvious that he does not try to establish any kind of empathy with
the protagonists of his book, on whom he projects everything that he intends to
ridicule in early modern Spanish society. The belligerent discourse against the
infidel, which is latent in Cervantes's *Don Quixote*, is exacerbated grotesquely
in Fernández de Avellaneda's version, which often intermingles it with Sancho's
openly xenophobic expressions. For instance, in a hamlet near Sigüenza, one of
the authorities compares Don Quixote's appearance to the figure of Jews in a
tableau in the local church, to which he reacts by invoking the crusaders' spirit
as found in Castilian and Carolingian epic cycles; later, when they arrive in
Sigüenza, he identifies with Ferdinand II of Aragon to declare the death of the
Muslims in the ballads: "¡Muera Muza, Zegrí, Gomel, Almoradí, Abencerraje,
Tarfe, Abenamar, Zaide, y la demás gente galguna, mejor para cazar liebres que
para andar en las lides!" [Death to Muza, Zegri, Gomel, Almoradi, Abencerraje,
Tarfe, Abenamar, Zaide, better at hunting rabbits than battling!].[5] In some cases,

Islamophobia is entangled with anti-Semitism, as when Sancho exclaims, "¡Oh, reniego de los zancajos de la mujer de Job!" [Oh, curses on the heel bones of Job's wife!], an idiosyncratic idiom in which execration against Jews mixes with the allusion to the "zancajo de Mahoma" (Muhammad's heel), as the prophet's relics were often disparagingly known in Spanish texts.[6] This proliferation of xenophobic expressions in Fernández de Avellaneda's text is one of the features that have repelled the admirers of Cervantes's *Don Quixote*. Yet, the fact that all these xenophobic comments are expressed exclusively by ridiculed versions of Don Quixote and Sancho reveals that Fernández de Avellaneda used them as straw men to discredit the ethnocentric discourses underlying the apologies for the expulsion of the Moriscos.[7]

What then is Cervantes's Sancho really contesting about his characterization in Fernández de Avellaneda's continuation? By asserting that he must be respected because he hates Jews, Sancho paradoxically identifies with Fernández de Avellaneda's anti-Semitic character to some extent, even while he claims to refute it. Thus, Cervantes's Sancho both eats his cake and has it too: he wants to be recognized as an Old Christian because he could potentially insult Jews, but because such an insult never materializes in his speech, he is set apart from Fernández de Avellaneda's Sancho. The position of the nonpracticing insulter holds because it is sufficient to state that one is part of a slanderer community. Sancho's social ambition could explain his ambiguous insulting behavior; his racist candor makes explicit the underlying social logic of cementing one's reputation by scorning a third person. Agustín Salucio, in his *Discurso sobre los estatutos de limpieza de sangre* (1599), writing precisely about blood purity and Spanish racial discourse, criticizes the belief that one could generate honor by slandering other people: "Los pobres escuderos de corto entendimiento, viendo que apenas tienen otro caudal, sino la afrenta agena, essos son los que atizan estas differencias" [The wretched squires of short understanding, seeing that they have no other wealth than someone's else affront, they are the ones who incite these differences].[8] Thus, according to Salucio, ritual insulting of Jews and conversos might be a way to perform an Old Christian identity for the lower echelons in society, but the use of such crude xenophobic language would not be considered appropriate for those of a certain social status. Hence Sancho's ambivalence toward slandering, which allows him to assert his belonging to two disparate social categories at once, because being Old Christian (which requires the slander of Jews to identify and be identified as such) and belonging to nobility (which requires a certain linguistic restraint) do not necessarily overlap.

Thus, the contrast between the characterizations of Sancho in the two continuations of *Don Quixote* reflects the cultural dynamics about the limits of humor and how slandering defines social identity. The interrelationship of class and ethnoreligious criteria reveals the heterogeneous and always changing nature of slanderer communities, as well as the existence of larger debates about what should be the central insult that articulates society, with competing narratives about the exact composition of the injurious landscape of early modern Spain.

THE COMMUNITY OF THE AFFRONTER

Although *Don Quixote* seems to lack the ethnocentric slurs that abound in other early modern texts, Cervantes's body of work contains one of the crudest insults against other ethnic minorities of his day. In the novella *La gitanilla*, the first piece included in his *Novelas ejemplares* (1613), the narrator begins with a long tirade against Gypsies before introducing the main character, a Gypsy girl who at the end turns out to be an Old Christian:

> Parece que los gitanos y gitanas solamente nacieron en el mundo para ser ladrones: nacen de padres ladrones, críanse con ladrones, estudian para ladrones, y, finalmente, salen con ser ladrones corrientes y molientes a todo ruedo, y la gana de hurtar y el hurtar son en ellos como accidentes insepara-bles, que no se quitan sino con la muerte.

> [It would seem that Gypsies, both male and female, were born into this world to be thieves: they are born to thieving parents, are raised among thieves, study to become thieves, and finally end up becoming full-fledged thieves, through and through; for the urge to steal, and stealing itself, are, as it were, ingrained tendencies in them that never go away until they die.][9]

Scholars have long debated whether this statement is a straightforward repro-duction of common stereotypes about Gypsies in early modern Spain or whether it is intended as an ironic representation of that stereotype.[10] There are several elements in this passage supporting the ironic interpretation. For instance, the opening expression "parece que" ("it seems that") casts doubt on the stereotype of Gypsies it apparently reproduces—and such an interpretation is emphasized by Michael Harney, who translates it as "it would seem that." Which interpre-tation is meant is not easy to determine, because the plot of the novella, although it offers glimpses of noble traits of Gypsies and romanticizes their wandering life, also largely reproduces the stereotype about them being thieves.

What interests me here is not determining whether Cervantes was pro- or anti-Gypsy (or his narrator for that matter) but rather to point out that this pas-sage exemplifies the uncertainty about how to anchor one's voice in its social milieu through insult. This tirade is prominently placed at the very beginning not only of the novella but of the entire collection of "exemplary" novellas, which begs the question of how the narrator is trying to situate himself within the dis-cursive practices of his own community. Is the narrator looking for his readers' empathy because he insults Gypsies, thus inserting himself into a community that defines itself in opposition to this people? Or, quite the contrary, does he make fun of precisely those racial slurs by coining a tirade in which the term "thief" is repeated over and over like an obsessive litany? In the latter interpretation, the narrator would thus annul the injurious term not by explicitly contesting it but rather by eroding its semantic force through overkill. Although reconstructing intentionality is a slippery task, what remains in this passage, regardless of how we decide to read it, is that it overkills its target. Even if we conclude that the narrator indeed intends to insult Gypsies, then he turns out to be a clumsy insulter who can only achieve his goal by hammering the same slur over and over. Therefore, if the narrator intends to distance himself from the community of insulters, he does so by mimicking the slur, but if he intends to join the community of insulters, he would be probably recognized as a newbie, unable to craft a witty insult other than by ceaseless iteration.

Even when the most basic form of insulting is seen as a communication between just two people, the speaker and the receiver, it actually entails the existence of a larger community beyond the object of scorn. As Didier Eribon points out, "One of the consequences of insult is to shape the relation one has to others."[11] Although Eribon focuses on the targets of the insult, his statement is also true for how producers of the insult shape their relationship with community through this act. As Marta Madero notes, "La injuria revela un intercambio. Es un mensaje destinado inevitablemente a un tercero" [Insulting reveals an exchange. It is a message inevitably addressed to a third person].[12] Thus, the real question is how insulters insert themselves within the community with their speech act. In the case of Cervantes's La gitanilla, is insulting a way to create sympathy with readers sharing the same values? Or is it supposed to be a mechanism of narrative distance by setting readers against a biased narrator? Some cases are easier to discern than others, but whatever our interpretation, when confronting insults, we immediately generate ideas about what kinds of bonds the addresser is trying to make within the community.

Injury and Morality

Moralists and lawmakers condemned and persecuted slandering for a variety of reasons, mostly because it threatened to subvert the social order.[13] As moralists often claim, insulting entails the social death of the perpetrator and thus is a risky speech act: the abuse of injurious terms can easily boomerang against the speaker. For instance, Jerónimo de Urrea cites Aristotle in his Diálogo de la verdadera honra militar (1566) in asserting, "Malamente injuria, el que injuria, porque siempre injuria sin razon, y por tal queda, como dize Aristotiles, injuriado" [The one who insults always insults with no reason, and as such he himself becomes insulted, as Aristotle says].[14] Similarly, Luis de Torres claims in his Veintiquatro discursos sobre los peccados de la lengua (1590) that the slanderer "como la abeja muere picando y haziendo poco mal, assi mueren los tales injuriando a sus proximos; y assi es necessario compadecernos dellos" [like bees, they die when they bite, doing little harm, and thus they die when they injure those close to them; and thus we need to pity them].[15] All these comments suggest that slanderers, through the act of insulting others, do not put themselves beyond the system of infamy but rather reinsert themselves into the category of the defamed. In categorizing verbal offenses, what sets slanderers apart is that they constitute a meta-vituperation category. Moralists do not chastise slanderers because others exclude them (as is mostly the case for the other categories analyzed here); rather, slanderers exclude themselves from the community because of the form of insult they perform. Yet this is quite probably a rhetorical move with no actual social basis. As Marta Madero points out, the moralists' theoretical definition of injury as an act of social self-destruction does not correspond to actual social practice.[16] What the gap between the moralists' definition of insult and its actual societal impact shows are instead the anxieties and desires about how infamy should be wisely administered.

Probably one of the reasons why conspicuous slanderers are seen as destroying themselves is that insult as a tool of social control is more effective in its potentiality and somehow annuls itself in its iteration. The emotional charge of insults lies in their potential and imagined materialization, because what happens when an individual is indeed insulted (which happens relatively rarely) is different from what occurs when people imagine that they can be insulted in specific situations (which is the most dynamic life of insults). The power of insults resides in their "psychic life" (to freely paraphrase Judith Butler), rather than in their materialization. Occasionally, actual insulters serve as reminders of the potentiality of social exclusion, but by the same token, their proliferation may actually undermine the original efficacy implicit in the threat of social exclusion.

Throughout the early modern period there is an abundant production of moralist and juridical material about insults, which is very often centered on gossiping and reputation.[17] By the end of the fifteenth century, Hernando de Talavera published his *Breve y muy provechosa doctrina de lo que debe saber todo Christiano* (1494), which includes both the *Tractado muy provechoso contra el común e muy continuo pecado que es detraher o murmurar y decir mal de alguno en su absencia*[18] dealing with gossip and several sections in the *Confessional* addressing aspects of verbal aggression such as swearing and gossipping.[19] Similarly, Martín de Azpilcueta publishes in 1544 a *Commento sobre el capitulo Interverba XI q. III* (Coimbra 1544), which he later revises and publishes as *Tratado de alabanza y murmuración* (Valladolid, 1572). As Michèle Estela-Guillemont points out, the first version was written to support his application for a position at the University of Coimbra, whereas the later 1572 version seems to be an intervention in the trial against the former archbishop of Toledo, Bartolomé Carranza.[20] This work focuses on defamation, which Azpilcueta broaches both from the juridical and confessional angles. However, in most of the cases that he discusses, he refers to individual reputation; this material is intermingled with anecdotes, most of which are references to his own personal circumstances and the slander that he suffered while competing for his position at the University of Coimbra. Azpilcueta distinguishes between gossip ("murmuración") and harsh language ("contumelia"), depending on whether the affront takes place in the absence or the presence of the target.[21] Thus, as Claude Chauchadis points out, Azpilcueta classifies injurious words not only by their content but also on where they are pronounced: whether in front of the insulted person or in his absence.[22] Because the main focus of his treatise is on gossip, Azpilcueta barely refers to insults uttered in front of the target; he does so only when he defends the need to correct inferiors, such as children and slaves.[23]

In other instances, in their debates about duels, authors write about insults, trying to sort out when and how it is appropriate to be offended and to seek revenge. This is, for instance, the subject of Jerónimo Sánchez de Carranza's *Cinco libros sobre la ley de injuria de palabra o de obra*, written toward the end of the sixteenth century.[24] Sánchez de Carranza's main goal is to delimit in which cases offenses should be solved through secular justice, arguing that no one should take justice into his own hands to seek revenge for affronts and dispelling the societal myth that retracting a defamatory statement is itself a form of infamy—especially for nobles, who were never supposed to retract or apologize for offenses against others.[25]

Yet the aspects of verbal offense on which most moralists focused are swearing and blasphemy, which are often considered related phenomena, such as in Domingo de Soto's *Institución de cómo se ha de evitar el abuso de los juramentos* (1551), Bartolomé Carranza de Miranda's *Comentarios sobre el catechismo christiano* (1559),[26] Tomás de Trujillo's *Libro llamado reprobación de trajes, y abuso de juramentos* (1563), Felipe de Meneses's *Tratado de juramentos* (1569), Diego de Ojea's treatise on swearing, printed as an appendix to his *Breve instrucción de la devoción, cofradía e indulgencias y milagros del Rosario* (1589), Luis de Torres's *Veintiquatro discursos sobre los peccados de la lengua* (1590), and Nicolás de Ávila's *Suma de mandamientos* (1596). Most of these works were composed following the foundation of the Confraternity of the Name of God around 1550, which was created precisely to eradicate swear words.[27]

The significance of blasphemy in early modern Europe has been the object of heated historiographical polemics. The two poles of this debate are exemplified by Johan Huizinga, who asserts that blasphemy presumes the utterer to be a believer, even if a peculiar one, and Jean Delumeau, who contends that blasphemy is a transgression of social and religious norms.[28] Although this larger debate is beyond the scope of the present study, this book hews closer to Delumeau's position in considering not so much the theological aspect of blasphemy but the specific social milieu in which it takes place.[29]

What is relevant to our discussion is that the category of blasphemy includes not only direct insults to God and other religious figures but also many other sacrilegious statements that are not necessarily insults in the proper sense. More importantly, blasphemous insults do not generate the ghost of a community that identifies with the insult. Religious authorities certainly pondered hypothetical divine responses to blasphemy, which could range from bearing it with patience to punishing either the utterer or even the entire community that allowed the blasphemy to take place—but imagining God and other religious figures as identifying with the insults targeted at them seems like an inconceivable theological premise, and therefore their theorizations did not follow the path I do. Yet it is important to discuss blasphemers here because their existence is used to cement Catholic identity: publicized blasphemies could serve to galvanize the Christian community in response, in what were known as "fiestas de desagravio" (reparation festivals)—chapter 5 considers how they play a role in societal formation in response to blasphemy.

When moralists posit that the Christian community should be constructed in opposition to blasphemy, to the insult uttered against God, they indirectly recognize the existence of a parallel and widespread social code of defiance that is articulated around blasphemy. Thus Domingo de Soto complains that "el jurar es a unos hombres como ornamento de su lenguaje, con el que piensan que añaden gravedad y severidad a su razón" [swearing is for some men like the ornament of their language, with which they add gravity and severity to their reasoning].[30] Nicolás de Ávila follows Soto, reproducing his words verbatim but adding the observation that blasphemous swearing is an initiation to manhood and homosociability: "los moçuelos, para dar a entender que ya son hombres, refieren la primera licion, que tomaron de sus desventurados padres" [the youngsters, to send the message that they are men, repeat the first lesson that they learned from their unfortunate fathers].[31] As many moralists point out, blasphemous swearing occurs very often in the context of gambling; for instance, as Francisco de Luque Fajardo states in his *Fiel desengaño contra la ociosidad y los juegos* (1603), "El que mas sofisterías dice y hace en la materia, entre ellos es tenido por más discreto. . . . Su más jurar es mayor valentía, haciendo bramona de las blasfemias; sus bordoncillos son juramentos y votos contra el cielo" [He who says more sophistries is held among them as the most well-spoken. . . . His superior swearing demonstrates his greater bravery, interspersing their discourse with blasphemies; their adornments are filthy words and curses against heaven].[32] Such a parallel code of blasphemy is not identified with practitioners of Judaism or Islam, who would be naturally conceived as the expected offenders, but with Old Christians who use it to create bonds through a particular form of social distinction.[33]

Thus, blasphemy serves a social purpose: it binds together those who defend a militant view of Christian identity when they respond to explicit offenses against religious symbols and those who (without necessarily being non-Christian) insert themselves into a subculture of defiance. Although the body of early modern juridical and moralist literature on injury certainly illustrates societal concerns about how to polish insults and reputation, it tends to adopt a normative approach that sheds little light on the theoretical issues explored in this book. Given the spread of infamy, the debate about the role of insults in informing cultural identity can be traced to other kinds of documents, such as lexicographical works.

INSULTING LANDSCAPES

To what extent are insults a window onto early modern Spanish society? As Javier Salazar Rincón points out, "El repertorio de bromas ofensivas y alusiones injuriosas preferido por una comunidad nos descubre las líneas maestras de su estructura social y de su mentalidad colectiva" [The repertoire of offensive jokes and injurious allusions preferred by a community reveals to us the master lines of its social structure and its collective mentality].[34] Although I largely agree with Salazar Rincón, we should not analyze such repertoires as if they were homogeneous. Within the same period and society, different observers may construct diverging injurious landscapes that reveal both different conceptions of how insults are supposed to structure society and competing agendas for mapping the location of honor and injury, as this section argues.[35]

The treatment of infamous terms in early modern encyclopedic and lexicographical works is especially useful in illustrating this diversity, because when analyzed and compared to each other, they offer a variety of perspectives about the place of insult in the linguistic system of early modern Spanish, most notably in the works by Diego de Guadix, Francisco del Rosal, and Sebastián de Covarrubias. Of these three lexicographical projects, the one that undoubtedly has had the greatest impact is that of Covarrubias. Unlike his immediate predecessors, Covarrubias did manage to publish his *Tesoro de la lengua castellana o española* (1611) [Treasure of the Castilian or Spanish Language], which presents a closed and coherent corpus. His dictionary has thus become one of the foundations of Spanish lexicography: it served as the model for the *Diccionario de Autoridades* composed by the Real Academia Española in the eighteenth century and has become an indispensable tool for historians and literary scholars trying to reconstruct the meaning of early modern Spanish. For the sake of clarity, I analyze each of the encyclopedic and lexicographical works by Guadix, del Rosal, and Covarrubias in chronological order, although some back and forth is needed to point out the similarities and differences between them regarding their treatment of insults.

The Franciscan Diego de Guadix was a prominent Arabist in the sixteenth century. Because of his knowledge of Arabic, he was appointed as translator of the Inquisition of Granada in 1587 and was summoned to Rome in 1590, where he obtained a license to print his work in 1593; however, it was never published and circulated only in manuscript form until its recent publication.[36] The title *Recopilación de algunos nombres arábigos que los árabes pusieron a algunas ciudades* is misleading, because this lexicographical work goes beyond place names to serve as an encyclopedia about Arabic influence in Spanish culture.[37] Guadix, in spite of his condemnation of Islam, divorces religion from language, as stated explicitly in his goal: "para que ... salga del error que algunas personas tienen ... pensando que siempre anduuieron a vna la maldita seta de Mahoma y la lengua arábiga" [so that ... some people do not make the mistake ... of thinking that the damned sect of Muhammad and the Arabic language were always the same thing].[38] Although he claims that he learned Arabic as a child, quite likely among the Moriscos, his knowledge of formal Arabic is rudimentary, and his etymologies are based on capricious phonetic similarities rather than on exhaustive philological work.[39] Yet he offers useful information about the meaning of certain words in early modern Spanish and hints at a conception of the system of insults that is quite different from the one we often attribute to early modern Spanish society.

The special feature of Guadix's project is that he empties his definitions of their racial and ethnoreligious terminology that was common in early modern Spain. That operation becomes clear regarding the overcharged term "raza." Guadix's discussion of this term is quite succinct, merely stating that "llaman en España a la casta o linage" [in Spain they name the caste or lineage], and he offers its alleged Arabic etymology: "Es *raç*, que, en arábigo, significa cabeça, i., caput; assí que dezir a uno que es de buena o mala raça significa y es dezirle qu'es de buena o mala cabeça, i., de buena o mala cepa" [It is *raç*, which in Arabic means head, i.e., caput; thus to say to someone that he is of good or bad race means that that person is of good or bad head, i.e., from good or bad lineage] (*Recopilación*, 911). Guadix keeps silent about the fact that "raza" was most commonly used as a negative term to mark the descendants of Jews and Muslims; that is, Old Christians were those who had no "raza."[40] His insistence on applying the term to lineage ("cepa") and on making the term taxonomic rather than purely derogatory, seems to imply that it is used only to designate class difference. Rather than providing a definition of the term that reflects its most common use, Guadix seems to be offering a description of what the term should mean according to his own ideological position.

Similarly, in his entry "marrano," Guadix provides in the first place the meaning of "pig." Although this is certainly the proper referential meaning, "marrano" was used most commonly as a term of disparagement for Christian converts of Jewish origin. Guadix acknowledges that connotation but only in a very oblique way when he writes,"Marrano también llaman en Italia a el mal christiano que guarda mal la ley de Dios y preceptos de la Sancta Madre Iglessia"

[In Italy they call *marrano* the bad Christian who does not properly keep the law of God and the doctrine of the Holy Church] (*Recopilación*, 780). Guadix's definition performs a twofold operation: on the one hand, it sanitizes the potential insulting connotation of the term by attributing it to Italy and omitting that it was also commonly used in Spain[41]; on the other hand, he ignores the term's limitation to conversos of Jewish origin and applies it to the innocuous "mal christiano" [bad Christian]. The way he frames it, "marrano" would also include any Old Christian who does not follow the Catholic doctrine strictly, a significant reading that reveals his intention to convey a particular version of the injurious landscape of his own time.

The relative absence of "racial" insulting terms in Guadix's work does not mean that he is the defender of an egalitarian society. Quite the contrary, he emphasizes class difference throughout his work, placing commoners as the object of social exclusion. In contrast to the semantic cleansing of racial terms such as "marrano" and "raza," Guadix emphasizes the injurious value of words referring to peasants and rural people. For instance, he defines "zahareño" as a

> hombre áspero, esquivo e intratable. Viene y es deducido d'esta palabra, *çahara*, que, en arábigo, significa peño o peñón, y de aquí deduzen y componen, a la castellana, este adgetiuo *çahareño*, que significará peñasquino, i., hombre nacido y criado en peña o en peñasco, vale y significa tanto como este nombre, *serrano* o *montesino*.

> [rude, unsociable, and intractable man. It comes from this word *çahara*, which in Arabic means crag, and from hence the Castilian adjective *çahareño*, which means "craggy," that is, a man born and raised among boulders, meaning the same as mountain-dweller and wild.] (*Recopilación*, 467–468)

This meaning of "montañés" (wild, from the mountain) as an insult is also found in the entry "çafio": "Llaman en España a un villano para motejarle de muy villano. Es *çafi*, que, en arábigo, significa puro, i., no misturado con otra cosa; assí que dezir de un hombre qu'es villano çafio significará villano puro, i., sin alguna parte o mistura de hidalgo" [Thus, they call peasants in Spain to insult them as rustic. It is *çafi*, which in Arabic means pure (i.e., not mixed with any other thing): thus, saying of a man that he is a rustic *çafio* means pure rustic, with no part or mixture of noble] (*Recopilación*, 466). Once again, Guadix takes an oblique approach in defining this word. In principle, and against the expectations of a reader versed in the early modern Spanish social system, he attributes to "zafio" a connotation of purity. Yet his idiosyncratic concept of "purity" is a significant inversion of the connotation of purity of blood in his own time. Instead of referring to purity as the absence of "mixture from Jews and Moors," as it was commonly understood in his day, Guadix conceives of "purity" as the absence of social mixture, by which he probably means the lack of social upward mobility: he points out that the peasant is that individual "sin alguna parte o mistura de hidalgo," thus displacing the emphasis of genealogical purity from the ethnoreligious to the social discourse.

Despite the fragmentary nature of Guadix's encyclopedic project, we can glimpse his attempt to rewrite the system of ethnoreligious exclusion by erasing or minimizing the injurious connotations of several terms usually regarded as insults against Jews and Muslims or even by deflecting them as insults scorning Old-Christian ethnocentrism. The effect of both simultaneously emptying the most common ethnoreligious slurs while emphasizing insults against commoners is to displace the logic of exclusion from the confrontation with the descendants of Jews and Muslims to the criteria of social distinction.

Somewhat similar to Guadix's work is the serendipitous lexicographical project by Francisco del Rosal (1537?–1611?). In 1601 del Rosal was granted the license to publish a work titled *Origen y etimología de la lengua castellana* [Origin and Etymology of the Castilian Language], but it was never printed—quite probably because of the author's health issues in his final years and of the publication of competing similar works, such as Bernardo Aldrete's *Del origen y principio de la lengua castellana* (1606) and Sebastián de Covarrubias's *Tesoro de la lengua castellana, o española* (1611), which might have decreased the potential market value of del Rosal's work.[42]

The entry that is most useful for our understanding del Rosal's lexicographical mapping of insults in his own society is the one for "judío" [Jew]:

> Esta palabra Judio dice el Vulgo en Castilla por denuesto a los descendientes de Judios, como el Aragones llama Moros a los que de Moros descienden; ambos usan de rigor, y mas propriedad guarda el Andaluz, que al descendiente de Judio llama Confeso, y al que deciende de Moros Morisco. . . . Y en esta materia es cosa dura, que apenas nos hemos servido de una ropa un año, y ya es vieja; y apenas ha cumplido un hombre quarenta años, y le llaman y aun es viejo; y esta pobre o rica gente no acaba de envejecer aunque tengan diez abuelos Christianos, ni el tiempo hace en ellos el estrago que en las demas cosas.

> [The commoners in Castile use this term "Jew" as an insult for the descendants of Jews, in the same way that the Aragonese call "Moors" those who descend from Muslims; both use some sort of rigor, and the Andalusian is more accurate when he calls the descendants of Jews "confeso," and those who descend of Muslims, "Morisco." . . . And this is a difficult topic, because we have barely used one garment for one year, and it is already old; and we already call old a man who has barely reached forty (and he is); and these people, whether poor or rich, never become "old," even if they have ten Christian granparents, and time does not affect them as it does with the rest of things.] (*Diccionario*, 402)

Despite his appeal to terminological precision, del Rosal betrays a certain chauvinism in claiming that Andalusians (like himself) are being more accurate when they equate the terms "converso" (which properly speaking refers to the descendants of Jews who converted from Judaism to Christianity) with "confeso" (which refers to those who were tried by the Inquisition and therefore "confessed" their sins in a public ceremony).[43] Although this conflation is not correct, there is some truth to it, because the only reliable sources of tracing Jewish ancestors were the trials of the Inquisition—meaning that the descendants of Jews who were never persecuted by the Inquisition quite probably had no problem passing as Old Christians after a few generations. Yet, even when del Rosal acknowledges that the term "Judío" is used as an insult, it is hard to find such use in his own discourse. Instead of the usual deprecation against Jews, what we find is a roundabout comment about how the term "old" is used as an insult when referring to someone's age. If he acknowledges at first that the adjective "old" is applied to any man who surpasses forty years, when he refers to Moriscos and conversos he points out, quite to the contrary, that the insult consists in treating them as if time had no effect on them, as they were called "cristianos nuevos" (New Christians) even several generations after their ancestors' conversion.[44] In his oblique phrasing, del Rosal seems to suggest that the injurious connotation of a term depends not on its lexical meaning but on its context of production, reminding the reader that "old" is usually used as a derogatory term and pointing to the linguistic exceptionality of the expression "Old Christians," the only context in which "old" has a positive connotation.

In his entry for "marrano," del Rosal begins by reproducing the opinion of one of his sources, according to which "es vocablo Arábigo, con que el Moro llama al Judío" [it is an Arabic word, with which the Muslims name Jews]. He then points out that its current meaning is different: "Marrano es nuevo o reciente, y así será como recién convertido" [Marrano means new or recent, and therefore would mean newly converted] (*Diccionario*, 402). Thus del Rosal follows the same strategies as Guadix regarding this term: (1) deflecting it to people outside Spain (in this instance, attributing it to Muslims), as if it were an alien word in Castilian, and (2) offering a vague definition of converting from one religion to another that does not entirely convey the specific meaning that it actually had in early modern Spanish society.

In his definition of "raça," del Rosal begins by reproducing Nebrija's etymological hypothesis: "falta en el paño, es Ráritas, y así la llamaron Raléa que era rareza de pelo, y después pasó a significar la falta de linage, que así también decimos hablando del linage: en el mejor paño cae la mancha. Después pasó a significar el linage y descendencia indiferentemente" [a defect in the cloth; it is *raritas* (scarcity), and hence they said *ralea* (bloodline), that was thinness or scarcity of fur, and later it came to mean the lack of lineage. In this way we say, speaking about lineages: in the best cloth there is a defect/stain. And later it came to mean lineage or ascendancy with no distinction] (*Diccionario*, 528–529).

Thus, like Guadix, del Rosal emphasizes the taxonomical connotation of the term "raza," and when he alludes to its derogatory connotation, he applies it to a vague understanding of "lineage," which could refer to either ethnoreligious ancestry or class difference. There are other entries, such as "linage" and "mancha," in which we would also expect to find a mention of the doctrine of blood purity, but it is conspicuously absent.[45] In other terms related to the *auto de fe*, del Rosal tellingly emphasizes their etymology but refrains from defining their meaning; for example, "coroza," the cone-shaped hat worn by those condemned by the Inquisition, and "sambenito," which he succinctly defines as "el hábito del penitenciado" [the garment of the penitent] (*Diccionario*, 207, 555). There are certainly some entries that reflect ethnoreligious slurs, such as "alárabes" (Arabic), which he defines as "gente rústica y servil" (55) (rustic and menial people), and "gitanos" (Gypsies), which he characterizes as vagrants (351), as well as several terms referring to racial mixture such as "burdegano" and "çaíno."[46] But these cases are a minority (at least when we compare the proportion of ethnoreligious slurs in his lexicographical work with that in Covarrubias, as I analyze later).

Like Diego de Guadix, Francisco del Rosal's brevity when defining the terms referring to blood purity contrasts with the special emphasis he places on the insults referring to class difference, most notably against plebeians. For instance, in the entry "Behetría," del Rosal establishes a clear opposition between commoners and *hidalgos*, to the benefit of the latter:

> Cosa de escándalo y alboroto ... procede de la antigüedad, que en Castilla hai unos lugares ... que tienen el privilegio de las Behetrías, que es no admitir Hidalgos, o que todos contribuyan en un cuerpo y voz sin distinción.... Y así dize bien el Andaluz, quando muchos hablan y no escuchan a algún hombre honrado, que dice quejándose ser aquella Behetría, donde los bien nacidos no tienen voto ni mandan. Mejor me parece que decimos Behetría a la confusión y vozes, como si dixésemos trato y plática de gente Bauna y Villana, como en bodegón ... contrarios de los equestres o Hidalgos, cuya conversación es concertada y modesta, sin vozes ni alborotos.[47]

> [It is a thing of scandal and racket.... It comes from the past, since in Castile there are some places ... that hold the privilege of *behetrías*, which consists in not admitting *hidalgos*, or that everybody can contribute as one body and one voice with no distinction.... And hence the Andalusian rightly complains, when too many speak at once and none listen to an honorable man, that that is *behetría*, in which those of noble birth have no vote nor rule. Even better, I think, is that we call *behetría* confusion and voices, referring to the

behavior and speech of vile and rustic people when in a tavern . . . which are
the opposite of knights or *hidalgos*, whose conversation is well-thought and
modest, with no shouting or racket.]

In many other entries, he repeats his insults against rustics.[48] Thus, as does Guadix, del Rosal draws a map of injury in which class difference is the central
motivation for insults, and in comparison, blood purity is but a secondary criterion of social exclusion.

Sebastián de Covarrubias y Horozco's *Tesoro de la lengua castellana o española* (1611) makes the most familiar intervention in the injurious repertoire, at
least to any reader who is relatively well versed in early modern Spain.[49] Covarrubias's lexicographical project vividly differs from the vision crafted by his
immediate predecessors, from whom he diverges substantially when dealing
with insults. The comparative approach helps demonstrate how each of these
works represents a particular ideological intervention and highlights that
Covarrubias's project is only one among many, even though we tend to grant
his a degree of representativeness of the early modern period that may be over-
stated or that should at least be contextualized.

In Covarrubias's *Tesoro*, certain injurious terms have a prominent place, in
some cases taking up most of the lexicographical entry. This is especially the case
with insults referring to conversos of Jewish origin. The entry for "confesso"
shows the shift from merely reflecting the common meaning of this term as a
synonym of converso—"El que deciende de padres judíos o conversos" [He who
descends from Jewish or converted parents]—to surreptitiously introducing what
is a personal opinion about their religious sincerity: "digamos que confesso es lo
mismo que judío" [let's say that confesso is the same as Jew] (*Tesoro*, 348). In the
entry "marrano," Covarrubias gives as its first definition, "el rezién convertido
al christianismo, y tenemos ruin concepto dél por averse convertido fingidam-
ente" [he who recently converted to Christianity, and we think of him as despicable because he has faked his conversion]; it is only when he goes on to explain
the possible etymology that he alludes in passing to the proper referential meaning of "pig" (791).

His definition of "Christiano viejo" is "El hombre limpio que no tiene raza
de moro, ni de judío. Christiano nuevo, por el contrario" [The pure man who has
no trace [*raza*] of Moor or Jew. New Christian is quite the contrary] (*Tesoro*, 371).
And he defines "Raza" as "La casta de cavallos castizos, a los quales señalan
con hierro para que sean conocidos. Raza en el paño, la hilaza que se diferencia de los demás hilos de la trama . . . Raza en los linages se toma en mala
parte, como tener alguna raza de moro o judío" [*Raza* (stain) in the cloth, the
thread that differs from the other threads in the weft . . . Race, when speaking
about lineages, is taken as a bad term, as having some *raza* (trace) of Moor or
Jew] (896–897). Covarrubias is certainly more accurate than Diego de Guadix

and Francisco del Rosal in defining *raza* as a negative mark that Old Christians lack, thus conveying how the Spanish early modern racial system was not taxonomical. Yet, although the derogatory connotation is the most widely documented, Covarrubias makes sure to suffuse his lexicographical work with racial terminology, which, unlike his predecessors, he never questions.

Thus, in his entry "Judío," he explains the meaning of "almagre," a red ochre used for branding livestock:

> En tiempo del rey don Enrique, cerca de los años de mil trezientos y setenta . . . se mandó que los judíos que habitavan en el reyno, mezclados con los christianos, truxessen cierta señal con que fuessen conocidos y diferenciados de los demás. Estos se llamaron judíos de señal. . . . Y de aquí entiendo les vino el llamarlos los enalmagrados, porque parecía señal de almagre, qual se pone al ganado para distinguir un hato de otro, y dende a tres años mandaron traer a los moros otra señal de paño açul.

> [During the time of King Henry II of Castile, around 1370, it was ordered that Jews who inhabited the kingdom and mingled with Christians should wear a certain sign in order to be recognized and differentiated from the others. They were called "marked Jews." . . . From this I understand that they came to be called "enalmagrados," because it recalled the mark made of *almagre* (red ochre), used for livestock to distinguish one flock from the other, and three years later they ordered that the Moors should wear another sign, of blue cloth.] (*Tesoro*, 719–720)

He insists on this meaning of "almagre" in other entries, such as "almagre" and "enalmagrado" (94, 510). Although the term "almagre" was still used in seventeenth-century Castilian in the context of branding livestock, the discriminatory connotation retrieved by Covarrubias was not current in his own time—Guadix does not allude to such a discriminatory connotation in his entry for this word.[50] Even Covarrubias acknowledges that it is a medieval term that no longer has connotations of social exclusion, yet he insists on retrieving it repeatedly in three separate entries, as if it were an essential element of the medieval lexical heritage that should be preserved. Thus, he invokes the need to keep the medieval practice of differentiating ethnoreligious communities using distinct marks, which had evolved from the physical marking of bodies to the genealogical, administrative register.

As Claude Chauchadis points out, in Covarrubias's *Tesoro*, terms referring to infamy are disproportionately abundant in comparison to those referring to praise and honor.[51] Indeed, Covarrubias even turns language itself into a synonym for insulting, as glimpsed in some metalinguistic entries. In his entry for "palabra" (word), among several other connotations, he is careful to include its defaming one: "Palabras mayores, son las injuriosas, como ladrón, corduno, etc"

[Insulting names, are those that are injurious, such as thief, cuckold, etc.] (*Tes-oro*, 845). Under "lengua," which in Spanish means both "tongue" and "language," he also mentions, "Ay algunas frasis vulgares, como poner lengua en alguno, hablar mal dél. . . . Irse de lengua, hablar demasiado en perjuyzio de tercero. Des-lenguado, el que tiene costumbre de hablar mal de los otros" [There are some vulgar idioms, such as "to put one's tongue on somebody," to speak ill of some-one. . . . "To leave the tongue speak," to speak harmfully of a third person in excess. "Foul-mouthed" (Literally "He whose tongue is unreined"), he who habit-ually speaks ill of others] (760). Thus, in Covarrubias's lexicographical world-view, language is primarily a tool for defamation, and the insult occupies a central position as the foundation of social discourse.

His definition of "famoso" (famous) is also illustrative of how Covarrubias situates insult and infamy on the lexicographical axis of cultural identity: "Aquel a quien ha divulgado y publicado la fama; hombre famoso, cuento famoso, vellaquería famosa, hecho famoso. Famoso vellaco, el conocido por tal. Libelo famoso, el escrito por incierto autor, que trata de la honra de alguna persona y le infama. Afamado. Infamado. Infame. Infamar. Disfamar" [He whose name has been divulged and publicized by fame; famous man, famous tale, famous trick, famous deed. Famous scoundrel, the one who is known as such. Famous libel, the one written by unknown author, dealing with the honor of a person and defaming him. Famed. Infamed. Infame. To infame. To defame] (*Tesoro*, 583–584). Thus, even an adjective that could, in principle, be conceived as positive—for example, one could be famous because of one's good actions—turns into the emblem of infamy. His definition of "famoso" is very tellingly one of the most confused entries in his dictionary. Not only there is no clear explana-tion about the progress from fame to infamy but also there is a convoluted enu-meration of terms that ends up not even respecting grammatical categories, duplicating lexemes, and piling up nouns, adjectives, and verbs as synonymous, as if Covarrubias had let the reins loose on his otherwise elaborate discourse and let his stream of consciousness speak.

Insults against women are also abundant. In two of those entries, he seems to criticize the slandering of women. In the entry "muger" (woman), Covarru-bias succinctly and enigmatically writes, "Muchas cosas se pudieran dezir en esta palabra; pero otros las dizen, y con más libertad de lo que sería razón" [Many things could be said about this word; but other people say them, and with more liberty that it would be convenient] (*Tesoro*, 818). Similarly, the entry "hembra" (female) reads, "Mala hembra, es todo quanto malo se puede dezir; y en fin naz-imos de hembras, y sea hi de mala el que dixere de propósito mal dellas" [Bad female synthesizes all the bad things that could be said about anything; yet we are all born from females, so may he who says bad things about them on pur-pose be the son of a bad female] (681). In these two entries Covarrubias seems to defend women's reputation, pointing out that they constitute a common target of slander. Yet throughout the *Tesoro* there is a flood of derogatory terms referring to "bad women," which he minutely registers not only in entries that may be directly related to this concept but also in others in which he merely digresses to scorn women; these latter entries do not seem to reflect the contemporary meaning of these terms but are saturated with his own misogynistic worldview.[52] This tension between the defense of women's reputation and recurrently chastising them reveals the untenable position of the moralist who tries to distance himself from a certain use of slander while belonging to the same male community that strengthens its bonds through the scorn of women.

Covarrubias devotes a significant amount of ink to animals, quite probably because of the symbolic value that literary tradition has imbued in them and because of their emblematic features—indeed, Covarrubias also penned a book of emblems, *Emblemas morales* (1610). It might also be argued that he devotes a lot of attention to animals because of the socioeconomic value that they had in Spanish society.[53] Because of the combination of these factors, and in marked contrast with the minute registering of insults in almost any other lexical field, Covarrubias is strikingly oblivious of animalizing insults, even though they formed a privileged lexicographical repertoire for insults in seventeenth-century Spanish—as in many other cultures. His entry for "asno" (ass) is unusually long, full of erudite references to this animal, yet he merely points very briefly to the very common insulting connotation: "Comúnmente con este nombre de asno afrentamos a los que son estólidos, rudos y de mal ingenio" [We often use this name of ass to affront those who are stupid, rude, and slow] (*Tesoro*, 157).This concise reference is buried in the definition and is easily missed. More strikingly, when dealing with "perro" (dog), he does not allude to any derogatory connotation, even though it is one of the most common (and crudest) insults in early modern Spain.[54]

More significantly, and in marked contrast to the works of Guadix and del Rosal, terms in Covarrubias's project that refer to rustic people are usually devoid of disparaging connotations. His dictionary certainly contains a wealth of terms referring to peasants, but in general, they are circumspect entries without the negative connotations emphasized by Guadix and del Rosal.[55] That absence of disparaging connotations is most obvious in those entries in which Covarrubias dialogues with Guadix's earlier work, to whom he explicitly refers several times—there is no evidence that Covarrubias knew of del Rosal's work.[56]

In the entry for "behetría," Covarrubias recognizes the common meaning of this term in his own time, which was "donde quiera que dan vozes confusamente" [wherever people shout, causing a confusion] (*Tesoro*, 204). But this meaning is buried in a long exposition of legal and historiographical erudition about the consolidation of towns in medieval Castile, thus emphasizing the importance of this concept for the political formation of the kingdom of Castile and in the process downplaying the actual pejorative meaning that it had acquired in his own time.[57] Something similar happens in the entry for "çafio," in which Covarrubias acknowledges that "comúnmente llamamos çafio al villano descortés y mal mirado" [we usually call the rude and bad-looking commoner *çafio*] and in which he cites Guadix explicitly: "El padre Guadix dize ser nombre arábigo, de *çafi*, que vale puro y simple, sin doblez ni mixtura" [Father Guadix says that this is an Arabic name, from *çafi*, which means pure and simple, with no sophistication or mixture] (389). Yet Covarrubias disregards Guadix's negative qualification of "purity": "dezir de un hombre qu'es villano çafio significará villano puro, i., sin alguna parte o mistura de hidalgo."[58] In his *Tesoro*, he is therefore careful to omit Guadix's particular conception of "purity" as a lack of nobility, framing rusticity instead as a form of candor.

Covarrubias's selection of specific segments of Guadix's entry perfectly fits with his overall attempt to convey ethnoreligious opposition as the central element of social exclusion in early modern Spain. Chauchadis claims that, in doing so, Covarrubias is merely reflecting the opinion of his contemporaries.[59] Although I am indebted to Chauchadis's article for my own analysis of Covarrubias (and for other sections in this book), I must add some nuance to his observation regarding Covarrubias's representativeness: Covarrubias does not merely reflect but also emphasizes the defamatory lexical heritage. I am not claiming here that Covarrubias's picture is inaccurate (indeed most of his definitions are quite probably accurate), nor am I trying to diminish the overall usefulness of his work. Rather, I wish to point out how he puts more emphasis on some elements of the insult system in early modern Spain while downplaying others. Although the semantic systematization offered by Covarrubias is the most common point of entry to study the set of insults in early modern Spain, when we put it in dialogue with the unfinished lexicographical projects by Diego de Guadix and Francisco del Rosal, we can observe the existence of alternative, diverging visions of the vituperation landscape. Within this larger context, Covarrubias's stands as only one intervention among others.

In principle, the absence or minimizing of ethnoreligious insults in the lexicographical works by Guadix and del Rosal may look like a form of political correctness when contrasted to Covarrubias's *Tesoro*. Yet the way they compensate for that lack with the denigration of the plebeian (while Covarrubias eliminates the insulting terms for plebeians at the expense of saturating ethnoreligious derogatory terms) shows that the three lexicographers share a similar underlying premise: to structure social meaning, someone has to be insulted. Their respective projects thus reveal the many ways in which communities of insulters can be articulated against alternative objects of scorn—without ever questioning the logic of constructing social hierarchies on the exclusion and defamation of some group or another.

Insults, Sociability, and Distinction

The way that the act of insulting informs community belonging becomes clear in its festive and socializing aspect, which intends to create a bond between the addresser and the addressed.[60] For instance, in chapter 13 of the second part of *Don Quixote*, Sancho engages in a dialogue with the squire of the Knight of Mirrors (unaware that his interlocutor is, in fact, his neighbor Tomé Cecial in disguise), to whom he confesses his delusional expectations that one day his daughter will become a countess. When Tomé Cecial asks about his daughter's age, Sancho says that she is only fifteen years old, but she has other qualities: "Es tan grande como una lanza, y tan fresca como una mañana de abril, y tiene una fuerza de un ganapán" (II: 13, 669) [She's tall as a lance, and as fresh as an April morning, and as strong as a market porter] (Trans. Rutherford 565). In response to this description, Tomé Cecial comments in a praiseworthy manner, "Partes son esas . . . no sólo para ser condesa, sino para ser ninfa del verde bosque. ¡Oh hideputa, puta, y qué rejo debe de tener la bellaca!" (II:13, 699) [With those assets . . . she could be not just a countess but a very nymph of the greenwood. Oh, the little whore, what muscles the little bastard must have on her!] (Trans. Rutherford 565). Sancho does not take well Tomé Cecial's compliment of his daughter, urging him to temper his tone: "Ni ella es puta, ni lo fue su madre, ni lo será ninguna de las dos, Dios quiriendo, mientras yo viviere. Y háblese más comedidamente; que para haberse criado vuesa merced entre caballeros andantes, que son la mesma cortesía, no me parecen muy concertadas esas palabras" (II:13, 699) [She isn't a whore and nor is her mother and, God willing, neither of them ever will be while I'm still alive. And you'd better watch your language—considering you were brought up among knight errants, who are courtesy itself, I don't think those words of yours were of very good taste] (Trans Rutherford 565). Tomé explains to Sancho that, what might look like an insult is but a common way of praising people:

¡"Oh, qué mal se le entiende a vuesa merced . . . de achaque de alabanzas, señor escudero! ¿Cómo y no sabe que cuando algún caballero da una buena lanzada al toro en la plaza, o cuando alguna persona hace alguna cosa bien hecha, suele decir el vulgo: "¡Oh hideputa, puto, y qué bien que lo ha hecho!"? Y aquello que parece vituperio, en aquel término es alabanza notable. (II:13, 669)

[How little you know . . . about the language of compliments, squire! Are you really not aware that when one of the horsemen in the bullring deals with the bull a good lance-thrust, or when anyone else does something with great skill, people say: "He's a clever bastard, look how well the bugger did that!" and what might seem like insults are, in this setting, high praise?] (Trans. Rutherford 565)

As their conversation continues, Sancho ends up acknowledging Tomé Cecial's opinion. Right after drinking up his wine, Sancho suddenly exclaims, "¡Oh

hideputa, bellaco, y cómo es católico!" (II:13, 672) [That little bastard's a drop of
the real stuff all right!] (Trans. Rutherford 568). When Tomé Cecial points out
that Sancho has just praised the wine exactly with the same expression with
which he earlier praised Sancho's daughter, the squire acknowledges that Tomé
was right: "Confieso que conozco que no es deshonra llamar hijo de puta a nadie
cuando cae debajo del entendimiento de alabarle" (II:13, 672) [I confess that I recognize that it isn't dishonorable for somebody to be called a bastard, when it
comes under the heading of meaning to praise him] (Trans. Rutherford 568). As
Castillo Lluch points out when he cites this passage among others in *Don Quixote*, in these instances the insult loses its referential value and acquires a conative-
expressive one.[61] As William Childers observes, Sancho does not recognize at
first that Tomé Cecial tries to establish a playful exchange of insults "which establishes solidarity on the basis of a mutual refusal to take offense at what would
normally be considered offensive."[62]

The expression most commonly used in early modern Spanish to refer to such
a festive exchange of insults was "dar pullas." Sebastián de Covarrubias defines
"pullas" (cutting remarks) as "dicho gracioso, aunque algo obsceno, de que
comúnmente usan los caminantes cuando topan a los villanos que están lab-
rando los campos" [witty remarks, although somewhat obscene, that passersby
usually say to the peasant when they are working their fields].[63] In *Días geniales
y lúdricos* (c. 1615–1626), Rodrigo Caro observes,"Cuando tan licenciosas fiestas
hace la gente rústica, no perdona los oprobios que la lengua puede decir, dán-
dose grita unos a otros" [When rustic people do their licentious parties, they do
not refrain their tongues from their usual slurs, shouting at each other].[64] Both
Covarrubias and Caro clearly attribute this cultural practice to commoners,
which might be one of the reasons why Sancho refuses to acknowledge its real
meaning.

In parallel (but sometimes in explicit opposition) to this popular form of
socializing, insults are noble versions of exchanging cutting remarks in formal-
ized settings. One of the ritualized forms of educated classes was the "vejamen,"
a highly conventionalized, public ceremony of scolding that candidates for a doc-
torate had to endure as their final requirement for receiving their degree; this
practice was also in use in literary academies.[65] There were also many situations
in which aristocrats were supposed to show a certain wittiness in gallantly mocking others and in enduring mockery.[66] Anthony Close has thoroughly documented how the manners and taste regarding humor and satire changed from
the sixteenth to the seventeenth century, with laughter and injurious jesters
increasingly being perceived as incompatible with an aristocratic ethos.[67]

For instance, Luis Zapata's *Miscelánea* (c. 1592) compiles a series of jests about
people who, at least according to him, abide by a certain norm of decorum.[68] He
ends up offering a prescriptive recommendation about jests, trying to differen-

tiate between those that are but sheer slurs and those that maintain propriety and therefore can be used to show wittiness:

> Mas en los dichos motes y recaudos falsos, concluyo que se han de guardar estos términos; que no sean sucios ni deshonestos, ni desacatados a Dios ni al Rey; ni de lástima ni malicia, ni contra la honra que en los hombres consiste en la valentía y en la honestidad de las mujeres, ni de cosa que se está ella dicha, ni contra el pobre, ni afligido, que es crueldad; ni al poderoso que no conviene, ni al amigo que no es razón y es perderle; ni al enemigo que es provocarle; ni al padre ni al hijo, ni al hermano ni a la mujer. . . . Que sean las cosas galanas, agudas y nuevas, y leves; que no toque en lo vivo, sino que solamente pasen por las plumas por alto. También se ha de considerar el tiempo y lugar, que sea de burlas, y también no siempre, porque una vianda continua enfada, y la miel a muchos les empalaga; y como a las gracias llaman sal, la sal ha de ser poca para que sea sabrosa y no amargue.

> [But regarding dubbing and fake calling, I conclude that everyone should abide by the following rules: that they are not dirty nor dishonest, nor sacrilegious against God or the king; nor of harm or malice, nor against reputation, which in men lies in bravery and in women in chastity, nor about something that has already been said, nor against poor people, nor against the unfortunate, which is cruelty; nor against the powerful, because it is doesn't work out, nor against your friend because it is not right and would be the cause to lose him; nor against an enemy because it would be a provocation; nor against the father or the son, nor the brother or wife. . . . That they are elegant, witty, and new things, and light; that they do not cut to the quick, but that they touch lightly like feathers flying high. The time and place for jesting should also be considered, which is not always the case, because a constant food bothers, and honey tires out many people; and since wittiness is called salt, it should be used sparingly to be savory and not bittering.][69]

It is very unlikely that anyone would abide by such a strict codification of jesting, which turns it into an almost impracticable form of humor.[70] Yet, in spite of the limited prescriptive value of such recommendations, which quite likely say very little about actual practices of humor, they reveal the increased awareness that certain kinds of humorous expressions are no longer considered compatible with courtly life and aristocratic identity.[71] Indeed, Zapata establishes a clear class difference when he criticizes libels and states that, instead, "las gracias son cosa de juego y de burla de caballeros y cortesanos" [wittiness is a matter of play and jesting among nobles and courtly people].[72]

There is certainly a huge difference between the doctoral candidate who has to endure a conventionalized lampooning before obtaining his degree and those ordered by the Inquisition to wear a sambenito and to be shamed in public in an auto de fe. The academic vejamen is the humiliating ritual of initiation to a promisingly successful career, whereas the auto de fe is the public humiliation that presages a future stigmatization of both penitents and their descendants. Yet, between these two poles, quotidian life is filled with a whole gamut of social interactions based on the exchange of insults, which can either turn violent or, quite the opposite, sublimate conflict. The social ubiquity of insults requires that early modern individuals be trained to distinguish their pragmatic connotations depending on the context. Although the circulation of insults such as "Jew" or "sodomite" certainly adversely affects the daily lives of their recipients by marginalizing actual individuals for real or alleged religious or sexual practices, it does not mean that all individuals interpellated with those terms were really considered as such nor that they felt such insults as an attack on their sense of identity. Certainly, some libels unmistakably sought to destroy the honor of certain members of the community involved in local conflicts.[73] Yet, in other contexts, especially in literary ones, those very same injurious terms were likely acceptable and brought with them a very different connotation. For instance, when poets call each other *marrano* or sodomite, it is unclear whether they are making an accusation that is intended to be referential or whether they are following a conventional rhetorical frame of literary slandering, in which a certain level of provocation is considered integral to the poetic conventions of the time. Based on these kinds of festive name exchanges, Layna Ranz raises an important point when he wonders about our limited ability as modern scholars to neatly distinguish the different contexts for insults in early modern Spain and whether we tend to conflate festive situations with repressive instances, or vice versa.[74]

Taking into account the class distinction inherent to the divide between *pullas* and *motes*, between a popular and an aristocratic version of exchange of insults, let us return to Sancho's refusal to recognize Tomé Cecial's use of the word "hideputa." The way Sancho finally acknowledges that Tomé was right in using that term indicates that there is something else at stake: "confieso que conozco que no es deshonra llamar hijo de puta a nadie cuando cae debajo del entendimiento de alabarle" (II:13, 672) [I confess that I recognize that it isn't dishonorable for somebody to be called a bastard, when it comes under the heading of meaning to praise him] (Trans. Rutherford 568). Rutherford's translation here conveys what we expect Sancho to say in this situation ("I confess that I recognize that you are right"), rather than what Sancho is literally saying ("I confess that I *know* that you are right"). Sancho's convoluted wording indicates his reluctant acknowledgment that he was already aware of such a praiseworthy use of insults but pretended not to know it to mark his social distance from his interlocutor, quite probably because of the delirium of social mobility induced by Don Quixote—until he is caught in the same kind of speech act and has to acknowledge that both interlocutors share the same codes of language use and therefore belong to the same social community after all. What is at stake is how the use of certain insults anchors the subject in a specific social space. The problem of this passage might not be that Sancho guilelessly thinks that Tomé Cecial really calls his daughter "hideputa," but that participating in such an exchange would remind him that he is not the noble figure he intends to be.

FROM THE COMMUNITY OF THE SLANDERERS TO THE COMMUNITY OF THE SLANDERED

As the previous examples have shown, imagined communities are articulated around insults, either as slanderers or as slandered, and their boundaries are redrawn in every instance. This chapter has explored how communities are constructed in relation to their object of scorn and how such articulation of the collective varies; it is always in flux depending on the target being selected. Rephrasing Benedict Anderson's well-known definition of the nation as an imagined community, we could say that different conceptions of nationhood are also different versions of imagined communities of insulters, shaping their boundaries around the selection of a certain category of exclusion (be it class, race, or sexuality) that is assumed to be central while downplaying other internal divisions.[75]

Yet the line separating the risky trade of the insulter and the no less risky search for an injurious place in social discourse is a very thin one, because the object of scorn might have an active role in the production of the injurious terms. Such tension between the satirist's trade and how the targets can demand to be insulted surfaces in Cervantes's novella *El licenciado vidriera*. Its main character Tomás Rodaja, after having lost his sanity, wanders around Valladolid chastising everyone. He scolds others without limit, including any profession, social class, or gender—such as poets, conversos, painters, and aristocrats—in his chastising, by which the novella seems to follow the conventions of literary satire.[76]

Strikingly, however, those who are not mentioned in Rodaja's chastisement actively seek his opinion about them. First, the litter bearers among the audience beg for what Rodaja has to say about them, to which he replies that litter bearers are all gossipers (*Novelas ejemplares*, 2:61). In the same vein, a muleskinner addresses Rodaja to ask his opinion about his trade: "De nosotros, señor Redoma, poco o nada hay que decir, porque somos gente de bien y necesaria en la república" (2:61) [Concerning us, Mr. Glass Jar, there is little or nothing to be said. For we are respectable folk, and necessary to the commonwealth] (Trans Harney 228). Not surprisingly, Rodaja responds with a tirade accusing muleskinners of being thieves, racketeers, and sacrilegious (2:61–62). Because his comments are always derogatory and the stereotypes about muleskinners were well known, the demand from the muleteer is not a sign of naive vanity but an

outright provocation.[77] Members of both guilds, until then ignored by Rodaja, do
not try to defend their honorability, because by that point in the narrative nobody
would expect to win good reputation by being mentioned; litter bearers and
muleskinners were instead claiming their own injurious name and their place in
the community of the insulted in Rodaja's speech. The universality of Rodaja's
public satire equalizes his audience, as they see themselves reflected in a parallel
society in which social existence is cemented on the received insult.

Certainly, Tomás Rodaja performs the role of the buffoon, which, as Sebastián de Covarrubias defines in his entry "chocarrero" (uncouth), is

> El hombre gracioso y truhán . . . porque es hombre de burlas, y con quien todos
> se burlan; y también se burla él de todos, porque con aquella vida tienen lib-
> ertad y comen y beven y juegan; y a vezes medran más con los señores que los
> hombres honrados y virtuosos y personas de letras. Dizen que los palacios de
> los príncipes no pueden passar sin éstos.

> [The funny and cunning man . . . because he is a man of mockeries, whom
> everybody taunts, and he also taunts everybody, because with this way of life
> he is free and can eat, drink, and gamble. The saying is that princes' palaces
> cannot live without them.] (Tesoro, 437)

Thus, Rodaja's insults are permitted because his voice is perceived as lacking
authority and is therefore placed out of the reach of social truth. It is a carnivalesque performance that momentarily releases the pressure created by the
honor system while at the same time reinforcing it in an illusion of social equal-
ity that assumes that we are all equal if we are all equally defamed. Yet, despite
the sanitized social space of Tomás Rodaja's satirical performance, the reactions
toward him indicate the existence of a demand for the injurious word as a site
of social visibility. Both the satirist and the affronter perform a social function,
and in their absence, the demand for the injurious place can only be achieved
either by impersonating their absent voice (as chapter 5 explores) or by provoca-
tive self-deprecation, as the following chapter analyzes.

CHAPTER 2

Self-Deprecation and Fame

Ningún hombre es tan perdido . . .
que se precie de parecer malo

[No man is so wretched . . . that he boasts of looking bad]
—*Pedro de Valencia,* Tratado acerca
de los moriscos de España

Pedro de Valencia, citing Quintilian, holds that "ningún hombre es tan perdido . . . que se precie de parecer malo" [no man is so wretched . . . that he boasts of looking bad].[1] This statement reflects the normative view of insults, which assumes that infamous categories are undesirable subjective positions and therefore everybody seeks honor and reputation as the only acceptable form of social existence. Yet the opposite may also be true, and precisely because of the narcissistic element that insults bequeath to their subjects, there is always the temptation to inhabit an infamous category as a form of attaining social visibility. For instance, Martín de Azpilcueta states in his *Tractado de alabança y murmuración* (1572) that, although in principle it is not a sin to expose our own sins, it can easily become one if people boast about them and offer themselves as a model for other sinners.[2] He makes explicit the very thin line separating humility from the arrogant assumption of marginalized categories, which can be the seed for social reversal. Although self-deprecating characters are common in satirical literature, they always constitute a risky resource, because even if objects of satire are supposed to represent archetypes of bad behavior to be avoided, they can easily be interpreted as models to imitate.

Literary examples abound of individuals boasting of their miseries and being proud of their involvement in infamous situations. For instance, in Alonso Fernández de Avellaneda's second part of *Don Quixote* (1614), the narrator describes the strange appearance of one knight during a burlesque joust in honor of Don Quixote:

Un mancebo recién casado, rico de patrimonio, pero grandísimo gastador, y tan pródigo, que siempre andaba lleno de deudas, sin haber mercader ni

oficial a quien no debiese; porque aquí pedía, acullá engañaba, aquí hacía una
mohatra, allí empeñaba ya la más rica cadena de oro que tenía, ya su mejor
colgadura, de suerte que siempre que el padre le faltó andaba tan empeñado,
que la necesidad le obligaba a no vestir sino bayeta, atribuyéndolo al luto y sentimiento de la muerte de su padre; y para satisfacer a la murmuración del
vulgo, traía pintada en el campo negro de la adarga una beata, cubierta también de negro, más obscura que el del campo de la adarga, con esta letra: Pues
beata es la pobreza, / cúbrame la mía bien: / bayeta y vaya me den.

[A newly married young man, wealthy by his inheritance but a great spend-
thrift, so extravagant that he was always in debt and there was no merchant
or official to whom he didn't owe money. He made requests in one place; in
another he cheated, elsewhere he committed fraud; now he pawned his most
valuable gold chain, then his best tapestry. In consequence, after his father was
gone he was so burdened with debts that he was obliged to wear nothing but
baize, making the excuse that he was in mourning and sorrow for his father.
In order to satisfy the gossip of the common people, he had a nun painted
on the black field of his shield. She was also clothed in black, darker than
that of the shield, and the inscription was: Since poverty is blessed, / Let mine
cover me well: / Give me baize and bid me go.][3]

The rider's motto, which denounces his own miseries "to satisfy the gossip of
the common people," indicates the existence of an epic of social self-destruction,
according to which, instead of protesting against gossip or deflecting its content,
the affected individual may embrace it and be infamous in the most conspicuous way. These performances of self-deprecation, although they are recognized
as self-destructive, are also sometimes celebrated: these performers' audacity
in resisting the normative process of subjective formation is admired. These
instances are always presented as exceptional, yet when we gather them together,
it shows a constellation of infamous identifications that speak volumes of the cultural admiration for this kind of subjectivation.

This passage is one of the many instances in which Fernández de Avellaneda's book may have influenced Cervantes to explore in greater depth the
mechanics of insults in his own second part. When Sancho discovers that the
continuation of Don Quixote by Fernández de Avellaneda is circulating in print,
he is angry. As analyzed in the previous chapter, his initial reaction is to define
himself in relation to a potential community characterized by its insults against
Jews. Yet he stops defending his reputation once he decides that fame is a more
desirable goal, even if attained through infamy: "Por verme puesto en libros y
andar por ese mundo de mano en mano, no se me da un higo que digan de mí
todo lo que quisieren" (II:8; 633) [So long as I'm in books and being handed round
the world from one person to another I don't care a fig about whatever they want
to say about me] (Trans. Rutherford 534). In an effort to correct Sancho's atti-

tude, Don Quixote resorts to a repertoire of anecdotes about historical figures who also sought notoriety through infamous acts (among them the paradigmatic figure of Herostratus, who burned the temple of Artemis for the sole purpose of perpetuating his name for posterity).[4]

Even though Don Quixote's examples are taken from classical antiquity, he starts his tirade with an anecdote borrowed from contemporary popular wisdom:

> Eso me parece, Sancho . . . a lo que sucedió a un famoso poeta destos tiem-
> pos, el cual, habiendo hecho una maliciosa sátira contra todas las damas cor-
> tesanas, no puso ni nombró en ella a una dama que se podía dudar si lo era o
> no; la cual, viendo que no estaba en la lista de las demás, se quejó al poeta
> diciéndole que qué había visto en ella para no ponerla en el número de las
> otras, y que alargase la sátira, y la pusiese en el ensanche; si no, que mirase
> para lo que había nacido. Hízolo así el poeta, y púsola cual no digan dueñas,
> y ella quedó satisfecha, por verse con fama, aunque infame. (II:8; 633)

> [This seems to me, Sancho . . . rather like what happened to a famous poet of
> our time, who wrote a malicious satire against all courtesans but did not
> include or name a certain lady about whom it could be doubted whether she
> was one of them or not; and seeing that she wasn't on the list she complained
> to the poet, asked what he thought was wrong with her to make him fail to
> include her with the others, and told him to extend his satire and put her into
> the extension—and if not, he'd better watch out for himself. The poet did what
> she had demanded, and threw mud at her to his heart's content, and she was
> pleased to find herself famous for being infamous.] (Trans. Rutherford 535)

Thus, Sancho quickly moves from a position in which he expects to be treated with respect to claiming quite the opposite—a social existence based on "infamous fame," which would constitute a more desirable form of reputation than oblivion. This anecdote about the demand to be insulted to attain a form of social existence is analogous to similar demands we analyzed in chapter 1 in the novella *El licenciado vidriera*. The large number of these anecdotes reveals that there is an underlying, recurrent anxiety about what happens when an insult is set in motion and its affective force takes on a life on its own.

Such fear can be glimpsed in Sebastián de Covarrubias's entry for "canalla" (riffraff), which he defines as "Junta de gente vil" (gathering of vile people), stating that "la gente de canalla es innominada y sólo la referimos con este nombre genérico, sin hazerles tanta honra que los nombremos y queden famosos, aunque sea infamándolos" [the despicable people are unnamed, and we only refer to them with this generic name, so that we don't award them so much honor by naming them and thus they become famous, even if that would be by defaming them].[5] Covarrubias's wording is so confusing in this case that I needed to expand my translation to spell out what I believe he is trying to say. Here, we can argue, he is indirectly recognizing that many people look for social existence through infamy and that the only way to counteract this trend is by referring to them with nouns that scorn them but without designating them individually, thereby preventing them from appropriating the affective force of the insult. Although this theoretical practice of insulting is quite likely untenable, it reveals Covarrubias's awareness of the potential inefficacy of insults and his subsequent desire to find the perfect infamous formula that can attack its target without allowing it the option of appropriating the potential narcissistic component of insults.

CERVANTES'S SELF-PORTRAIT

Literary invectives were common in early modern Spain, and Cervantes participated in the exchange of insults between writers as part of the literary system in which he is inscribed. On the one hand, Cervantes criticizes other authors in his own works, mostly in the scrutiny of Don Quixote's library in chapter 6 of the first part and in his *Viaje del Parnaso* (1614)—although the high degree of ambiguity in both texts makes it difficult to determine whether he intends to insult or praise. On the other hand, Cervantes is also the target of other poets' satires.[6] However, what makes his participation in the exchange of insults unique is that it is Cervantes himself who provides the elements for the satires against him. In the prologue to his *Novelas ejemplares* (1613), a self-fictionalized Cervantes ruminates about the comments that a hypothetical friend could say about him, as he ponders the idea of having a portrait engraved with the following captions:

> Este que veis aquí, de rostro aguileño, de cabello castaño, frente lisa y desembarazada, de alegres ojos y de nariz corva, aunque bien proporcionada; las barbas de plata, que no ha veinte años que fueron de oro, los bigotes grandes, la boca pequeña, los dientes no menudos ni crecidos, porque no tiene sino seis, y ésos mal acondicionados y peor puestos, porque no tienen correspondencia los unos con los otros; el cuerpo entre dos extremos, ni grande, ni pequeño, la color viva, antes blanca que morena; algo cargado de espaldas, y no muy ligero de pies; éste digo que es el rostro del autor de *La Galatea* y de *Don Quijote de la Mancha*. (1:51)

> [This fellow you see here, eagle-like of visage, with chestnut-colored hair, a forehead smooth and clear, with merry eyes and the nose a bit hooked but well proportioned; the beard all gray, although not twenty years ago it was all of gold, with a long moustache, a small mouth, and the teeth neither too small nor too big, because only six remain, and those are in bad condition and not well situated, for they do not match up with one another; the body, between two extremes, neither too big nor too small; the coloring, lively, although

rather more pale than swarthy; a bit hunched-over in the shoulders, and not very spry on his feet; this, I affirm, is the face of the author of *La Galatea* and *Don Quijote de la Mancha*.] (Trans. Harney 9)

The hypothetical portrait mixes conventional praise with physical defects, such as the lack of teeth or the impediments to mobility typical of old age. To these defects, Cervantes then adds his being one-handed, which could be considered the scar of a heroic deed, given that he was wounded in the symbolic battle of Lepanto against the Ottoman Empire (1571), as the description goes: "Perdió en la batalla naval de Lepanto la mano izquierda de un arcabuzazo, herida que, aunque parece fea, él la tiene por hermosa, por haberla cobrado en la más memorable y alta ocasión que vieron los pasados siglos, ni esperan ver los venideros" (1:51) [In the naval Battle of Lepanto he lost his left hand, taken off by a shot from a harquebus, a wound which, although it seems ugly to look at, he considers beautiful, on account of its having been won in the most memorable and exalted occasion ever witnessed in past ages, nor ever to be seen in ages to come] (Trans. Harney 10). The allusion to being one-handed is linked shortly afterward to the alleged moral exemplarity of his novellas, which Cervantes defends in an ambiguous way: "Si por algún modo alcanzara que la lección destas novelas pudiera inducir a quien las leyera a algún mal deseo o pensamiento, antes me cortara la mano con que las escribí, que sacarlas en público" (1:52) [If the reading of these novellas might somehow induce some evil thought or desire in any reader, I would rather cut off the hand with which I wrote them than release them to the public] (Trans. Harney 10). Threatening to cut off the hand that penned his book is already a hyperbolic disclaimer, which can only be ironic coming from someone who has just described himself as one-handed. He even adds a comment using another wordplay with "mano" (hand) when he complains about his old age, "Mi edad no está ya para burlarse con la otra vida, que al cincuenta y cinco de los años gano por nueve más y por la mano" (1:52) [At this age, I am no longer inclined to play games with the hereafter, for I am nine years past fifty-five, and still getting on] (Trans. Harney 11). As Sebastián de Covarrubias explains, "ganar por la mano" is an expression meaning "adelantarse a otro" (to overtake someone) and would be equivalent to the English "sleight of hand."[7] Yet, although Cervantes states that he should not joke about death, this is precisely what he does by using a play on words regarding the hand that he lacks and turning that lack into whatever time he has left of life.[8] The ironic description of himself that Cervantes writes in the prologue of his *Novelas ejemplares* belongs to the genre of "autovejamen" (self-deprecation).[9]

Such a self-deprecating description serves as the basis for the description of Cervantes published by Alonso Fernández de Avellaneda in his continuation of *Don Quixote* in 1614, when he claims that his version of the Manchegan knight's story

se prosigue con la autoridad que él [Cervantes] la comenzó, y con la copia de
fieles relaciones que a su mano llegaron; y digo mano, pues confiesa de sí que
tiene sola una, y hablando tanto de todos, hemos de decir dél que, como soldado tan viejo en años cuanto mozo en bríos, tiene más lengua que manos.

[is continued as authoritatively as he began it, with a copy of the faithful records which came into his hand (and I say "hand" because he himself admits
he has only one, and while we are talking so much about everybody, we should
say of him: "As a soldier as old in years as he is youthful in courage, he has
more tongue than hands.")][10]

Fernández de Avellaneda's reference to Cervantes being one-handed is followed
by a series of wordplays with "hand" that mimic Cervantes's own plays of words
and accuse him of having "more tongue than hands"; that is, of being foul-
mouthed rather than brave.

In the prologue to the second part of *Don Quixote* (1615), Cervantes reacts to
Fernández de Avellaneda's comments by stating that he will not respond to
insults, yet he immediately contradicts himself when he confesses that he cannot help but defend his physical defects:

Lo que no he podido dejar de sentir es que me note de viejo y de manco, como
si hubiera sido en mi mano haber detenido el tiempo, que no pasase por mí,
o si mi manquedad hubiera nacido en alguna taberna, sino en la más alta
ocasión que vieron los siglos pasados, los presentes, ni esperan ver los venideros. (II:573)

[What I couldn't help resenting is that he attacks me for being old and one-
handed, as if it had been in my power to halt time and prevent it from ravag-
ing me, or as if I had been maimed in some tavern brawl rather than at the
greatest battle that past and present ages have ever seen or that future ages
can ever hope to see.] (Trans. Rutherford 483)

Scholars have devoted much attention to analyzing how Cervantes attacks both
the alleged author of the spurious second part of *Don Quixote*, whom he might
have identified, and Lope de Vega—because some claim that Lope himself wrote
the prologue to Fernández de Avellaneda's book.[11] Yet certain elements in Cervantes's response indicate a solipsistic play on how to control reputation, rather
than an engagement with his alleged literary and social foes. We can wonder
whether Cervantes intended his prologue to the second part of *Don Quixote* to
be read as sincere indignation, because it has a rather farcical tone.

First, when Cervantes pretends to be upset by Fernández de Avellaneda's
description of him, he fails to mention that this author merely reproduces what
Cervantes had already said about himself in the prologue to his *Novelas ejemplares* (1614). Second, despite the defense of the honorable reasons for being

ideologically charged, because it relates to the ubiquity of Moriscos within *Don Quixote*. When Sancho returns from his ill-fated government in Barataria, he encounters the Morisco Ricote, a former neighbor from his hometown who had to leave Spain with the expulsion of the Moriscos in 1609–1614 but has returned with a group of foreigners disguised as pilgrims. Despite Ricote's unlawful return, Sancho declares that he will not denounce him and partakes of the supposed pilgrims' food and wine. In their conversation, Sancho and Ricote explicitly address the expulsion of the Moriscos ordered by Philip III. Ricote strikingly praises the expulsion of his own people because "no era bien criar la sierpe en el seno, teniendo los enemigos en casa" (II:54, 994) [it's unwise to nourish a viper in your bosom and keep enemies in your house] (Trans. Rutherford 854). Ricote repeats the same position when he reappears several chapters later in Barcelona, praising the Count of Salazar for not sparing any Moriscos from the expulsion while searching for them "como raíz escondida, que con el tiempo venga después a brotar, y a echar frutos venenosos en España" (II:65, 1085) [like a root buried in the ground that later sprouts and bears poisonous fruit in Spain] (Trans. Rutherford 933).[14] As Julio Baena has thoroughly analyzed, Ricote's deprecation of his own people and his praise of Philip III are acts of ventriloquism in which the Moriscos' appropriation of the insult undermines the very ideologies of representation promoted by the apologists of the expulsion.[15]

There is certainly a huge difference between the self-deprecation by the fictionalized Cervantes of the prologue, who is fashioning his own public persona in a farcical literary dialogue, and that of the more distantly ventriloquized Morisco Ricote, who is dealing with the tragic expulsion of an entire community from Spain. Yet they both are among the notable proliferation of instances of self-deprecation presented in the second part of *Don Quixote*. As we have seen, both the fictionalized Cervantes of the prologue and the character Sancho react in outrage to the publication of Fernández de Avellaneda's *Don Quixote*. Yet the second part of Cervantes's *Don Quixote* goes beyond a customary response to an attack on one's honor to constitute a larger reflection on insults and how they affect the subjectivity of the individual uttering them by creating a sense of belonging in their target; thus, the second part gestures toward a deeper exploration of vituperation. Although the instances analyzed here deal with how to react to insults from the perspective of individual reputation, the rest of the second part goes beyond the personal to craft a literary exploration of the role of insults in the formation of collective identity and the ambiguous place of infamy as a form of social existence, the object of my analysis in the remaining chapters of this study.

THE FRAGILITY OF SELF-DEPRECATORY EXISTENCE

Quite probably because infamous identities are not as well structured and codified as are models of honorable civic identity, they are always fragile and prone

one-handed, Cervantes resorts again, as he did in the *Novelas ejemplar*
wordplay with "mano": "como si hubiera sido en *mi mano* haber deten
tiempo." Last but not least, the vindication of the battle of Lepanto as the
edly honorable cause of his injury merely repeats verbatim his own words i
Novelas ejemplares, in a blatant case of self-plagiarism that underscores the
ventionalities of memorialization rather than evoking a sincere glorificati
past deeds. Therefore, Cervantes does not seem to be responding to Ferná
de Avellaneda but rather is using the words of this author to establish a dial
with himself and to mock the very same deprecating description of himse
had crafted two years earlier. Even so, regardless of the intended tone of
exchange, Cervantes makes a perverse use of the normative communica
structure of personal insult. He describes himself as old and one-handed,
providing the injurious terms that, once reproduced by Fernández de Avellan
Cervantes seems to attribute exclusively to that author, omitting to mention
he was the one who first circulated them. Thus, the victim here is somek
Fernández de Avellaneda, who has swallowed the bait offered by Cervantes w
he was demanding the insult that would grant social legitimacy to his own p
lic self-fashioning.[12]

In an indirect way, we could also consider Hamete Benengeli, the fictio
original author of *Don Quixote*, as practicing another variant of self-deprecati
Within the fiction of *Don Quixote*, Cide Hamete is supposed to be the author
the original manuscript; thus, we must conclude that it is indeed Cide Hame
who puts in the mouths of Don Quixote and Sancho the words that they spe
against him. In the second part, the two protagonists find out about the pub
cation of the first part of their adventures penned by Cide Hamete. Sancho ima
ines a phonetic similarity between the surname of the author (Benengeli) ar
the eggplant (*berenjena*), saying that Muslims are fond of eggplants (II, 2: 596
This is not just any insult, because "eggplant eater" (*berenjenero*) was the popu
lar nickname used for the inhabitants of Toledo, precisely the place where th
manuscript of *Don Quixote* was allegedly found and translated into Spanish;
is also rife with ethnoreligious connotations because eggplants were eaten b
Jews and Muslims as a substitute for pork.[13] Meanwhile, Don Quixote complain
that Cide Hamete must be a liar like any other Muslim (II:3, 597). If we recon
sider those insults in the light of the alleged authorship, we should refigure Cide
Hamete Benengeli as the original author who allows his characters to call him
a lying eggplant eater. Cide Hamete's attitude matches that of the fictionalized
Cervantes of the prologue of the second part of *Don Quixote*, who complains
about receiving from Fernández de Avellaneda's pen the same insults he had
given himself in the prologue to the *Novelas ejemplares*.

Yet such a recurrent theme goes beyond playing around with public self-
fashioning. Having the fictional Morisco author allow his characters to insult
him gestures toward another form of self-deprecation that is exceedingly

to disintegrating. Identifying with the insult as a form of resistance is quite likely a short-lived strategy that cannot be sustained over time; it is limited to producing in the subject a temporary sense of control over the process of interpellation. This dilemma is explored in Cervantes's novella *La ilustre fregona* [The Illustrious Kitchen Maid] in its presentation of the young noble Carriazo, who is attracted to the literary fashioning of the *pícaro*.

The novella begins by describing the exploits of two noble young men from Burgos, Avendaño and Carriazo, but soon focuses on the latter, who flees his comfortable aristocratic life to wander throughout Spain as a *pícaro* (*Novelas ejemplares*, 2:139–143). Though we may first think that his penchant for this kind of low life is merely an idiosyncratic literary fantasy, there is historical evidence that noble young men were attracted to the picaresque.[16] Thus, the novella supports Martín de Azpilcueta's fear that infamous characters can indeed become models of conduct, as this aristocratic character molds his conduct on a literary model that scolds lowlifes. After some time, Carriazo decides to return home, only to soon get bored again of the noble life. Carriazo then decides to return to his old ways and convinces his friend Avendaño to embark in the picaresque way of life with him. When the two young men are sent to study at the University of Salamanca, they take the opportunity to flee from their mentor by pretending that they are joining the army of Flanders, which would certainly be a more honorable excuse than the real reason for their departure. However, Carriazo is soon frustrated in his desire to return to the picaresque life, because his friend Avendaño lingers in Toledo after overhearing about the beauty of Costanza, "la ilustre fregona," with whom he soon falls in love. This sudden development is an inconvenience for Carriazo, because love stories do not fit his picaresque expectations.

To avoid being identified as a vagrant and to entertain himself while his friend courts Costanza, Carriazo (now adopting the name Lope Asturiano) rents a donkey and works as a water seller in Toledo. During a game of cards with other water sellers, Carriazo loses all his money; he then bets on his donkey by quarters until he also loses the entire animal. When he seems to have nothing left, he claims that he has not bet the "fifth quarter" of the donkey yet, which is his tail (which, as he explains, extends to the entire backbone). The other water sellers at first laugh at his ludicrous reasoning but allow him to bet the hypothetical "fifth quarter" of the ass after Carriazo turns violent and threatens to kill them. With this move, Carriazo performs a prodigious sleight of hand that enables him to recover all his losses and even fleece the other water sellers. Carriazo is satisfied with having won back all his money and, in an act of generosity, returns their money to his colleagues. All the elements of bravado that would increase the kind of reputation Carriazo is seeking are there: he wins back in an astonishing sleight of hand all the money he had lost, when all odds seemed to be against him; he does so by defiantly imposing on the other players the fallacious idea that the tail of the donkey should be counted as a fifth quarter; and he nonetheless compensates for his gaming feat by sharing the winnings with the losers, thus emphasizing his magnanimity.

The anecdote soon spreads throughout Toledo, but despite its possibilities as the story of a noble *pícaro*, the rumor crystallizes instead as a sexualized mockery when people focus on the demand for the tail:

> No quedó taberna, ni bodegón, ni junta de pícaros donde no se supiese el juego del asno, el desquite por la cola y el brío y la liberalidad del Asturiano; pero como la mala bestia del vulgo, por la mayor parte es mala, maldita y maldiciente, no tomó de memoria la liberalidad, brío y buenas partes del gran Lope, sino solamente la cola; y así, apenas hubo andado dos días por la ciudad echando agua, cuando se vio señalar de muchos con el dedo que decían: "¡Daca la cola, Asturiano!" (*Novelas ejemplares*, 2:183)

> [There was not a tavern, or inn, or gathering of rogues that remained uninformed regarding the affair of the donkey, the artful dodge of the tail, and the spirit and generosity of the Asturian. However, since that evil beast, the populace, is, for the most part, mean-spirited, depraved, and slanderous, Lope's generosity, spirit, and good character were little remembered, leaving only the matter of the tail as the thing most widely recalled. And so, scarcely two days had gone by, as he went about delivering water, when he saw himself pointed out by many as "the water carrier with the tail."] (Trans. Harney 340)

The derogatory expression used to defame Carriazo is difficult to translate. Although Harney's translation properly conveys its meaning, it leaves out many of its negative connotations in seventeenth-century Spanish. "Daca" is an archaic imperative form of the verb "dar" (to give), and it seems to have fossilized to mean a more aggressive demand than the regular imperative form "da." Therefore, from the perspective of pragmatic linguistics, "daca la cola" is a strong demand, which reinforces its demeaning connotation. Furthermore, Carriazo is asked to provide the "tail," a very obvious analogy with the male organ. Given that Carriazo has repeatedly expressed his lack of interest in women throughout the novella, this can be easily interpreted as an accusation of sterility or even of homosexuality. Rather than committing to one of these interpretations, I argue instead that it is precisely the vagueness of the "daca la cola" demand, full of potential sexual readings, that shames Carriazo—not because of any of its potential sexual implications, but because it is a reminder of how public opinion selects from the anecdote precisely the sexual element that Carriazo had been careful to exclude from his self-fashioning. Therefore, this phrase is also a reminder of how easily one can lose control of one's public reputation, even if it is infamous.[17]

Although the novella starts and finishes with Carriazo, the title does not refer to him but to the other subplot involving the elusive Costanza, "la ilustre fregona"—the silent girl who serves at the inn of El Sevillano and with whom everybody seems to be in love, even if she does not respond to any of them. Even though Carriazo and Constanza barely interact with each other, there are several parallels between them. In the first place, the title that she receives is an oxymoron. Translations usually convey some of its contradictory meaning, such as Harney's "the illustrious kitchen maid," which juxtaposes the noble status conveyed by the adjective "illustrious" with the low working-class status of her trade. Yet the oxymoron "illustrious"—"fregona" is even sharper in early modern Spanish, because "fregona" is a term replete with sexual and derogatory connotations that almost approximates a synonym of "prostitute."[18]

Tragic as Carriazo's ending may be, it pales in comparison with the parallel case of Constanza's reversed infamy. As noted, there is not one single explicit sexual reference in Carriazo's self-fashioning nor in the female character's behavior that could justify Constanza's nickname. Both lack any recognizable sexual desire, yet both are sexualized in the public discourse as a way to make them intelligible, as a first step to integrating them in a social system in which neither of them has ever shown any interest in belonging.

The denouement shows how both characters are forced to inhabit an imposed identity that is defined in both class and sexual terms. Although Costanza is apparently awarded noble status with the sudden discovery of her alleged noble origin and her subsequent marriage to Avendaño, her voice is never heard. Yet her silence cannot be implicitly taken as consent, as most scholarship does. She is confronted by an entrenched, powerful male hierarchy of power that engineers her sudden marriage with an unknown teenager; it is embodied by the innkeeper who guards her and the noble (Carriazo's father) pretending to be her father, accompanied and reinforced by the forces of law and order. Assuming that Costanza simply could have rejected her marriage to Avendaño means ignoring the enormous imbalance of power between a shy, orphaned, ostensibly working-class girl and the combined structures of patriarchy, civil justice, and nobility and the social discourse about desirable upward mobility.[19]

In contrast (but not by much), when Carriazo's father forces him into a blatantly undesired marriage, the young man is also forced to reinhabit the noble social position he constantly tried to escape; as in Costanza's case, nobody asks his opinion about this marriage. Yet, he cannot even enjoy the preeminence of his allegedly prestigious position. The last line of the novella refers to how Carriazo, who by then is old and has fathered three sons, still fears the infamous demand: "Apenas ve algún asno de aguador, cuando se le representa y viene a la memoria el que tuvo en Toledo, y teme que cuando menos se cate ha de remanecer en alguna sátira el '¡Daca la cola, Asturiano! ¡Asturiano, daca la cola!'" (*Novelas ejemplares*, 2:198) [No sooner does he catch sight of some water carrier's donkey than there appears before him, as if summoned to his memory, the image of the one he bought in Toledo. And he lives in constant apprehension of hearing himself, when he least expects it, made the butt of some satiric ditty in which can be heard the cry: "Give us the tail, Asturiano! Give us the tail!"] (Trans. Harney 355). The insult thus makes up the last words of the novella. Carriazo, the character whose true desire was to follow a way of life considered infamous, instead lives as a noble forever wary of being confronted by the "daca la cola" demand, thus always unable to enjoy any of the two options of subjectivation available to him. He is clearly not only uncomfortable inhabiting the aristocratic identity that he rejected throughout the story but he is also haunted by the form of sexualized infamy attaching to him, instead of the virtuous *pícaro* that he had tried to construct for his own persona. *La ilustre fregona* thus reflects on the difficulty of controlling an infamous reputation, which is a state that can only be inhabited temporarily, because it can easily morph into a different manifestation of infamy.

Carriazo certainly fails to form an infamous community with both his friend Avendaño and the water sellers in Toledo, but the narrator recalls his previous life in the *almadrabas* (tuna fishing factories) when he had successful relationships with others, imitating a well-known literary model among unruly nobles. Although all the cases analyzed in this chapter focus on the individual process of subjectivation, they also gesture toward the collective, because no individual reputation exists in social isolation without the gaze of the Other.[20]

"This Place Should Have a Cuckold Quarter": Cuckoldry as Individual Infamy

Of all the social categories of infamy, the one that seems most unacceptable (and yet is the object of most recurring social fantasies) is that of the cuckold, the man who, willingly or not, allows his wife to have sexual intercourse with other men. Sebastián de Covarrubias has several entries referring to cuckoldry, such as "cabrón" (male goat, but also a synonym for cuckold in early modern Spanish) and "cuerno" (horn).[21] In the entry "cornudo," Covarrubias shows the various kinds of cuckoldry, which are defined by whether the husband is aware of his wife's infidelity, the worst case being that of the husband who purportedly consents to her wife's infidelity for monetary gain. He points out that, in the medieval legal code, consenting cuckoldry was punished with the death penalty and laments that in his own time public punishment for this crime has become a rather symbolic act:

> Comúnmente los sacan con un casquete de cuernos en la cabeça y una sarta
> al cuello de otros; y se usa alguna vez irle açotando la muger con una ristra de
> ajos, por diversas razones. La primera es, porque siendo la condición de la
> hembra vengativa y cruel, si le dieran facultad de açotarle con la penca del ver-
> dugo, le abriera las espaldas, rabiosa de verse afrentada y habilitada por él; o

porque los dientes de los ajos tienen forma de corneçuelos o porque la ristra
se divide en dos ramales en forma de cuernos. . . . Para los que han perdido la
vergüença, esta pena . . . no es pena, sino publicidad de su ruin trato, para que
sean más conocidos y freqüentados; pero si tras esto los embiassen a galeras,
no se iría todo en risa.

[They usually parade them with a horned helmet on their heads and sometimes a string of horns as a necklace; and sometimes the woman whips them
with a string of garlic, for several reasons. The first of them is because, since
women are vengeful and cruel by nature, if they were allowed to flog them with
the butchers' whip, they would tear their backs apart, enraged by seeing themselves affronted and humiliated because of him; or because cloves are shaped
like little horns or because the string is split in two branches with the shape
of horns. . . . For those who have lost their sense of shame, this penance . . . is
not such a penance, but publicity for their despicable trade, so they are well
known and visited; but if after all this they sent them to row in the galleys, it
would not be such a laughable act.][22]

The iconographic rendition of the punished cuckold in the illustration of Seville
in Georg Braun's *Civitates Orbis Terrarum* (1572–1618, first included in the 1598
edition) seems to confirm Covarrubias's lament: we see a man wearing horns
while being whipped with garlic strings by a woman (Fig. 2.1). According to
Covarrubias's account of civil punishment given to consenting cuckolds in his
own time, civil justice was lenient, and pimping husbands even mocked their
own ceremony of public humiliation, using it as an opportunity to promote their
trade. Accurate or not, Covarrubias conveys the imaginary that cuckolds formed
a category for which interpellation did not work as it should, because the threat
of social shame did not cause them to desist from their infamous behavior—as
if cuckolds had a special inclination, at least compared to other criminals, to create a resilient identification with the signs of infamy.

The text that has become more emblematic of this figure is the anonymous
Vida de Lazarillo de Tormes, the first known edition of which dates from 1554.
The *Vida* is a tale told in the first person by the narrator, the adult Lázaro de
Tormes, who addresses an anonymous recipient who has asked to hear his story
"pues Vuestra Merced escribe se le escriba, y relate el caso muy por extenso"
[since your Honor has written me asking me to write and tell my case at length].[23]
He starts recounting his life from his early childhood in an effort to explain how
he finally became successful, thus announcing that his story is one of social
climbing from very humble origins. The reader finds out only in the denouement
of the story that the "case" to which he refers at the beginning is that he was
accused of being a cuckold and that his master, the archpriest of San Salvador, has
forced Lázaro to marry his mistress to cover up their affair. Lázaro alludes to
these arrangements only indirectly by describing the presents that the archpriest,

Figure 2.1. Seville. Detail with punishment of cuckold. Georg Braun and Franz
Hogenberg, *Civitates Orbis Terrarum* (Coloniae Agrippinae, Petrum a Brachel, 1612–1618),
vol. 5, plate 8. Library of Congress, Geography and Map Division. G1028.B7 1612.
https://www.loc.gov/item/2008627031/

who lives nearby, often brings to his house, and describes this as an idyllic situation. He complains about the gossip that circulates about his wife visiting the
archpriest too often but reports that both his wife and the archpriest have
promised that such rumors are unfounded (*Lazarillo*, 132). Therefore Lázaro
silences his friends when they try to speak against his wife. Despite the naive
justification, it is clear that Lázaro knows that the rumors are true, yet he still
describes his as a life of success.

Because the names of those accused of bigamy and adultery were often posted
on local churches, we can clearly see the compromising situation of Lázaro's wife
and of Lázaro himself, given that consenting cuckoldry was also penalized.[24] Part
of his job as a town crier was to engage in the public denunciation of defamed
individuals, a category in which he would himself be included. Through the narrative failure in which the same voice exposes the infamy that the act of writing
is intending to deny, the text criticizes the cynical position of the messenger of
infamy, whose position allows him to elude it.

The denouement of *Lazarillo* has been traditionally analyzed as a form of symbolic punishment for low-born individuals' social ambition in sixteenth-century Spain. Such interpretations are based on the premise that, because cuckoldry is considered an infamous category in Lázaro's society, he can only inhabit such an identity with shame. Therefore, when he claims to have ascended socially, he is either merely a cynic or sacrifices honor and endures an infamous situation for the sake of having some economic standing.[25] Anthony Close wonders who would disclose cuckoldry so openly, given the prejudices about honor in his society, and concludes, "Clearly, nobody would, other than in the extravagant world of comic fantasy."[26] Even though I do not agree with Close's view because it does not consider the possibility of stubborn attachment to an infamous reputation, he raises the important point that the possibility of individuals boasting of an infamous social existence is coded as a "fantasy." That the literary imagination conceives the assumption of cuckoldry as an inexplicable subjective position speaks more of the ideological frame underlying the representation of honor than of social reality itself, especially when we consider that this fantasy recurs very frequently.

What is rarely considered is how Lázaro may identify cuckoldry as a category of recognition and social existence. This interpretation is confirmed when we return to the opening words of the tale. Despite his apparent active role in hiding the case, the fact is that the addressee "vuesa merced" (as well as the reader) finds out about Lázaro being a cuckold precisely through his storytelling: he proposes at the very beginning that his deeds "vengan a noticia de muchos" [are known to everybody] (*Lazarillo*, 3). This defiant exposition seems to be the sign of a clear instance in which the subject can appropriate the injurious name as a narcissistic form of subjectivation, as we saw in the introduction.[27] When Lázaro establishes his "case" as the trigger for his speech, he not only assumes the injurious name addressed to him but also reiterates and publicizes an identification that should have been silenced and dissimulated.

If we consider Lázaro to be an unreliable narrator, we assume that his speech betrays itself, revealing both the reality of his life situation and the idealization that he tries to elaborate about it. Yet, if we interpret such self-betrayal as conscious, we should then wonder what the purpose must be of conspicuously pretending to be covering his sins but doing it in such an imperfect way that it actually reveals the truth; we could only consider how a narrator can self-fashion himself as a bad liar. The recurrence of the narrative slip becomes more unlikely when we consider that most of the trades that Lázaro has performed throughout his life are related in some way or another to rhetorical skills, which have turned him into a "professional persuader," as already noted by Shipley.[28] There is therefore a virtuosity in slippage. Butler notes, following Althusser, that the acquisition of consciousness is linked to the acquisition of a certain linguistic and professional mastery.[29] The ability to speak well is a social skill through which the subject acquits himself of the potential accusation by reproducing the linguistic code: "To acquit oneself 'conscientiously' is, then, to construe labor as a confession of innocence, a display of proof of guiltlessness in the face of the demand for confession implied by an insistent accusation."[30] Lázaro's persistent self-deprecation, even when all his duties are related to rhetorical skills, entails a rejection of the commandment to acquit oneself through linguistic mastery. This is why Stephen Gilman labels Lázaro's narrative voice as "an act of stylistic self-destruction."[31] Julio Baena proposes a "heretical" Christological reading to Lázaro's case, in which salvation can only be achieved through infamy, and therefore "será precisamente el salvado/infame el que se convierta en chivo expiatorio, puesto que, por ser tal salvado/infame, es susceptible de convertirse en modelo de otro en cuanto a la salvación" [it is precisely the saved/infamous one who can become the scapegoat, because, being the saved/infamous, he is susceptible to become a model of others toward salvation].[32]

Yet it is not easy to categorize Lázaro's narrative because it shows both the rejection of the injurious name and its appropriation. At the same time that Lázaro writes his own story so his deeds "are known to everybody," which supports the interpretation that he identifies with the infamous name by contributing to its dissemination, he also takes the opposite attitude, presenting himself as rejecting with violence the potential insult when he claims that

> Cuando alguno siento que quiere decir algo della, le atajo y le digo:—Mirá si sois mi amigo, no me digáis cosa que me pese. . . . Que yo juraré sobre la hostia consagrada que es tan buena mujer como vive dentro de las puertas de Toledo. Quien otra cosa dijere, yo me mataré con él.

> [When I feel that somebody wants to say something bad about her, I cut him short and say: "Look, if you are my friend, don't tell me anything that will do me harm". . . . Because I will swear over the Holy consecrated host that she is a woman as good as any other who lives in Toledo. Whoever says otherwise, I will fight to the death with him.] (*Lazarillo*, 134)

Even if we consider this moment as a farce of honorable manhood, it indicates that subjectivation toward the injurious name may not be an either–or issue. What is at stake is the control over infamous self-fashioning. As we have seen with the case of Carriazo in *La ilustre fregona*, even when the subject embraces an infamous category, this subjective attachment is always prone to changing and to triggering unexpected interpellations. Lázaro takes control by both rejecting insinuations about cuckoldry with his friends and by exposing it in writing through his own narrative voice. Contradictory as these two actions are, it is precisely the strategic combination of the two possible responses to interpellation that makes Lázaro the master of his own infamy.

Such mastery over self-deprecation in the original *Lazarillo* is precisely what is denied to Lázaro in the *Segunda parte de la vida de Lazarillo de Tormes*, published in 1620 by Juan de Luna, who was exiled in Paris, quite probably for religious reasons.[33] Despite the title of Luna's work, there is another earlier *Segunda parte de la vida de Lazarillo de Tormes*, published in 1555, merely one year after the publication of the first known edition of the *Vida de Lazarillo de Tormes*; Luna refutes this work as a spurious continuation.[34] In his own continuation, Juan de Luna crafts a well-oiled form of interpellation as a fantasy of power and subjectivation. Luna's work begins when Lázaro heads to the war in Algiers and is shipwrecked, finding himself swimming with a school of tunas. The earlier second part of *Lazarillo* begins in nearly the same way: Lázaro is transformed into a tuna and lives under the sea in a fantastic tale. Luna, however, gives a realistic turn to this plot; when Lázaro is captured by fishermen, they wonder, "¿Qué pescado es este que tiene las facciones de hombre?" [What kind of fish is this whose face looks like a man?][35] The fishermen decide to profit from Lázaro's strange visage and spread the rumor that they have found a sea monster, even requesting the Inquisition's permission to exhibit "un pez que tenía cara de hombre" [a fish that had the face of a man] (Luna, *Segunda parte*, 293).[36] The fishermen make sure to transform Lázaro's body into such monster by tying up his arms and legs and submerging him in water:

Atáronme las manos y pusieron una barba y casquete de moho, sin olvidar los mostachos.... Envolviéronme los pies en espadañas.... Pusiéronme en una media cuba hecha al modo de un bergantín, que, llena de agua y yo sentado en ella, me llegaba hasta los labios; no me podía levantar en pie por tenerlos atados con una soga ..., de suerte que si por malos de mis pecados pipeaba, me hacían dar un zamarujo como rana.... Cerraba la boca hasta que sentía que el que tiraba aflojaba.

[They tied my hands and they placed a beard and a helmet made out of moss on me, without forgetting the mustaches.... They wrapped my legs with bulrushes.... They put me in a half-barrel in the shape of a boat, in which, when full and with me seated in it, the water reached my lips; I could not stand up because my feet were tied with a rope ..., in such a way that, if I made the mistake of moving my lips, they forced me to plunge as if I was a frog.... So I closed my mouth until I felt that the one pulling the rope stopped.] (294–296)

Lázaro endures this torture for several months. As he states, the worst part of his situation was that the setup was designed to prevent him from talking (297). The silence imposed on Lázaro in order to make him accept his new identity is reminiscent of how recalcitrant blasphemers and heretics were usually gagged during the auto de fe to prevent them from spreading their offenses in public.[37]

Only in this situation, trapped in a device preventing him from speaking, can Lázaro conform to an apparently ideal form of interpellation.

Yet, interpellation requires the opportunity to respond to it, so it can be interiorized by the subject through practice. Such an opportunity is offered in a limited form while Lázaro is not being exhibited to the public:

> Cuando caminábamos por despoblados me permitían hablar.... Pregun-
> tábales quién diablos les había puesto en la cabeza me llevasen de aquella
> manera puesto en picina. Respondíanme que si no lo hacían así moriría al
> punto, pues siendo como era pescado, no podía vivir fuera del agua. Viéndo-
> los tan porfiados, determiné de serlo, y así me lo persuadía, pues que todos
> me tenían por tal, creyendo que el agua de la mar me habría mudado, siendo
> la voz del pueblo, como dicen, la de Dios.

> [When we walked through deserted areas, they allowed me to talk.... I asked
> them who the hell told them to carry me like than in a pool. They answered
> that, if they did not do it like that, I would immediately die, because being a
> fish, I could not live outside of water. Seeing that they insisted so much about
> me being a fish, I determined to be one, since everybody had me as such,
> believing that the seawater had transformed me; being the people's voice, as
> they say, God's voice.] (Luna, *Segunda parte*, 299–300)[38]

This idealized subjective interpellation, in which the subject is physically impeded from responding, fades away only with the intervention of two university students who swear that he is not a monster but a man (300–301). The students' opinion is the only dissonant voice about his identity that Lázaro hears during several months of confinement, when he believed himself to be a fish-man. Yet for Lázaro his retrieved awareness of humanity is immediately associated with the figurative animality of the cuckold: "Confirméme en que era hombre, y por tal me tuve de allí adelante, aunque mi mujer me había dicho muchas veces era una bestia, y los muchachos de Toledo me solían decir: 'Señor Lázaro, encasqué-tese un poco su sombrero, que se le veen los cuernos'" [I then confirmed to myself that I was a man, and as such I regarded myself from then on, although my wife used to say to me that I was a beast, and the young boys in Toledo used to tell me, "Mr. Lázaro, pull on your hat, because your horns can be seen"] (301). That is, the rediscovery of his own humanity is linked to the other mark of animality with which Lázaro had been identifying, when he based his social identity on being a cuckold, a metaphorically horned man.

Such animality as a mark of humanity is negotiated when, during the subsequent inquisitorial trial to determine Lázaro's true identity, his wife Elvira (as she is named in this version) refuses to recognize him: "Entró mi mujer ... y, mirándome atentamente, dijo ser verdad que parecía en algo a su buen marido; mas que creía que no era él, porque, aunque había sido una gran bestia, antes había sido mosquito que pez, y buey que pescado" [My wife came in . . . and, care-fully looking at me, said that it was true that I somehow resembled her good husband; but that she believed I was not him, because, even though I had been a great beast, I was rather a mosquito (i.e., drunkard) than a fish, and rather an ox (i.e., cuckold) than fished]. (Luna, *Segunda parte*, 309). His monstrosity is thus constantly negotiated by a myriad of voices, yet it is invariably linked to some form of animality or another.

Because the original *Lazarillo* described his state of cuckoldry (or at least the perks that come with it) as "la cumbre de toda buena fortuna," Juan de Luna can only continue the story by introducing a conflict that prevents Lázaro from rein-tegrating into the original structure with his wife Elvira and the archpriest. As Lázaro soon discovers, he has been replaced during his absence by Pierres "el gabacho" (the French), and both Elvira and the archpriest refuse to recognize him. There is also a sudden change in Lázaro's subjective position that precludes his return to his previous state of consenting cuckoldry. When he later receives from Elvira an offer to reconcile, Lázaro is tempted to accept but rejects it, influ-enced by his friends who push him to sue the archpriest instead; this legal pro-cess culminates with the confiscation of Lázaro's wealth and his forced exile from Toledo (Luna, *Segunda parte*, 313–314). Lázaro regrets having allowed his friends to convince him to pursue such a disastrous course of action, which occurs pre-cisely at the very moment in which Lázaro heeded normative subjectivation, defending a conventional conception of honor and manhood through legal action. He then mourns his previous state, when, thanks to his wife, "había empezado a alzar cabeza y a ser conocido de muchos, que con el dedo me señal-aban diciendo: 'Veis aquí al pacífico Lázaro'" [I had begun to succeed and be known by everybody, who pointed to me with their finger saying "There you are the meek Lázaro"] (317). In Luna's version, the stubborn attachment to cuckoldry is hence located in the past, as a place of nostalgia in which he had control over the kind of horned monster he performed in the social space, until the ceaseless process of interpellation threw him back to a chain of animalizing meanings in which he lost a sense of self-fashioning.

Lázaro is literally exhibited as a monster in Juan de Luna's continuation. By relying on the etymological root of "monster" from Latin *monstrare* (to show), Harry Vélez-Quiñones claims,

In a semantic field that extends from the prodigious to the abject the mon-strous stands, above all, as a sign—a being, an artefact, a construct or an event—that demands to be seen and, simultaneously, to be read . . . ; the monster is both abominable and enticing. . . . It strikes viewers as offen-sive, in so far it presents itself as outside what is held to be normal or acceptable, yet it concurrently demands to be approached, to be voiced, to be understood.[39]

Lazarillo and its continuations (at least Luna's) are only an extreme materialization of a larger cultural impulse to exhibit cuckolds as social monsters in both
visual and literary culture. Cuckolds are conceived of as monsters not because
they depart from a normative corporality (although the symbol of the horns precisely reinscribes them into that field of thought) but because they seem to be
immune to the subjectivation process. Indeed, most of these representations of
the cuckold imagine them in relation to the potential failure in the subjectivation process, emphasizing both their monstrosity and animal individuality.
Cuckolds become one of the most prominent categories of satire precisely because
men named as such are always conceived as individuals who are not supposed
to create bonds among themselves. Such individualism is probably the feature
that explains why the cuckold becomes such a successful figure in which poets
can test the failure of the subjectivation process.[40] The cuckold constitutes a safe
target of scorn because, as the most seemingly individualistic of the infamous
categories, the cuckold cannot be imagined as a model spreading into society.

Indeed, when Francisco de Quevedo repeatedly imagines cuckolds as creating communities, he is showing his wittiness in fabricating an unaccountable
situation. For instance, in his poem "Que pretenda dos años ser cornudo" (That
He Pretends to Be a Cuckold for Two Years), Quevedo outlines precisely that
potentiality and then proposes the measures that should be taken in such a case:

> Y sepan desde hoy que hay diferencia
> de un cristiano a un cornudo de cuantía,
> y que fuera muy grande providencia
> que, como en Roma tienen judería,
> para apartar esta nación dañada,
> tuviera este lugar cornudería.

> [You should know, starting today, that there is a great difference between
> a Christian and a prestigious cuckold [*de cuantía*], and that it would be a
> great benefit that, in the same way that there is a Jewish quarter in Rome,
> to set aside this damned people, this place should have a cuckold quarter.][41]

The poem further proposes applying specific marks of infamy to cuckolds:
"aunque fuera, por Dios, muy acertado / que, como al toro hierran una nalga, /
un cornudo anduviese señalado" [and it would be, for God's sake, very convenient to mark them, in the same way that bulls are branded in the rear].[42] Such
proposed marking is not entirely farcical, considering that Jews and Muslims
were required to wear signs to declare themselves as such during the medieval
period. The use of the term "nación" to define cuckolds suggests that this category could potentially form a community that could even form genealogical and
hereditary ties. This fictional community is a blatant comic exaggeration carrying an obvious moralistic air of condemnation.

Such explicit condemnation is diluted in another satirical text by Quevedo, "El siglo del cuerno: carta de un cornudo a otro" (The Age of the Horn: Letter from One Cuckold to Another); it insists on the same fictional community by repeating some of the jokes of the previous poem ("como hay lencería y judería hay cornudería" [because there is a cloth shop and a Jewish quarter, there is a cuckold quarter]) and expanding other possible connections with the language of social stratification: "hay agora casta de cornudos como de caballos" [there are races among cuckolds as there are among horses].[43] Although in the poem that hypothetical community is predicated in the third person, in the letter there is a more complex communicative system in which the addresser self-identifies as a cuckold and writes to another individual using the same terms, thus enforcing the alleged bonds of solidarity and the sense of belonging to the same community.

Quevedo's reductio ad absurdum illustrates precisely, in its exceptionality, what the category of the cuckold is not and cannot be imagined to be: even if an individual assumes the subject position of cuckold, that position, unlike other stigmatized categories, is never imagined as constituting a model for an alternate community. Cuckolds were never conceived as forming a "nación" or "casta," and there were never real proposals to create "cornuderías." Certainly, we could say that they form a "textual community" because of the iterative ubiquity of the figure in the literary tradition, but it is always (except in Quevedo's parody), a constellation of individuals, myriad isolated representations that express again and again the loneliness of cuckolds. The importance of the figure of the cuckold in early modern Spanish literature is likely tied to its particular conception vis-à-vis individual subjectivation. It can be used to theoretically demonstrate an individual stubborn attachment to the injurious term, yet it is always presented as a sterile case, in the sense that it does not translate into a collective formation that may reverse the social order. Literary fantasies about cuckolds are thus safe manifestations of the cultural anxiety about how the Other may appropriate insult. Focusing on this literary figure avoids the risks of venturing into more unsettling fantasies in which such assumptions of infamy may lead to the formation of alternate collective identities, the subject of the remaining chapters.

CHAPTER 3

Dystopias of Infamy

*Siendo ya infinita la gente, a quien toca la afrenta de lo passado . . . es forçoso
que no sea ya tan grande el miedo desta afrenta en lo por venir, porque mal de
muchos (como dizen) consuelo es. Y comunmente qualquiera de los que oy son
penintenciados se contentara antes de su afrenta.*

*[Since there are already too many people affected by past affronts . . . there will
be necessarily less fear about such affront in the future, because, as the saying
goes, "misery loves company." And logically those who are punished today will
rather be happy with their infamy.]*
    —Agustín Salucio, Discurso sobre los estatutos de limpieza de sangre, 41v

The tension between the theoretical rationale for infamy and its practical application is seen most clearly in relation to the *conversos* of Jewish origin. The coex-
istence of Christianity, Judaism, and Islam in medieval Iberia, along with its
unsettling at the beginning of the early modern period, has been one of the most
prominent subjects in Hispanic studies. The Black Death prompted violence
against Jews throughout Europe; in the Iberian Peninsula, pogroms against Jewish communities began at the end of the fourteenth century and continued
until their expulsion in 1492.[1] In 1478, the Catholic monarchs established the
Inquisition in Castile to monitor the orthodoxy of converted Jews, usually called
conversos or *cristianos nuevos.*

The mass conversion of Jews in 1391 and 1492 (along with that of Muslims in
Castile in 1502 and in Aragon in 1526) did not result in their full integration into
Christian society. In fact, although those who converted were labeled *cristianos
nuevos* (literally, New Christians), in contrast to *cristianos viejos* (Old Christians,
those who boasted of a lineage that had been Christian for many generations),
the early modern segregationist discourse continued to justify itself through religious difference but added a new element. The integration of New Christians
was increasingly hindered from the fifteenth century on by the emergence of
"estatutos de limpieza de sangre" (statutes of blood purity), which required genealogical proof that an individual was "limpio de sangre" (of pure blood) or had

no "raça de moro o judío" (taint of Moor or Jew); a person who was so tainted
was not permitted to enter various private and ecclesiastical institutions or to
travel to the New World.[2] Thus, the ethnic boundaries constituted by religious
differences in the Middle Ages were reshaped in the early modern period around
genealogy.

In the early years of social change, there was some uncertainty about which
institution should be in charge of recording and managing infamy. As Jean-
Pierre Dedieu points out, by creating a register of those punished in the *autos
de fe* and maintaining the *sambenitos* hung in local churches, the Inquisition
ended up as the archivist of those defamed even though those actions were not
supposed to be part of its original task, which was to monitor religious orthodoxy.[3] One important nuance that is very often overlooked—both by early modern sources and contemporary scholars—is that such registers mostly included
those who had been punished by the Inquisition and who were "inhabilitados"
for certain offices and even wearing silk: they were not lists of descendants of
Iberian Jews, whose lineages were preserved only in public memory, which naturally started to fade toward the second half of the sixteenth century.[4] Because
"only" some Spanish Jews were tried by the Inquisition and their lineages were
the only ones that were remembered as being of converso origin, the vast majority of descendants of Jews were able to pass themselves off as Old Christians
after a few generations.

This observation is not intended to minimize the impact that the doctrine of
blood purity had in early modern Spain and on the persecution of Iberian Jews.
Statutes of blood purity still affected a sizable portion of the population, which
in turn resulted in a large number of people engaging in the trade of tracing genealogies. Thus, we can speak of an "economy of infamy" in its most literal sense.
On the one hand, the legal practice of social discrimination was often intended
as an indirect fiscal penalty.[5] The Inquisition very actively persecuted those who
were "inhabilitados" and their descendants quite probably because selling dis-
pensations was one of their main sources of income.[6] On the other hand, the
search for reputation and genealogical information generated an array of related
occupations. Although the Inquisition was not the main instrument in applying statutes of blood purity, it turned its secret listings of penitents into a profit-
able enterprise because many institutions requested "informaciones de limpieza
de sangre" (blood purity background checks). But there was soon competition
for the Inquisition in the economy of infamy. Because both popular memory and
the sambenitos were ephemeral, toward the second half of the sixteenth century
they were complemented by the "libros verdes," which listed names of converso
families, and the "tizones," which focused on noble families.[7] The social obsession with blood purity also led to the proliferation of "linajudos" (lineage search-
ers), professionals who profited from compiling genealogical information and
very often extorted those attempting to receive certain honors.[8] Beyond the

El número de progenitores		Los grados.		
	2	1. padres.	2.048	11
	4	2. abuelos	4.096	12
	8	3. bifabuelos.	8.192	13
	16	4	16.384	14
	32	5	32.768	15
	64	6	65.536	16
	128	7	131.072	17
	256	8	262.144	18
	512	9	524.288	19
	1.024	10	1.048.576	20

Figure 3.1. Agustín Salucio, *Discurso sobre los estatutos de limpieza de sangre.* n.p., [c. 1599], 3r. BNE, R/29688. Courtesy of the Biblioteca Nacional de España.

materialistic interests created around the management of infamy, the expression "economy of infamy" can also be understood in the sense that the compulsion to record genealogical information was permeated by economic discourses dealing with accounting and the management of risk—most significantly when the debates about the reform of blood purity statutes addressed the adequate proportion of defamed individuals that would ensure infamy would work properly as a means of social control.

The danger of the unchecked generalization of infamy as a disciplinary tool is clearly formulated in Agustín Salucio's *Discurso sobre los estatutos de limpieza de sangre* (c. 1599) (Discourse about the Statutes of Blood Purity). According to Salucio, the doctrine of "blood purity" is but a social fiction, a point that he tries to demonstrate through a historiographical, statistical argument applied to the logic of genealogical inquiry. Based on his own calculation, if we would trace each individual's stemma back 600 years, each one would have more than one million ancestors, and among such a large pool, it would be mathematically impossible not to find Jewish, Muslim, or heretical people (Fig. 3.1).[9]

Most scholarship interprets Salucio's treatise as a critique of the statutes of blood purity and generally assumes that his apparent defense of those statutes is but a subterfuge to avoid criticism. Scholarship focuses on his description of contemporary Spanish society and his historical calculation about the impossibility of having "blood purity," precisely at the time toward the end of the sixteenth century and the beginning of the seventeenth in which several voices were complaining about the abuses of a rigorous application of the statutes of blood purity.[10] What has received less attention is how Salucio also projects his argument into a probable future, which shows that his proposal of reform may not be intended to eliminate the statutes of blood purity and their exclusionary logic but rather to preserve and protect them from their own entropic drive.

As Salucio frames it, the original objective of the statutes of blood purity was not to look for the hidden *raça* (stain) in the people, but rather to force them to dissimulate it: "El afligir a esta gente con el rigor de infamia perpetua en todos sus descendientes, fue por apretar los cordeles, para que sintiessen la afrenta: y en sintiendola, sanaron de la infidelidad" [The purpose of threatening these people with the rigor of perpetual infamy was to put pressure on them so they could feel the threat of affront; and when they felt it, they were cured from the unbelief] (Salucio, *Discurso*, 17r). Salucio's concern is that, based on his calculation of genealogical expansion, if the statutes of blood purity are not limited most of society would end up being considered as "impure," a moment that he seems imminent as he writes, "Los escluydos paresce que es ya grandissima parte de la gente que ay en España" [It looks like those excluded are now most of the people in Spain] (2r). Salucio conceives the social division created by the statutes as a civil war in which the side of the defamed is the only one that grows: "Cresciendo siempre el numero y fuerças de los descontentos" [The number and strength of disgruntled people are always growing] (6v). Indeed, their numerical superiority is exaggerated as the treatise proceeds, so that a few pages later the number of the defamed is simply infinite (21v). Such a line of argument leads him to project an uncertain future in which those defamed through the statutes of blood purity will far exceed those who are considered Old Christians:

Otro peligro en alguna manera mayor es, que entre la gente onrada y rica de España es forçoso, si no ay limitacion de los estatutos, que a toda priessa se vaya apocando el numero de los limpios, y cresciendo (como espuma) el de los que tienen alguna raça. Y assi dado que entre los ricos, y onrados y poderosos fuessen oy sin comparación mas los limpios, evidencia moral es que dentro de pocos años a de ser al trocado.[11]

[There is another danger which is somehow bigger, which is that, among honored and rich people in Spain, and if there is no limitation of the statutes [of blood purity], the number of those "cleaned" will decrease while the number of those tainted will grow like foam. And given that among rich, honored, and powerful people those "cleaned" were nowadays the majority, the moral evidence tells us that within a few years, the numbers will be reversed.] (25r)

Even though he seems to focus on the elite in this passage, he later extends this proportional tendency to the entire population of Spain. Salucio observes that in 1547, when the statutes of blood purity were implemented in the Cathedral of

Toledo, they affected "la milessima parte de la gente de España" [one of every one thousand people in Spain], whereas in his own time, toward the end of the sixteenth century, "toca ya por ventura a la mitad" [it probably affects half of them] (*Discurso*, 29r). Facing this estimated exponential growth of infamy, he wonders, "Pues quien no ve que el numero de los que descienden dellos y de sus parientes, y de los que despues se an castigado, a de ser infinito?" [Don't you see that the number of those who descend from those people and their family, and those who have been punished since then, will be infinite?] (29r).

Salucio is vague about the dystopian moment that structures his entire argument, but the consequences are implicit in his warning to the monarch. He points out that "no ay cosa que mas apure la paciencia de los vassallos y los aúne a desobediencia, que el sentirse muchos agraviados" [there is nothing wearing more on our subjects' patience and uniting them to revolt than that most of them feel defamed], thus wondering in military terms "quantos exercitos harian los que tienen raça en España" [how many armies could be made by those who have a genealogical stain in Spain] (*Discurso*, 29v, 30r). What Salucio theorizes is the potential moment of inflection in which infamy could lose its role as a dissuasive social tool because of its extensive, nondiscretionary use.

Salucio raises over and over again the idea that the discrimination imposed by blood purity statutes against conversos actually reinforces their sense of belonging to a separate community, which induces them to relapse: "No judayzaran sin duda, si no supieran que descienden de judios: y para que lo olviden seria eficacissimo remedio la universal limitacion en todo genero de gentes" [They would surely not Judaize, if they did not know that they descend from Jews; and in order for them to forget, it would be a very efficient remedy the general limitation [of the statutes of blood purity] on all sorts of people] (*Discurso*, 37v). He follows a commonly used argument that points out the paradox of the repressive law, which at times seems to preserve its object rather than to eradicate it. For instance, in a letter written between 1535 and 1540 López Villalobos had already protested the implementation of the blood purity statutes in the Franciscan order, accusing their proponents of forcing the descendants of Jews and Muslims to turn back to their original religion: "Cuanto en vosotros es, todo se trabaja porque se tornen judíos o moros" [All your effort is to make them become Jews or Muslims].[12] In addition, a memorandum sent to Philip III claims that one of the unintended consequences of the blood purity statutes is that "a los conversos no se les deja olvidar los yerros y secta de sus antepasados, porque la rigurosa separación en que se les mantiene les hace recordar continuamente su origen, lo que ocasiona no pocas caídas" [conversos are not allowed to forget the mistakes and sect of their ancestors, because the rigorous separation in which they are held reminds them constantly about their origin, which is the cause for many relapses].[13]

What Judith Butler observes about the libidinization of the repressive law regarding homosexuality could be applied to the persecution of conversos as Salucio presents it:

> Prohibition reproduces the prohibited desire and becomes intensified through the renunciations it effects. The "afterlife" of prohibited desire takes place through the prohibition itself, where the prohibition not only sustains, but is *sustained by* the desire that it forces into renunciation. In this sense, then, renunciation takes place through the very desire that is renounced: the desire is *never* renounced, but becomes preserved and reasserted in the very structure of renunciation.[14]

Therefore, Salucio proposes instead that "para acabar de apurar las reliquias del judaismo, conviene que con la limitacion se olvide en España . . . el nombre de judios; y los que dellos descienden, no lo sepan" [in order to completely eradicate the remnants of Judaism, the appropriate thing is that the name of Jews be forgotten in Spain with the limitation (of the statutes of blood purity); and that those who descend from them be ignorant about their origin] (*Discurso*, 37v). According to him, then, a wiser combination of social amnesty and a moderate application of the blood purity statutes would circumvent the potential, paradoxical dangers of the repressive law.

Seen in this light, his proposed amnesty does not eliminate the statutes of blood purity but rather is a means to invigorate them, because he suggests imposing harsher measures on those who relapse after such amnesty:

> Pues que remedio para que la afrenta sea mucho mas terrible de aquí adelante sino echar tierra a lo passado, y reduzir a toda España a tal onra y reputacion, que los que de aqui adelante fueren penitenciados, vean claramente que ellos solos son los viles y baxos, y los que afrentan a sus hijos y descendientes, y que como tales son señalados con el dedo de todos, y no se puedan consolar con la desonra de muchos.

> [Because there is no greater measure to make infamy more terrible from now on but to forget the past, and restore to all Spain its honor and reputation, so that, those who were punished from now on, could clearly see that they are the only vile and low people, and that they shame their sons and descendants, and as such they are pointed at by everybody, so that they do not feel satisfied with the idea that everybody is dishonored.] (*Discurso*, 41v–42r)

Further, he recommends preserving repressive measures for some cases, especially for the descendants of those who were recently condemned by the Inquisition, and he also sets the Moriscos apart, at least "mientras que no se desprecian de su casta" [as long as they don't abhor their lineage] (37r). Thus he still defends the need to defame some individuals, so they set the example against which the rest of the population will seek to maintain public honor: "Y quiça esta ecepcion . . . seria invencion saludable, para que la emulacion y embidia del favor comun, y la nota particular, los provocassen y obligassen a hazerse dignos de que adelante se les comunique el beneficio de la limitacion, y alcancen onra como los demas fieles" [And maybe this exception . . . would be a healthy invention, so that emulation and envy of common opinion and individual reputation, move them and force them to make themselves worthy of being favored by the limitation, and they rise to honor like the rest of the believers] (37r).

Therefore, his solution is to limit the statutes by considering the adequate proportion of those affected by them: "Siendo forçoso que la infamia (si no se ataja) inficione a casi toda España, mejor le esta al Santo Oficio que no sea tan grande la multitud de los lastimados: porque nunca es buen consejo, que no sean siempre mas los favorescidos y onrados" [Since it will surely happen that, if infamy is not limited, it will infect most of Spain, it would be more convenient for the Inquisition that there is no such multitude of affected people; because it is never good advice, not to propose that the number of privileged and honored people be larger] (Discurso, 42v). It is in these dialectics of proportionality between the honored and the defamed that he situates the harmony of the state: "Siendo ya infinita la gente, a quien toca la afrenta de lo passado . . . es forçoso que no sea ya tan grande el miedo desta afrenta en lo por venir, porque mal de muchos (como dizen) consuelo es. Y comunmente qualquiera de los que oy son penintenciados se contentara antes de su afrenta" [Since there are already too many people affected from past affronts . . . there will be necessarily less fear about such affront in the future, because, as the saying goes, "misery loves company." And logically those who are punished today will rather be happy with their infamy] (41v).

These explicit passages defending infamy as a practical social tool are usually glossed over by those scholars analyzing this treatise, who suggest that Salucio includes them as a form of rhetorical caution. Although such a selective reading of his treatise might legitimately make him a precursor of certain contemporary debates on social rights, his statements about preserving the statutes of blood purity as a tool for social discrimination may indeed be sincere. His treatise is certainly not a vindication of Jewish and Muslim lineages, even though he leans toward a Pauline doctrine of evangelization according to which baptism is true birth in the Christian community. Yet, his ultimate goal is not to prevent all the people in Spain from becoming infamous, but rather to preserve the efficacy of infamy as a tool of social regulation. As he points out repeatedly, the issue is that the exponential growth of infamy would make defamed individuals into the majority, and thus the terms of what constitutes as infamous categories would be diluted and lose their original marginalizing purpose. The danger is that the infamy that institutions are recording in a cumulative, bureaucratic way could turn into the seed of a potential strengthening of collective identification.

The ghost haunting Salucio's treatise is a dystopian Spain in which most of its inhabitants would have been marked as descendants of Jews or Muslims, and they would realize that their genealogical stain is the social norm in the kingdom, causing them to identify with the religion of their ancestors, even if they no longer observed it. Hence, strict and unchecked implementation of the statutes of blood purity would end up triggering the rebirth of Jewish and Muslim Spain, a dramatic social revolution created, paradoxically, by the repressive law itself. Therefore, Salucio's main recommendation is to establish an effective regulation of infamy, following the principle that more is less: the fewer the defamed, the more powerful stigmatization can be.

When talking about dystopias imagined in the past, such as Salucio's, it is important to contrast what was proposed could happen with how events actually developed, because that gap reveals the real efficacy of infamy. Obviously, given the benefit of hindsight, we see that the apocalyptic scene imagined by Salucio never took place. I make this point to emphasize not only that his apocalyptic image is a mere exaggeration or an instrumentalization of prefabricated fears but also that the extent of such exaggeration illuminates the distance between the theory and the actual practice of dynamics of infamy. Agustín Salucio does not consider (consciously or otherwise) the gap that exists between the discourses of exclusion and the practices of exclusion: the former always dreaming about a totalizing application, and the latter being more reduced, strategic, and limited in scope. Salucio ignores the ability of regimes of infamy to regulate themselves and correct entropic tendencies by setting the right proportion of defamed individuals that the system can absorb before it collapses. It would be hard to determine whether Salucio is simply unaware of the self-regulating mechanisms inherent to the regimes of infamy or whether he consciously ignores them for the sake of building his argument.

Yet such conflation of discourse and practice in his impossible fantasy is the central piece of his treatise for a very good reason. Salucio deploys a ghostly future that may be unlikely to be realized but yet cannot be disputed directly by his potential opponents; that is, because the only way to dispel the demagogical component of Salucio's dystopian horizon is to make explicit that the actual practice of implementing the doctrine of blood purity is arbitrary, restricted, and contingent, driven by reasons and criteria that have very little to do with their initial goal. This is a fact that the defenders of the blood purity statutes cannot acknowledge publicly, even if they are aware of the many cases in which the potential extension of infamy had to be curtailed arbitrarily to keep the system going.

This regulatory need becomes evident precisely in those cases in which the excess of zeal of certain inquisitors threatened to dissolve the social fabric. In

Murcia, uncontrolled inquisitorial persecution unleashed against alleged crypto-Jews during the 1550s and 1560s provoked the intervention of both the Supreme Council of the Inquisition and Philip II.[15] The ensuing negotiations between these parties tried to repair the excesses committed by the previous inquisitor while also keeping up appearances and preserving the Inquisition's authority. One of the proposals considered was hanging the sambenitos as usual, but omitting the names of the indicted individuals. Because this potential solution undermined inquisitorial protocol, the final agreement was to hang the sambenitos in an inaccessible place of a local church while the Inquisition granted "habilitaciones" to most of the individuals previously condemned to erase the memory of their infamy.[16]

Something similar happened in Mallorca with the "xuetas," as the descendants of Jews were known there, who experienced a long history of social discrimination beginning in the fifteenth century and continuing well into the twentieth century. Between 1675 and 1693 the Inquisition of Mallorca increased the persecution of local Jews, condemning several converso families in reinvigorated autos de fe. The stigmatization of those families was even harsher than usual: the sambenitos of their ancestors were renovated for decades, as was generally the case, but they even circulated in print to ensure their wide circulation, which was not part of normal inquisitorial practice. These hostilities toward a specific group of families continued, at the same time, the decision not to renew the sambenitos of the people condemned before that period, thus effectively erasing the memory of their lineages.[17] In the case of Mallorca, as Christiane Stallaert points out, the reinvigoration of genealogical exclusion was tenable precisely because the size of the target group was reduced.[18]

As these two cases show, whenever the restraining gears of the mechanics of infamy fail and persecution becomes rampant—thus upsetting the balance by increasing the proportion of defamed individuals within society—the system always ends up readjusting and preserving itself by starting over with a clean slate. Thus, the solutions proposed by Salucio—periodic, institutional erasing and limitation of the memory of the infamous memory—were already in place, even though they were never recognized as such because that would entail acknowledging the arbitrariness of the application of blood purity statues.

Although the Inquisition had its own implicit mechanisms of self-restraint, the fear of an unchecked spread of infamy is clear in the attempts to control the privatized memorialization of converso families through the "libros verdes," which evaded royal and inquisitorial control and were thus prohibited by Philip III in 1606.[19] As John Beusterien points out, the popular success of the "libros verdes" indicates the rupture between the credit that their readership granted those listings of converso families and the censure of civil and inquisitorial institutions that wanted to have a monopoly over the management of infamy.[20]

A similar recognition of the arbitrariness of ethnic cleansing can be found in the case of the Moriscos. Although their expulsion forced the migration of thousands of families, it did not remove the entire community.[21] The expulsion of the Moriscos was considered as complete after five years by the Council of State, even though it acknowledged that removing the entire community was an impossible task, that many expelled Moriscos were already returning, and there-fore that the process of ethnic cleansing was fictional. It therefore ordered those in charge of the expulsion to stop their efforts: "porque si esto no se ataja, es cosa que nunca tendrá fin" [because if this is not stopped, it will never have an end].[22] These kinds of limitations illustrate that infamy as a tool of social control is only efficient to the degree that it affects limited numbers of people.

Ethnocentrism thus survives as a well-greased system by incorporating (and even actively generating) a series of exceptions to its own theoretical formula-tion. Christiane Stallaert interprets these kinds of moments as the turning point in which Spanish ethnocentricsm slides towards self-destruction or, as she labels it, "self-genocide."[23] Yet, if self-genocide refers to the self-destructive dynamics in a society involved in an incessant drive for physical purging, "self-ethnocide" is the subsequent fantasy that imagines that the process of social self-destruction may not necessarily entail the physical erasure of the community members but rather a transformation of ethnocultural patterns of collective identification. Another part of that fantasy is that transformation can be imagined to be para-doxically provoked by the same dynamics of infamy that are allegedly designed to prevent it.

Salucio focuses on the descendants of Jews and only alludes to the Moriscos to suggest that they should be temporarily excluded from receiving social hon-ors, at least until they attain a certain level of cultural assimilation (*Discursio*, 11v, 18v–r, 23r). In contrast, Pedro de Valencia's *Tratado acerca de los Moriscos de España* (1606), while following Salucio's line of argument, focuses on the Moriscos and claims that assimilation and evangelization can only be effective once the practice of insulting them as "Mahometan dogs" is eradicated.[24] Valen-cia implies that infamy has ceased to be effective and thus calls for the deroga-tion of infamy for all the Moriscos. Instead, he recommends a clean slate like the one proposed by Salucio that would provide the basis for their true assimi-lation and enable them to no longer fear infamy: "Hay otro modo de acabarse una nación . . . , no que se acabe materialmente, sino quedando los hombres, y el linage de ella se pierda el nombre, y no haya ninguno conocido, y mezclado con otras, y pasar con el nombre de ellas" [There is another way to eradicate a nation [people] . . . not to eliminate it materially, but leaving their people and erasing the name of their lineage, so nobody could be known as such, and mixed among the other people, they pass as the latter with their name]. (Valencia, *Trat-ado*, 138). His ultimate goal is "que se borre y olvide de todo el nombre de Moros" [to eliminate and forget once and for all the name of Moors] (139). Like Salucio,

Valencia holds that, if Moriscos forget their lineages and mix with Old Christians, they "se preciarán de cristianos, y de honrados y se querrán encubrir" [will boast of being Christian, and, being honored, they will try to hide their origin] (137). This willingness to dissimulate is the central way to conform to the normative idea of honor, which the repressive law, with its perverse preservation of the object of prohibition, precludes achieving. Like Salucio, Valencia does not advocate for the eradication of the doctrine of blood purity, but for a new application that would reinvigorate its original social purpose.

Both Salucio's and Pedro de Valencia's arguments are based on a denial of fact, but Valencia's is quite different. Whereas Salucio ignores, for the sake of his apocalyptic argument, that the vast majority of the Jews who converted to Christianity by the fifteenth century had already turned into Old Christians by the end of the sixteenth century, Valencia proposes a utopia of forgetting for the Moriscos that is impractical by the beginning of the seventeenth century: in contrast to conversos, there were extensive records of Morisco lineages. In addition to the inquisitorial register of individuals relapsing to Islam (similar to the record of Judaizers and Old Christians tried for different crimes against the faith), there were a whole gamut of additional lists. Parochial birth certificate books indicated whether a newborn was Morisco, and more importantly, Phillip II ordered the systematization of censuses of Moriscos.[25] Indeed, without those censuses, the expulsion of 1609–1614 would have been nearly impossible.

Salucio (and to some extent also Valencia) instrumentalizes the ghost of infamy as an unerasable memory that is always expanding; he does so to promote a reform of the blood purity statutes. Other authors use a mild version of this ghost to illustrate the problems caused by allowing some Moriscos to remain in the Iberian Peninsula. This is the case of Pedro Aznar Cardona's apologetic defense of the deportation, *Expulsión justificada de los Moriscos Españoles* (1612) [Justified Expulsion of Spanish Moriscos]. As Aznar Cardona argues, allowing the sons of Moriscos to stay in the peninsula would perpetuate their infamous position in society, thus prolonging the existence of the Morisco community even after the official expulsion:

> Despues de grandes, aviendola recibido sin proprio consentimiento y contra
> el gusto y opinion antigua de sus padres, cuya mala sangre los llamaria siem-
> pre, y los lleuaria tras si el siluo de su secta seguida de su obolorio, y los
> despechara la memoria y remembrança de la Expulsion y priuacion de padres
> y bienes, por donde siempre tuuieran ojeriza entrañable contra los Christia-
> nos, de quienes oyeran por largos años, el nombre de Moriscos, llamandolos
> assi por injuria, como ha sucedido con los Iudios: y esta infamia se estendiera
> a muchos Christianos viejos que cassaron con las Moriscas, o los Moriscos
> con Christianas, inficionando por este camino la sangre sana, y dando suce-
> sion, a que nunca se acabaran tan auiesas plantas.

[When growing up, after having received [Catholicism] without their consent and against the will and customs of their parents, whose bad blood would always call them, and the sound of their sect would always carry them with its flute, and they would be sad because of the memory and celebration of the expulsion and deprivation of their parents and wealth, and would therefore hate Christians, from whom they would hear for a long time the tag of Morisco against them, as a form of injury, as it has happened with Jews: and this infamy would be extended to any Old Christian men who married with Moriscas, or Morisco men with Old Christian women, thus infecting clean blood, and renovating their lineage, so these bad weeds would never cease to exist.][26]

Aznar Cardona's position on this matter has a telling contradiction in his line of argument. Whereas in the rest of his treatise he characterizes the Moriscos as an inherently resilient community, which is the sole reason for the failure of their Christian evangelization, in this passage he attributes the persistence of Morisco collective identity to the insults they received from Old Christian hegemonic society, thus suddenly adopting the opposing view of Salucio and Valencia. The theorization on insult emerges precisely when Aznar Cardona needs to project into the future the possibility that some Morisco children would remain in Spain so that he could craft a hypothesis to refute the proposal allowing some of them to stay. This instance, in which Aznar Cardona unexpectedly changes his line of reasoning, further shows how imagining how the Other may respond to the insult from hegemonic society provides the space to negotiate the formation of the political body by creating dystopian fantasies of alternative social orders that should be avoided.

Some years later, Fernández de Navarrete's *Conservación de monarquías* (1626), at the same as it applauds the expulsion of the Moriscos, warns that ethnoreligious tensions were caused by a clumsy assimilation policy and an ill-fated administration of infamy:

Tengo por cierto que si a los principios se hubiera tomado algún modo de no tener señalados con nota de infamia a los moriscos, hubieran procurado reducirse todos a la religión católica; que si la tomaron odio y horror, fue por verse en ella abatidos y despreciados y sin esperanza de poder con el tiempo borrar la nota de su bajo nacimiento.

[I believe that, if some measure had been taken not to mark the Moriscos with infamy, all of them would have tried to conform to Catholicism: and that, if they took it up with hatred and horror, it was because they saw themselves wretched and despised in it, and without the hope that time would erase the stain of their low birth.][27]

Thus, Fernández de Navarrete states that it was the strict application of the doctrine of blood purity that caused the failure of the assimilation projects of the Moriscos:

Los de diferentes costumbres y religión no son vecinos, sino enemigos domésti-
cos, como lo eran los judíos y moriscos; con todo eso, me persuado a que si antes
que estos hubieran llegado a la desesperación que les puso en tan malos pensa-
mientos se hubiera buscado forma de admitirlos a alguna parte de honores, sin
tenerlos en la nota y señal de infamia, fuera posible que por la puerta del honor
hubieran entrado al templo de la virtud y al gremio de la obediencia de la Iglesia católica, sin que los incitara a ser malos el tenerlos en mala opinión.

[Those of different customs and religion are not neighbors, but domestic enemies, like Jews and Moriscos were; yet, I believe that if, before they had reached
that point of desperation that induced bad thoughts in them, we had looked
for a way to admit them to their share of honor, without dishonoring and
defaming them, it would have been possible that through the gate of honor
they would have entered the temple of virtue and the guild of obedience of
Catholic Church, instead of being incited to be bad by the bad opinion that
we had of them.] (*Conservación*, 466a)

Although Fernández de Navarrete justifies the expulsion as a historically inevi-
table measure, he exculpates the Moriscos for their alleged resistance to acculturation. He uses this case to warn Spanish society that it should in the future
avoid similarly defaming certain social minorities as a group, because "todos los
reinos en que hubiere muchos excluidos de honor están en grande riesgo de
perderse" [all the kingdoms in which there were too many people excluded from
honor are at great risk of being lost] (466a). Salucio's argument resonates both
as a counterfactual of what could have happened with the Moriscos had infamy
been managed differently and as a warning for the future, portraying a dystopian horizon in which self-genocide triggers self-ethnocide.

Despite the different consequences that these authors attribute to the collective infamy derived from blood purity statutes, all (most notably, Salucio) perceive the paradox that these social engineering methods may end up heightening
the awareness of their origins in those individuals who would have otherwise
adapted to hegemonic Old Christian society under more accommodating circumstances; their strengthened ethnic awareness perpetuates the very religious
difference that social discrimination tries to eradicate. This social fantasy of a
self-ethnocide somersault is formulated in literary form in one of Cervantes's
most well-known theatrical pieces, *El retablo de las maravillas*, in which two
actors seeking to exploit social anxieties about blood purity end up unleashing
a potential reversal of collective identification.

INFAMY AND ENTROPY IN *EL RETABLO DE LAS MARAVILLAS*

In the short play *El retablo de las maravillas* [The Stage of Wonders], published
in *Ocho comedias y ocho entremeses* (1615), Cervantes reworks a traditional ori-

ental tale, today most well known as retold by Hans Christian Andersen in "The Emperor's New Clothes."[28] A probable source for Cervantes's play—and one similar to Andersen's fairy tale—is the medieval version of the tale in Don Juan Manuel's *Libro de los enxiemplos del conde Lucanor e de Patronio*. This work, composed toward the first half of the fourteenth century, is a compilation of tales with a moral and political frame in which the counselor Patronio uses each one (here called an "exemplo") to illustrate a polemical issue and advise Count Lucanor. Exemplo XXXII, titled "De lo que contesçió a un rey con los burladores que fizieron el paño" [What Happened to a King with the Tricksters that Made Cloth], tells how two tricksters, pretending to be weavers, offer to make a fabric for the king that can only be seen by those who are legitimate sons of their fathers. The king is amenable to the idea because "por esta manera podría acresçentar mucho lo suyo; ca los moros non heredan, cosa de su padre si non son verdaderamente sus fijos" [in this way he could increase his own wealth, since Muslims do not inherit from their fathers if they are not their true sons].[29] Although the lack of detail in the tale does not enable it to be pinpointed to a precise location, in Don Juan Manuel's time the Muslim kingdom of Granada was still in existence, and the Christian kingdoms of Castile, Aragon, and Portugal had Muslim vassals as well. The idea of a king—whether he is Muslim or Christian is never specified—instrumentalizing his Muslim subjects' reputation as an opportunity to increase his own patrimony was probably perceived in fourteenth-century Castile as a plausible royal action. Knowing the conditions that the king believes make it possible for subjects to see his clothing, his subjects pretend to see the nonexistent garments so as not to be regarded as illegitimate offspring. The illusion is maintained over and over until a Black man "que non avía que pudiesse perder" [who had nothing to lose], openly says that the king is naked; as a consequence "todos los otros perdieron el reçelo de conosçer la verdat e entendieron el engaño que los burladores avían fecho" [the others lost the fear of acknowledging the truth and realized the tricksters' hoax].[30]

In both Don Juan Manuel's and Andersen's tales, which are the most canonical versions, order is restored as soon as one single unsocialized voice dares to reveal the truth, thus conveying the message that social fictions are powerful devices that can nonetheless be easily rendered ineffective by an act of individual bravery or ingenuity. Cervantes's version of the tale, *El retablo de las maravillas*, diverges from those canonical versions in arguing that the truth cannot produce a revival of social harmony: he suggests that social fictions take on a life of their own, and that even those affected by them will defend them with the utmost violence.[31] Although this point has already been made by the scholarship on Cervantes's play, here I argue that the appropriation of the infamous logic by those affected by it is actually a literary reflection of the debates about how the spread of infamy can trigger unexpected futurities.

El retablo de las maravillas begins when two actors named Chirinos and Chanfalla and the musician Rabelín arrive at a Castilian town where they offer to the authorities to present a theatrical spectacle but only on a peculiar condition: "ninguno puede ver las cosas que en él se muestran, que tenga alguna raza de confeso o no sea habido y procreado de sus padres de legítimo matrimonio" (801) [no one can see the things revealed in it who has even one drop of non-Christian blood or who was not conceived and procreated within the bonds of legitimate matrimony] (Trans. Patterson 77). They are then invited to do a private performance at the house of the councilman Juan Castrado, who is celebrating his daughter's wedding that night. Before the performance, Chirinos and Chanfalla explain the criterion for spectators being able to see several scenes that will show on a white cloth while the performers describe them.[32] All the townspeople assert that they will see the figures in the show, because they all believe themselves to be Old Christians. As Benito Repollo brags defiantly, "Cuatro dedos de enjundia de cristiano viejo rancioso tengo sobre los cuatro costados de mi linaje" (803) [I've got four inches of Old Christian fat covering the four sides of my lineage] (Trans. Patterson 79).[33] The cloth remains empty during the entire play, yet each of the spectators pretends to see the nonexistent figures so they will not be questioned about their lineage. As the governor makes explicit in an aside, "Todos ven lo que yo no veo; pero al fin habré de decir que lo veo, por la negra honrilla" (806) [Everyone sees what I can't see. I guess I'll have to just say that I can see it to protect my damn reputation] (Trans. Patterson 82). The performance is interrupted by the arrival of a quartermaster (Furrier) who orders the townsfolk to provide lodging for his company. It is only when the quartermaster shows his surprise over the audience's fixation on the play with no actors nor visible figures that the townspeople can finally identify a scapegoat and accuse him of being a converso, which triggers the ensuing violence between soldiers and townsfolk that serves as the denouement of the piece (810–811). In the midst of the chaos, Chanfalla congratulates himself for the result of their performance and tells Chirinos that they are ready to perform the spectacle for a broader audience the next day.

Many scholars have analyzed how *El retablo de las maravillas* underscores the fictionality of the concept of blood purity.[34] They also see in the metatheatrical element of the play a critique of Lope's *comedia nueva* as a business and social illusion.[35] Although these contributions shed light on the social and literary reality that Cervantes is reflecting, the play's unresolved ending has received less attention. By establishing the timeline and stages in which the identity of this town is transformed and articulated around insult and the spread of infamy, we can observe how Cervantes's play reworks in literary form Salucio's apocalyptic horizon.

In the first place, the community that welcomes Chirinos and Chanfalla is being transformed as they watch the play. At the start of the play, this rural community is formed by people who say they regard themselves as Old Christians. There is nothing in the text indicating whether the villagers are Old Christians or not, and the reader has access only to their fears and anxieties about the possibility of not being regarded as such—after all, there is no essence in "being" Old Christian other than belief in being one and the reputation of being considered one.[36]

Then, as soon as all the spectators realize that they do not see the figures on the stage, they reconsider their own identity and fear that they are conversos. As Martínez López states, "Tanto si dejan de hacer como si hacen algo ante las acusaciones del retablo, la infamia les acosará, directamente o por rodeos, pero sin falta" [Even if they react or not to the accusations in the tableau, infamy will haunt them, directly or indirectly but with no haste].[37] That is, the tricksters' device is effective because it does not matter how the audience reacts to the performance: their sense of belonging has already been affected in some way. The tableau's interpellation is extremely powerful because it produces a chiasmus between individual self-esteem and public identity: if the members of the audience keep silent, all of them will individually believe themselves to be conversos, but if they speak out against the hoax, they know they will be publicly accused of being one. In other words, those who pretend to see the performance know that they are merely pretending and therefore believe they are conversos themselves, whereas those who openly acknowledge not seeing the performance are publicly regarded as conversos.

We cannot properly say that this town, whose members watched the play, has been transformed into a community of conversos: they do not disclose any memory of being descendants of Iberian Jews or of having converted themselves, and most importantly interpellation as conversos functions at an individual level. Because every one of them believes themselves to be conversos but is careful not to acknowledge it publicly, their silence prevents the formation of any sense of converso collective identity. Yet even though the text does not address this factor explicitly, we need to consider that all these town dwellers form a thick network of family relations. For instance, Juana Castrada and Teresa Repolla are the daughters of Juan Castrado and Pedro Repollo, respectively, and the two women are cousins (805). Therefore, at some point each of them will necessarily reach the conclusion that, if they themselves are conversos, then their relatives must be conversos as well.

Insults play an important role in how this community negotiates its own boundaries during the play, which begs the question of what the exact timeline of this construction is and whether we can trace the process of transformation. The play gestures toward the imminence of that inflection of collective identity when Chirinos describes Herodias's dance, even though it should actually be his daughter Salomé who is dancing after they bring her the head of John the Baptist. Benito Repollo expresses his admiration for the dance: "Hideputa, y cómo que se vuelve la mochacha" (809) [Sonofabitch! Look at the girl move!] (Trans. Patterson 84); he encourages his nephew to dance with the imagined figure whom Benito disparagingly calls "bellaca jodía" (rascally Jew girl) even while admiring her dancing. The use of the expression "hideputa" recalls the debate about the potential complimentary connotations of some insults in certain contexts, as we saw in Sancho's rumination about this term in chapter 13 in the second part of Don Quixote (see chapter 1); the potential affective value of insults also contaminates the expression "bellaca jodía" and makes us wonder whether the anti-Semitic insult should now be understood as a compliment. On the quartermaster's second arrival, Juan Castrado asks Chirinos and Chanfalla to make Herodias appear again so that his nephew can dance again with her (810). By immersing themselves in the performers' fiction, town dwellers interact with "Jewish" figures and simulate acts of brotherhood that would have been unthinkable for them before the performance began.[38] A brotherhood is thus attained through the use and overuse of insults.

Insult is a fiction both about the Other and the community that the insulters intend to delimit with their speech act. Yet those boundaries are malleable. As we have seen, when Sancho claims that he is a good Catholic and "enemigo mortal, como lo soy, de los judíos" (II:8: 633) [mortal enemy, as I am, of all Jews] (Trans. Rutherford 534), he defines himself as a nonpracticing insulter. In this anonymous town, quite on the contrary, at the same time as the townfolk are insulting Jews, they are actually becoming them in their imagination. In the scene of Herodias's dance, the behavior of the characters alters the supposed original performative force of the insult so that it sounds in this instance like an expression of admiration. The anti-Semitic insult was already there in its potentiality since the very beginning, but its first materialization is rather frustrating for the purposes of policing the community around it. Certainly, pre-Christian Hebrews are not considered "Jews" by anti-Semitic theology, because they lived before the revelation.[39] Yet it is doubtful that these rustic townspeople would draw such a sophisticated historiographical line between biblical Hebrews and pre-1492 Iberian Jews—which by the early seventeenth century were almost equally vague and remote historical figures in the popular imagination. This fledging confraternity between real and imagined dancers gestures toward one of the possible outcomes of the social tensions, even if they are left unresolved in the text, which would have led the town dwellers to assume a "Jewish" identity—even if there is no sign in the text suggesting that they were of Jewish origin and even if they are on the brink of becoming Jews only nominally, without the need to perform any specific religious or cultural practices associated with Judaism.

It is only the second anti-Semitic insult against the quartermaster ("De ex illis es" [You are one of them]), uttered with the most violent rage, that fulfills the requirement of drawing the boundaries of the Old Christian community through the disparaging of Jews. As Julio Baena observes, only when the quartermaster

has been labeled "de ex illis" can there be an "us."[40] Certainly, a sense of community is constructed on the excluded element, as Girard points out in his analysis of the scapegoat.[41] As a foundational moment, the insult against the Other is
the narrative element that structures the community: it is not so much about how
to be a Christian (there is no mention of Catholic rituals or doctrine in the play,
despite the multiple biblical references) but about how not to be a Jew (without
knowing anything about the Jewish rituals to which they should be opposed). Yet
this socializing insult comes too late, because by then this community has been
transformed into something different.

The tension created by the tableau can only be momentary. Without the erup-
tion of the quartermaster at the end of the play to serve as the scapegoat, social
tensions would have reached a climax in which two options were equally possible: either inter-ethnicidal violence among the town dwellers in their attempts
to find the conversos among them (while each believes individually that he or
she is a descendant of cristianos nuevos) or the apocalyptic turning point fore-
seen by Salucio in which the discovery of belonging to the infamous category
would trigger its assumption as the model for social articulation (that is, the revelation of the truth would not necessarily lead to denouncing the tableau as a
hoax but to the collective assumption that Old Christian identity is an illusion).
When all the tension is unleashed toward the quartermaster and his men as they
are accused of being Jews, the inhabitants of this anonymous town attack what
they now think they themselves are. The experience of watching the play has
transformed them into a converso community, because now every inhabitant
considers him- or herself as such—even if they had no Jewish ancestors and even
if no one really shares the conviction of being a converso.

The idea that the figure of the Jew serves as the scapegoat on which Old Christians construct their own feeling of identity is complicated when we consider
that there is a secondary scapegoat, Rabelín, against whom all the tension is
directed in several moments throughout the play. Rabelín, the musician who
accompanies Chirinos and Chanfalla, has a very limited presence and very few
lines; he is marked from the very beginning as the target of scorn for the rest of
the characters. Chirinos complains to Chanfalla about the poor decision they
made in hiring Rabelín, whom she describes as "desventurada criaturilla" (795)
[wretched little creature (Trans. Patterson 76)]. In his first entrance, Chirinos
tells him, "Cuatro cuerpos de los vuestros no harán un tercio . . . si no sois más
gran músico que grande, medrados estamos" (799–800) [Four bodies like yours
would not make up the third part of a body . . . if you are not more so a great
musician than you are of great height, we are screwed].[42] When the show is about
to start, Benito complains about the horrific presence of Rabelín. "Músico es este?
Métanle. . . . . detrás del repostero; que, a trueco de no velle, daré por bien
empleado el no oílle" (805) [You call that a musician? Put him behind the
curtain. . . . If I have to put up with hearing him, I might as well not have to see

him] (Trans. Patterson 81). Benito indeed complains repeatedly about Rabelín's musical skills (805, 807–808, 810). At the end of the play, after inciting the rebellion against the quartermaster instigated by accusing him of being a Jew, Benito does not aim his violence against him and his soldiers but against Rabelín: the stage directions indicate that, in the midst of the final chaos, Benito beats the musician (811). Thus, the alleged anti-Semitic uprising turns into the subterfuge for Benito's discharge of rage against Rabelín, who seems to be the real scapegoat, at least for this character. Thus, Rabelín not only serves to alleviate the tension but also to create a dialectical relation between the several scapegoats and minimize the danger of identifying with any of them.

Within such dialectics of identity, "Jew" becomes a flexible insult that could be instrumentalized strategically to refigure the boundaries of the community. The first instance of the insult "Jew" is quite explicitly "bellaca judía" applied to Herodias, but as we have seen, it is employed in the most tender way to a character with whom the town dwellers empathize and interact in a festive way. This suggests that they are in the process of re-semanticizing the insult "Jew." By contrast, the quartermaster is accused of being Jewish with the Latin formula "De ex illis es." Scholarship points out that this is a conventional expression to refer to Jews, as the ones external to the Christian community. Yet, properly speaking, this expression does not contain the term "Jew," and the townspeople were earlier characterized as not being very familiar with Latin expressions, which begs the question of what they exactly mean when they use it against the quartermaster. Do they really mean that the quartermaster is a Jew, or do they rather use the expression to suggest that he is external to a community that now believes itself to be of conversos, and for which the representative of the state is a figure against whom they feel entitled to rebel? As Baena argues, the moment the illusion takes a logic on its own is paradoxically the liberating moment, triggering the revolt against authority because "the villagers' mechanisms of self-delusion prove to be the mechanisms of *active* denial of an oppressive reality."[43] In this sense, the resolution of the social tension within the play is not interrupted by the fortuitous arrival of the quartermaster and his company but is rather crowned by his intervention, as Chirinos and Chanfalla congratulate one another on the success of the performance.

The denouement of the play offers an open ending, which suggests the mechanics governing the spread of infamy are still in motion even when the performance has come to an end, thus signaling the essential divergence from the traditional tale. Whereas in the traditional version of the story, the end of the tale largely constitutes the end of the illusion, in Cervantes's play the denouement is but the prelude to a larger project whose further development is merely glimpsed. Chirinos and Chanfalla leave the scene celebrating the success of the performance, talking about how they will repeat it for a general audience the next day and later, we might conjecture, throughout Castile. Therefore, the short play that we read is presented as being merely the first public rehearsal, the prelude of a more extensive endeavor in which Chirinos and Chanfalla will leave a trail of peasants believing they are conversos, even if they had regarded themselves as Old Christians until the arrival of the two tricksters. Certainly, Chirinos and Chanfalla are con artists with no explicit social agenda who are selling a nonexistent performance for profit, with the primary objective of exploiting social anxieties about blood purity. Yet, even if their motivations are purely economic, the exploitation of the audience's anxieties turns into a potential agent of social change, because it contributes to spreading the awareness of the "stain," even among those who may have had considered themselves as Old Christians until then. Through their performance, Chirinos and Chanfalla incarnate the entropic tendency of infamy feared by Agustín Salucio, which could transform a tool of social control into an agent of social change, if allowed to reach that critical point in which the infamous identity of the present becomes the hegemonic kernel of collective identity in the future.

CHAPTER 4

Fancy *Sambenitos*

THE ETHNICIZATION OF INFAMY

Pues si este, a quien por sus pecados le pusieron el sambenito, llamasse un sas-
tre, y le hiziesse poner guarniciones de seda y brocado, y saliesse muy pomposo
con el en publico, podriase tener por loco?

[If the person who has received the sambenito because of his sins, called a tailor
and had him adorn the sambenito with silk and brocade, and wore it conspicu-
ously in public, should he be considered a fool?]

—*Alonso de Villegas*, Fructus Sanctorum y
quinta parte del Flos Sanctorum, *1594*

Although the previous chapters explored verbal insults for the most part, the
management of infamy includes nonverbal manifestations as well.[1] Undoubtedly,
in early modern Spain, the most shameful occurrence was appearing in an *auto*
de fe, in which those punished by the Inquisition were paraded and their offenses
against the faith announced publicly.[2] The defaming ceremony culminated in
donning the sambenito, the garment in which those punished in the auto de fe
had to parade and, in some cases, were condemned to wear for a certain time,
ranging from a few days to several years. In other cases, the sambenitos were
hung in local churches so the descendants of those punished by the Inquisition
could be identified by the rest of the population: by looking at the garment, people
could remember not only the condemned individual but also his family, therefore projecting infamy through the entire lineage.[3] Thus, the sambenito was not
merely a garment but also a document that included an array of highly codified
information. It came in several versions, depending on the gravity of the alleged
offense, from the least important crime against the faith to the greatest: those
accused of the most serious offenses were condemned to be burned alive at the
stake.

Although according to written documentation sambenitos were produced by
the thousands, there are very few extant examples. The first reason for their scar-

city was their material fragility. The sambenitos were made of fabric and so were not durable objects—in general, very little clothing has survived from the early modern period. Inquisitors were already aware of their fragile nature and therefore requested local churches to repair the sambenitos periodically. For instance, we have a sketched copy of an old sambenito in Cordoba that was worn out and had to be repaired (Fig. 4.1). The second reason why sambenitos have not survived is that the individuals that they named and their descendants often tried to destroy them by any means.[4]

Only one set of sambenitos has survived in Tui, and only by accident, because they lay forgotten in a trunk for centuries. The extant sambenitos preserved in the Museo Diocesano de Tui show very clearly how they codified the information the Inquisition considered relevant to defame the individuals who wore them and their lineage (Fig. 4.2).[5] Capital punishment is conveyed in the drawing of the head in flames and the inclusion of the cross of Saint Andrew. It also includes the name of Andrés Duarte Coronel, informing the spectator that the person who wore it is a citizen of Tui, and also that he is absent—which means that he likely escaped and was burned in effigy. Finally, the sambenito lists the accusation—in this case, being a Judaizer—and the date of the auto de fe.

Public exhibition of infamy was the exemplary punishment for heretics and was intended both to reconcile them to the Christian body and to serve as a deterrent for the audience of the auto de fe. Despite the means of punishment at the disposal of the Inquisition (at least apparently) and the spectacular nature of the auto de fe, there was always the anxiety that the mode of interpellation would fail, as happened with the other forms of infamy analyzed in previous chapters.

One reason why this public exhibition of infamy might not achieve its purposes is that not everyone who witnessed it would be aware of the defaming meaning of the sambenito. For instance, in an inquisitorial trial in Tecamachalco (Mexico) in 1578 to find out who posted some forfeited sambenitos, thus appropriating the symbols of the Inquisition, several witnesses state that they were unaware of the meaning of the sambenito.[6] Whether the witnesses testified honestly or not, what is significant here is that their lack of knowledge about the sambenito could be considered an acceptable justification by the inquisitors, who thus acknowledged the limited reach of their symbols. The Morisco Ginés Pérez, accused of crypto-Islamism and traveling to North Africa, was condemned to wear the sambenito for two years in an auto de fe held in Granada in 1581.[7] Ginés Pérez shows up again in the next auto de fe in 1582, this time for questioning the previous sentence ordering him to wear the sambenito and for defying the authority of the Inquisition.[8] What is significant in this second accusation is a heretical statement attributed to him by the witnesses: "Fue testificado por tres testigos de aver dicho despues de reconciliado de que el habito no lo traya por cosa que ubiesse pecado sino porque se hizo ynquissidor" [Three witnesses

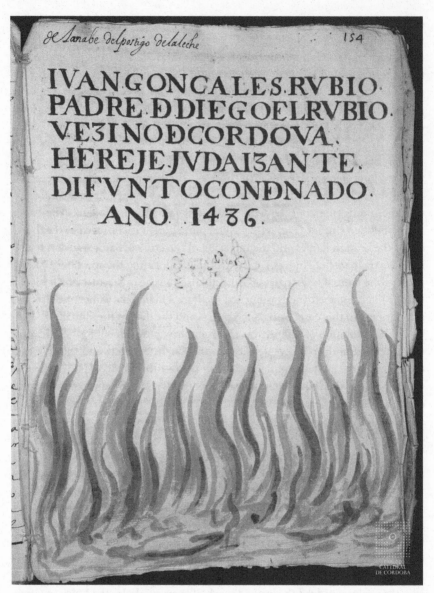

Figure 4.1. Copy of sambenito to be repaired. Archivo Capitular de Córdoba, Secretaría, Leg. 5278, doc. 1, 154r. Courtesy of Archivo y Biblioteca Capitular de la Catedral de Córdoba.

Figure 4.2. Sambenito. Museo Diocesano de Tui. Photograph by the author.

testified that, after being punished, he said that he was not wearing the garment because he was a sinner, but because he had become an inquisitor].[9] This does not seem to be a case of mental derangement, because Ginés Pérez denies the accusations and complains to the inquisitors about having to wear the sambenito, which means that he is well aware of its meaning. Ginés Pérez's fiction that the sambenito is the robe of the inquisitors was likely a joke to alleviate his humiliation, but we should not entirely discard the possibility that he was seriously trying to trick others, thinking that they might not be aware of what a sambenito really was.

The second reason for the potential failure of inquisitorial interpellation is that the defamed might appropriate the sambenito as a sign of honor. Because it was the most visible and shameful form of infamy in early modern Spain, it would be inconceivable that anyone would attempt this strategy. Yet, precisely such a possibility circulates in the form of cultural fantasy. Pedro Malón de Chaide's *La conversión de la Magdalena* (1588) critiques sartorial excess by

conceiving luxurious clothing as a sign of infamy and comparing ostentatious-
ness to the unimaginable situation of boasting of wearing a sambenito:

> Ha sido después tanta la vanidad de los hombres y ha crecido tan por extremo
> su malicia, que han llegado a hacer golosina del pecado, y que lo que se dio
> por sambenito y afrenta eso sirva de gala y honra, porque preciarse del ves-
> tido es como si uno se preciara de traer más galán y costoso el sambenito, que
> por sus culpas le puso la Inquisición.

> [Men's vanity and malice have grown so much that they have turned sin into
> taste, and what was given as a mark of infamy and affront serves now as a sign
> of elegance and honor; because taking pride in clothing is comparable to one
> taking pride in wearing a luxurious and expensive sambenito, which was
> imposed opun him by the Inquisition.][10]

Alonso de Villegas's *Fructus Sanctorum y quinta parte del Flos Sanctorum* (1594)
echoes this comparison between conspicuous expenditures on luxurious clothing and wearing the sambenito, which he expands by imagining the unthinkable situation in which its wearer would request that a tailor adorn that garment:
"Pues si este, a quien por sus pecados le pusieron el sambenito, llamasse un sas-
tre, y le hiziesse poner guarniciones de seda y brocado, y saliesse muy pomposo
con el en publico, podriase tener por loco?" [If the person who has received the
sambenito because of his sins, called a tailor and had him adorn the sambenito
with silk and brocade, and wore it conspicuously in public, should he be considered a fool?].[11] I selected this quotation for the epigraph of this chapter not only
because Villegas formulates very succinctly the social fantasy being explored here
but also because he raises the possibility of this being a form of madness, as is
analyzed later.

By the turn of the sixteenth century, the trope of the individual creating a
personal stubborn attachment to the sambenito evolves into a different kind of
urban legend that begins to take on some narrative form. Andrés Núñez de
Andrada's *Vergel de la escritura divina* (1600), when chastising ambition, refers
to an anecdote of how the sambenito could attain a productive value for a family
affected by infamy:

> Vi yo usar con un hombre rico, que en poco tiempo auia crecido su hazienda
> como espuma, y con la mucha hazienda estauan sus hijos tan soberuios, que
> competian con los mas principales caualleros: y viendo su padre, que no los
> podia humillar, saco un sanbenito del arca, que le auia costado hartos dine-
> ros, el quitarlo de la Yglesia, y dixoles: mirad quien soys, y humillaos.

> [I have seen the case of a rich man, whose wealth increased all of a sudden,
> and with his wealth his sons became so arrogant that they competed with the
> most illustrious noblemen. And his father, seeing that he could not humiliate

them, took the sambenito from a chest (which he spent a lot of money to take out of the church) and told them, "See what you are, and swallow your pride."][12]

The anecdote is most likely an apocryphal urban legend, if not invented by Núñez de Andrada himself. Indeed, his claim of having witnessed the event contradicts the circumstances of the story, which would have necessarily occurred in private.

Núñez de Andrada opines that seeing the sambenito "este es el mejor remedio contra la ambicion" [this is the best remedy against ambition] (Núñez de Andrada, *Primera parte del Vergel*, 53r). Yet the moral is ambiguous, because in this tale there are two types of ambition, of which Núñez de Andrada only explicitly censures one. Even though he begins the anecdote by pointing out that the father became rich in a very short amount of time, that kind of material ambition does not seem to be the object of his criticism, because the father knows his place in society despite his wealth. The kind of ambition that is disapproved of here is that of his sons, who boast of the economic position achieved by their father and act as if it should yield them an equally elevated social standing. This particular appropriation of the sambenito in which it is turned into a private object that can indeed be productive of family honor seems to have not been a unique formulation.[13] Sebastián de Covarrubias adds a colophon to his definition of the sambenito: "Aunque para el mundo sea ignominia y afrenta, si los que los traen reciben en paciencia lo que dirá el vulgo, pueden para con Dios merecer mucho" [Even though for everybody it is infamy and affront, if those who wear it take with patience others' opinion, they can become worthy to be with God].[14] When Covarrubias suggests that what has been constructed initially as a sign of infamy can indeed acquire a productive potential for the affected individual, he is likely arguing that he should accept the stigma and suffer silently. Yet such an exercise of humility also opens the door for the kind of perverse appropriations of infamy explored here.

As we have seen, many people affected by the defaming sambenitos did everything they could to remove them from local churches. Yet sambenitos were eventually taken down to be destroyed as a matter of course, thereby removing their testimony and thus rewriting collective memory. The case that Núñez de Andrada recounts is atypical because the sambenito, which is no longer public, is privatized as a disciplinary device to manage family honor and behavior. It thus reflects the unusual situation of a man who, after removing the sambenito from the church and thus erasing the family stigma from collective memory, nonetheless keeps the defaming garment as a family heritage and uses it strategically to defend the group's honor. The anecdote suggests that the signs of infamy, even when they have been taken out of the circuit of public information, can still have a series of formative values for the affected individuals themselves. In this case, the sambenito has been retired from public circulation so that the infamy that it was originally seeking to produce can be transformed into private capital for family management. This story largely gestures toward a new paradigm in which the management of infamy does not entail avoiding sin out of fear of public humiliation, but in making every possible effort to hide sin while retaining disciplinary measures within the family. Infamy is still imagined as a form of control, but only as far as those who could be publicly defamed can interiorize its logic—and no longer as a disciplinary regime in which the signs of infamy serve to identify and exclude the defamed individual publicly within the community.

The brevity of Núñez de Andrada's anecdote leaves many details unexplained, such as which family member originally wore the sambenito—it is not clear whether that person is the head of the family or one of his ancestors—and, more importantly, what kind of religious offense is being covered up. Those are precisely the gaps that become saturated in Alonso de Castillo Solórzano's novella *El obstinado arrepentido* [The Repentant Obstinate Man], published in his compilation *Jornadas alegres* (1626).

The narrator of *El obstinado arrepentido* is Doña Luisa, who presents the alleged moral of the tale at its beginning.[15] Although such moral prescription is common to Baroque tales, the narrator offers so many possible moral lessons that in the end it is uncertain which one is really the main object of the fiction, if there is any.[16] The similarities with Núñez de Andrada's anecdote suggest that either Castillo Solórzano is merely expanding it or that both authors are elaborating on the same urban legend. *El obstinado arrepentido* presents Don Alonso, a rich gentleman living in an unnamed Spanish city. Don Diego, one of his six sons, is always brawling, confident that his violent behavior will not jeopardize his social status. After one such quarrel in a gaming house, Don Alonso learns about his son's reckless behavior and summons him for a conversation. Don Alonso confesses to his son that he was also arrogant when he was young, until one day his own father summoned him on a similar occasion and shows him a box: "Conociendo mi padre y vuestro abuelo que eran estas propiedades ocasionadas para algún desdichado suceso, temeroso del peligro . . . me previno un antídoto que, si bien me costó sentimientos, su experiencia me fue el total remedio para mi reformación; de este me tengo de valer ahora para con vos" [My father and your grandfather, knowing that these properties were cause for some unfortunate event, fearing the danger . . . prevented it with an antidote, an experience that, although it caused me lots of pain, was the remedy for my reformation: I have to use it now with you] (*Jornadas alegres*, 196). The "unfortunate event" is that Don Alonso's own grandfather, after killing another gentleman in a duel, fled to England and Germany, where he converted to Protestantism and was subsequently punished by the Inquisition on his return to Spain:

En un acto público salió con otros delincuentes con las insignias que en esta caja veréis. Entonces, abriéndola, sacó de ella un sambenito cruzado con la aspa roja del glorioso apóstol San Andrés. Este—dijo prosiguiendo don Alonso—me mostró mi padre, que ya era nacido cuando el suyo—mi abuelo—delinquió en sus errores. Sabe Dios el sentimiento que tuve cuando le vi ignorando la ignominiosa ofensa que hizo contra su majestad y la obscura mancha que dejó en nuestra sangre. Este desengaño de quien era me templó los bríos, me allanó la soberbia y me hizo humilde, comedido y apacible con todos, conque granjeé tantos amigos que puedo bien decir ha habido muy pocos que en esta dicha me hayan excedido. Sírvaos, hijo, este antídoto para que hagáis lo mismo, considerando que si hasta aquí no os han advertido los que ofendéis de lo que sois, vendrá día en que lo oigáis de alguno y sea causa el vengaros, de que perdáis la vida.

[In a public trial, he appeared with other criminals with the signs that you will see in this box. Then, opening it, he took from the box a sambenito crossed with the red cross of the glorious Apostle Saint Andrew. This, continued Don Alonso, was shown to me by my father, who was already born when his [father] and my grandfather committed his crime: God knows the sorrow that I had when I saw it, not knowing the ignominious offense he committed against his Majesty and the dark stain that he had left on our lineage. This disenchantment about who I was, calmed my temperament, soothed my arrogance and made me humble, cautious and mild-mannered with everybody, with which I cultivated so many friends that I can well say that there have not been many people that have surpassed me in this joy. My son, I hope this works as an antidote so you do the same, considering that, if up until now those offended by you have not warned you yet about who you are, some day you will hear it from someone and you will seek revenge, thus risking your life.] (*Jornadas alegres*, 196)

In Castillo Solórzano's tale, Don Alonso explains that he succeeded socially and economically not despite the sambenito, but precisely because of it, because internalizing the fear of infamy motivates the family to hide its infamous past and avoid all potential occurrences in which dishonor may surface. At the same time, the private showing of the sambenito turns what was initially conceived as a public ceremonial into a family tradition that is passed from fathers to sons and therefore becomes a rite of initiation to adult life.

Even though Don Diego accepts at first his recently discovered identity, he soon returns to his old ways and provokes another altercation. When he finds out that his sister Blanca has run away with Don Fadrique de Ávalos, a noble from a rival family, he heads to the noble's house, where he kills one of his servants. Don Diego then flees the city in search of his sister and Don Fadrique. As is characteristic of the Baroque novella, *El obstinado arrepentido* turns at this point into a byzantine romance of serendipitous adventures, at the end of which Don Diego arrives in Barcelona after being arrested along with some Catalan bandits. The misunderstanding is soon cleared up, and this humiliating experience finally has an impact on Don Diego's attitude and behavior. During his imprisonment, as the title of the novella foresees, Don Diego repents of his worldly life and, after being freed through the intervention of Don Fadrique, enters a religious order, "tomando el santo hábito del glorioso patriarca San Benito en el monasterio de Nuestra Señora de Monserrate, con el cual pensaba acabar sus días en servicio de Nuestro Señor" [putting on the holy garments of the glorious patriarch Saint Benedict, in the monastery of Our Lady of Montserrat, with which he intended to end his days serving our Lord] (*Jornadas alegres*, 221). By expanding the tale, Castillo Solórzano elaborates a religious allegory with an unclear interpretation. As the narrator phrases it, when Don Diego puts on the "el santo hábito del glorioso patriarca San Benito," he seems to literally retrieve the sambenito that his father had shown him at the beginning of the novella as a symbol of religious faith—even if Don Diego's conversion is guided by a false homophony, because the term "sambenito" likely does not have a direct etymological relation with the name, Order of Saint Benedict (San Benito).

Arguably, Castillo Solórzano is able to give a positive moral spin to the appropriation of the sambenito because his expansion of this urban legend recognizes the "crime against Faith" as being the conversion of Don Diego's ancestor to Protestantism. Despite the swift punishment imposed by the Inquisition in the tale, the charge of Protestantism renders more acceptable the moral of the story. The social consequences would have been very different had Don Diego's ancestor been accused of Judaizing or Islamicizing—charges that would have made him a descendant of Jewish *conversos* or Moriscos. Although the Inquisition considered Protestantism a hereditary *raça* that extended to the descendants of those punished in the autos de fe that should therefore be memorialized through the sambenito—and thus would invoke the social discourse of blood purity—Protestantism was quite likely conceived as an individual sin that was not necessarily transmitted through lineage.

All these series of anecdotes—whether real or apocryphal—about individuals keeping or embracing the sambenito are always framed as unthinkable situations. Yet the motif's recurrence suggests a persistent underlying anxiety about the risky value of infamy as interpellation. For some authors, this riskiness threatens the entire system of infamy, whereas for others such appropriation can have an additional formative function beyond public punishment. What the cases analyzed in this section have in common is that they frame appropriations of the sambenito as individualized acts committed by deranged or extravagant persons. Meanwhile, in the case of the Moriscos a similar set of urban legends conceive that their alleged irreverence toward the sambenito is a collective trait that marks them as a separate community.

MORISCOS AND HONOR

The casuistic approach to the appropriation of the sambenito singles out certain groups as if their members were more prone to such behavior than Old Christians, as if they belonged to an incompatible but parallel system of honor and infamy. This biased interpretation is especially prominent regarding the Moriscos: most of the Christian authors dealing with this group point out how honor and social exclusion are essential elements to be addressed when either fostering their assimilation or promoting their expulsion. Muslims under Christian rule, also known as *mudéjares*, had been granted religious freedom during the Middle Ages; however, after the fall of the Nasrid kingdom of Granada in 1492, royal policy soon shifted to promoting cultural and religious homogenization, even in the face of protests by ecclesiastics engaged in conversion efforts. Castilian Muslims were forced to convert to Christianity in 1502 and those in Aragon in 1525. Around the same time, the monarchy passed a series of laws designed to eradicate cultural practices that were thought to be related to Islam. In 1526 Charles V banned Morisco cultural practices, such as the use of certain kinds of garments and the Arabic language, but a forty-year moratorium on its enforcement was granted when the Moriscos agreed to pay a levy. After forty years, Philip II refused to renew the moratorium in 1566, a decision that allegedly led to the uprising of the Alpujarras in 1568. By 1571 the uprising was repressed, and the Moriscos of the kingdom were deported from Granada and dispersed throughout the rest of Castile. Throughout this period, Moriscos were the target of several discriminatory practices; the most onerous measure was the imposition of a tax that treated them as if they were still Muslims living under Christian rule, which contradicted the evangelization theory assuming that they were now Christians, at least nominally.[17] Rising ethnic tensions culminated in 1609 with Philip III's decree ordering the expulsion of all Moriscos from Spain.[18]

Some authors argued that the acculturation and integration of the Moriscos would only be possible if they were granted the same access to the system of honor as Old Christians. Thus, Beltrán de Guevara, in a memorandum sent to Charles V in 1525, complains about not granting the Moriscos the honor that they should receive for converting to Christianity.[19] However, most of the authors state that the responsibility for the lack of assimilation lies with the Morisco community itself. In a 1597 memorandum addressed to Philip II, Martín González de Cellorigo also points out that a substantial factor preventing the assimilation of Moriscos is that they are proud to be considered as such; he therefore asks the king to order "que no se nombren, ni dexen nombrar moriscos" [that they are not called nor that they allow others to call them "Moriscos"].[20] González de Cellorigo suggests that Moriscos who do not react to insult in a normative way should also be subjected to punishment, thus proposing to legally criminalize the

appropriation of insult and revealing that this concern should be addressed in
a juridical manner.

Pedro de Valencia, in his *Tratado acerca de los Moriscos de España* (1606), suggests that insults against converts not only deter Moriscos from converting to
Christianity but also erect ethnic boundaries between both communities:

> No solamente no procuran ni quieren parecer Cristianos, sino que antes de
> propósito, y como cosa de que se precian hacen en todo por distinguirse, y
> apartarse de los antiguos Cristianos en la lengua, en el trage, en las comidas,
> en los casamientos, en el huir de las Yglesias y oficios Divinos, y siendo tan
> grande honrra en España el nombre de Cristiano Viejo ni aún quieren encu-
> brirse, y parecer que lo son. Que es esto sino que tienen por bueno el ser Moros.
> Porque ningún hombre es tan perdido (dice Quintiliano) que se huelgue de
> parecer malo.

> [Not only they do not want or try to look like Christians, but rather they do it
> on purpose, as they have pride in being different in everything, by setting
> themselves apart from Old Christians in language, clothing, food, wedding
> ceremonies, and avoiding churches and mass; and the title of Old Christian
> being such an honor in Spain, they do not even want to cover up what they
> are and to pretend that they are Old Christian. What is this but that they regard
> being Moors as a good thing. Because no man is so wretched, as Quintilian
> says, that he boasts of looking like he is bad.] (76–77)

Thus, in contrast, Valencia argues that the good Moriscos are "los que quieren
encubrir la nota de su linage" [those who want to hide the stain of their lineage]
(*Tratado*, 108). The main issue for him is not lineage itself or even the sincerity
of conversion, but rather providing the favorable conditions for Moriscos to seem
to be Old Christian; thus, he seems to acknowledge that what cements a sense
of collective identity is not an immanent set of religious beliefs but the willingness to agree on a common denominator of public reputation—and therefore on
a common denominator of social exclusion.

Valencia defends the dispersion of the Moriscos throughout Castile so that
they do not form compact communities, because if they keep together,

> tienen por teatro de su honra, y aplauso el corrillo de los de su nación, en él
> quieren parecer bien, y cuidan poco de la buena, o mala estimación con los
> cristianos. Quitados de entre los suyos, y que pierdan de vista la plaza, o teatro,
> donde les era afrenta no parecer Moros, ellos querran parecer cristianos, y en
> honrándose de lo bueno, y queriendo parecerlo, vendrán a serlo de veras den-
> tro de poco tiempo.

> [they have the applause and solidarity of those of their group as a theater of
> their honor, in which they desire to look well, and they do not care, or care

very little, about their reputation among Christians. If they are separated from their own people, losing sight of the public square or theater in which it was not an affront to look like a Muslim, they will desire to look like Christians, and being honored in the good thing, and wanting to look like it, they will truly become one soon.] (119)

Valencia's use of the expression "teatro de su honra" indicates his awareness that honor is a performative and situational concept that could adapt to the dynamics of consensus, much like Cervantes's *El retablo de las maravillas* analyzed in the previous chapter.

Anti-Morisco authors (and especially apologists for the expulsion), when looking for proofs that the Moriscos are not assimilable to Spanish culture, state that they take pride in wearing the sambenito and therefore appropriate signs of infamy to reinforce their own ethnic identity. In a memorandum addressed to Philip II, Francisco de Rivas holds that the main obstacle for their assimilation is that Moriscos lack the same concept of honor as Old Christians.[21] Juan de Pineda states in his *Tercera parte de la Monarchia Ecclesiastica* (1588) that the Moriscos who were punished by the Inquisition gained a higher reputation in their own community.[22] Agustín Salucio's *Discurso sobre los estatutos de limpieza de sangre* (c. 1599) also affirms that part of the assimilation problem is that the Moriscos are proud to be considered such.[23] Even an advocate of the Moriscos like Pedro de Valencia echoes this opinion in his *Tratado acerca de los Moriscos de España* (1606), in which he claims that "de los hábitos e infamias no hacen caso, porque antes causan honra que afrenta en ellos" [they don't care about sambenitos and other forms of infamy, because they cause honor rather than shame among them].[24] Similarly, in a 1606 letter addressed to the Inquisition, the curate of Hornachos accuses the Moriscos of taking pride in wearing the sambenito.[25] Such an opinion is emphasized by apologists for the expulsion such as Jaime Bleda, who in his *Corónica de los moros de España* (1618), observes, "Honrauanse de traer el sambenito, y quando estaua viejo, pedian que se lo diessen nuevo; estauan muy vfanos, quando en los autos de la Fe salian al tablado. Bueltos a sus casas los honrauan los otros Moriscos como nosotros reuerenciamos a los Santos canonizados" [They were proud to wear the sambenito, and when it was old, they asked to receive a new one. They were very happy when they went to the stage in the autos de fe. When they were back home, the other Moriscos honored them like we honor our canonized saints].[26] Finally, Damián Fonseca's *Justa expulsión de los Moriscos de España* (1612) makes a similar claim and adds an anecdote to illustrate it:

El primer indicio ... con que se prueua la Apostasia destos Mahometanos, es ver que no tenian por infames los que el tribunal del Santo Oficio mandaua açotar, degradar, sanbenitar, antes estos eran a los que mas honrauan, y estimauan ... andando los Inquisidores de Valencia echar un Sanbenito a una

Morisca por la obseruancia de la secta de Mahoma, quando se les vestian, rogo
al ministro, que le diesse otro para su hijo, porque padecia mucho frio, most-
rando gozo con aquel habito.

[The first sign . . . proving the apostasy of these Muslims, is that they did not
hold in infamy those who were whipped, degraded, or told to wear the sambenito by the Inquisition. Rather, those were the most honored and held in
high regard among them . . . When the Inquisitors in Valencia were about to
put a sambenito on a Morisca because she was declared a crypto-Muslim, she
begged for a second sambenito for her son, because it was cold, and she looked
like she was happy wearing said garment.][27]

As these passages show, there is an important difference between anecdotes that
circulated about the Moriscos and the similar ones in which Old Christians
embraced the sambenito, which are analyzed in the previous section. For Old
Christians, appropriating the sambenito is always framed either as a form of
individual madness or as a strategic tool for family honor deployed by individuals; when dealing with the Moriscos, it is construed as an essential collective
trait that marks them as a differentiated and resilient community.

This series of anecdotes has been the subject of disparate historiographical
interpretations. On the one hand, Charles Henry Lea interprets them as a bona
fide reflection of Moriscos' resilience.[28] On the other hand, other historians have
questioned the veracity of these tales; for instance, Rafael Carrasco believes that
Moriscos shared with Old Christians similar conceptions of honor and suggests
that their alleged identification with signs of infamy is part of the propaganda
strategy used by the apologists for the expulsion.[29] Both hermeneutical options
are not incompatible: even though Rafael Carrasco is probably right when pointing out the cultural similarities between Moriscos and Old Christians, given
that they likely shared a similar honor code, it is not entirely unthinkable that,
in some specific contexts, Moriscos could identify themselves with certain signs
of infamy as a form of resilience. As I have shown throughout this book, Old
Christians could also resort to identifying with infamous categories for a variety of reasons.[30] Indeed, some inquisitorial cases show that individual Moriscos
did identify with signs of infamy as a source of resilient identity, even if these
testimonies are filtered and should be taken with a grain of salt. Thus, the Morisco
Luis Carrillo is accused in 1576 of trying to convince other Moriscos "que era
un honor lucir hábito y sambenito, ya que era 'galardón de moros'" [that it was
a honor to wear the sambenito, as it was an "emblem of Moors"].[31] What would
be instrumentalized as a form of propaganda by the aforementioned inquisitorial and apologetic sources is not that some Moriscos may resort to this kind of
identity formation but that the stubborn attachment to signs of infamy was construed as if it were a privative trait of the Moriscos as a whole.

As I emphasized in the introduction, this is not a study about the target populations of infamy (nor about the Moriscos in particular) for two reasons. First, the methodological challenges of analyzing such potential identification in the early modern period make it very hard to document, because these cases are more often than not filtered by inquisitorial notaries or by apologists for the expulsion. But the more important reason is that the object of study of this book is the hegemonic social discourse that puts into circulation the signs of infamy and how that very discourse speculates about the effectiveness of the stigma. What interests me here is not so much to establish whether these anecdotes accurately reflect the opinion of certain Morisco communities or whether they distort or even fabricate Morisco voices with propagandistic goals. On the contrary, my focus is on the instrumentalization of those instances in apologetic texts defending their expulsion and what function they serve in how Old Christians imagined their relationship with Moriscos in regard to the honor code.

Determining whether Moriscos had a concept of social honor similar to that of Old Christians is a task fraught with disparate ideological underpinnings and biased comparisons. To begin with, Old Christians were not a homogeneous block of people sharing the same code of honor. Indeed, the proliferation of anecdotes about how the Moriscos react in a nonorthodox way to infamy serves as the foundation on which is built, by contrast, an idealized image of Old Christian society. The alleged lack of honor among the Moriscos serves as the subterfuge that explains the flaws in the mechanics of infamy, thus preventing a truly analytical approach to the logic that such projects of defamation set in motion and avoiding dealing with the traces they leave in hegemonic society. It is precisely such an analytical approach, although coined as literary expression, that we can find in the second part of Cervantes's *Don Quixote*.

Sancho's Sambenito

The debates over the regulatory force of the sambenito resonate in the second part of Cervantes's *Don Quixote*, published in 1615, right when the circulation of anecdotes about Moriscos embracing the sambenito was at its peak. After leaving Barcelona on his way back to his village, Don Quixote and Sancho become for the second time the victims of the Aragonese dukes. At the end of chapter 68, the knight errant and his squire are kidnapped by some men on horseback who throw at them a strange tirade of insults, as analyzed in the introduction.

As the reader soon finds out, they are taken back to the dukes' palace, in which a fake auto de fe has been set up; the knight errant and his squire are brought to a stage illuminated with torches and candles (II:69, 1102–1103).[32] The analogy with the auto de fe becomes clear when one of the dukes' squires puts a sambenito on Sancho:

Salió, en esto, de través un ministro, y llegándose a Sancho, le echó una ropa de bocací negro encima, toda pintada con llamas de fuego, y quitándole la caperuza, le puso en la cabeza una coroza, al modo de las que sacan los peni- tenciados por el Santo Oficio, y díjole al oído que no descosiese los labios, porque le echarían una mordaza, o le quitarían la vida. Mirábase Sancho de arriba abajo, veíase ardiendo en llamas; pero como no le quemaban, no las esti- maba en dos ardites. Quitóse la coroza, viola pintada de diablos, volviósela poner, diciendo entre sí:—Aún bien que ni ellas me abrasan, ni ellos me lle- van. (II: 69, 1103)

[Then a servant appeared from one side of the courtyard, and coming up to Sancho, he swathed him in a robe of black buckram with flames painted all over it, and removing his peasant's hood put in its place a cardboard cone like those worn by people condemned by the Holy Inquisition . . . Sancho looked himself up and down and saw that he was on fire, but since the flames weren't burning him he didn't care a hoot about them. He took off his cardboard cone, saw that it had devils painted on it and put it back on, saying to himself: Just as well the flames aren't hurting me and the devils aren't carting me off.]
(Trans. Rutherford 950)

The careful staging combines the elements of the auto de fe with other carni- valesque features, such as Altisidora's tomb or the ridiculous penance imposed on Sancho. One of the servants, disguised as Rhadamanthus, decrees that, to cure Altisidora, each of the people in the audience should inflict Sancho with "veinte y cuatro mamonas, y doce pellizcos y seis alfilerazos en brazos y lomos" (II: 69, 1105) [twenty-four fine fillips on his nose, twelves pinches on his arms and six pinpricks on his loins] (Trans. Rutherford 951). Strikingly, Sancho com- plains about all these corporal punishments, but does not say a word against hav- ing to wear the sambenito.

Literary criticism has focused on the allusions to the Inquisition and the auto de fe in this passage, which Doris Moreno Martínez labels as "la descripción menos 'ortodoxa' que tenemos de un auto de fe" [the least orthodox description we have of an auto de fe].[33] Cervantes's *Don Quixote* opens and closes with two parodic versions of the auto de fe; in both cases, they are organized by individu- als who lack the authority to stage them. In the episode known as the "donoso escrutinio" at the beginning of the first part, Don Quixote's niece attributes her uncle's madness to his reading his books, and she proposes to burn them in the public square as would be done with heretical literature heretics; her proposal is affirmed by the priest, who suggests "a fee que no se pase el día de mañana sin que dellos no se haga acto público, y sean condenados al fuego" (I:5, 67) [I swear that before another day has passed they'll be put on public trial and condemned to the flames] (Trans. Rutherford 50). This episode has often been interpreted as a parodic auto de fe.[34] Yet, as François Géal points out, the priest and the barber are not real inquisitors, and therefore they arrogate to themselves the authority to judge and redress lapses in orthodoxy.[35] This is an important observation that is often forgotten in the scholarship about this episode, because there is a general tendency to conflate the criticism of those who appropriate the Inquisition's symbols with a criticism of the Inquisition itself. The Inquisition never censured these two parodies of the auto de fe, quite likely because they were perceived as literary divertissements, but also because the object of criticism is not the Inquisition itself (at least not openly), but the abuse that some people made of its symbols.[36] In neither of the two cases would the "penitents" (Don Quixote's books in I:6; Sancho in II:69) be a matter of concern for real inquisitors, who would have punished instead the fake "inquisitors" for arrogating their authority. This is what happened, for instance, in a Mexican inquisitorial process analyzed by Luis Corteguera. In 1578 three forfeited sambenitos were hung in a church in Tecamachalco, accusing the merchant Hernando Rubio Naranjo of being a Jew.[37] In the subsequent trial, the Inquisition was not concerned with Rubio Naranjo's religious beliefs, but with the unlawful appropriation of its symbol of infamy par excellence and with finding the creators of the fake sambenitos so it could swiftly punish them.[38]

Whether we consider the fake auto de fe in *Don Quijote* a mockery of the Inquisition, it does reflect contemporary debates on the efficacy of infamy and more specifically on the cultural fantasy that the sambenito could lose its punitive value. When the mockery is finished, the duchess bids farewell to Sancho by promising him some of the duke's clothing. This scene portrays the act of giving livery to lackeys, although in this case even such an alleged honor is undone with the remark that the given shirts "Si no son todas sanas, a lo menos son todas limpias" (II:69, 1107) [If they are not all undamaged, at least they are all clean] (Trans. Rutherford 953)—which suggests that the shirts were pretty worn out and that the only positive thing that could be said about them was that they were clean. Sancho responds to the dukes' dubious magnanimity with a striking demand:

> Besóle por ello las manos Sancho, con la coroza en la mano y las rodillas en el suelo. Mandó el duque que se la quitasen, y le volviesen la caperuza, y le pusiesen el sayo, y le quitasen la ropa de las llamas. Suplicó Sancho al duque que le dejasen la ropa y mitra, que las quería llevar a su tierra, por señal y memoria de aquel nunca visto suceso. (II:69, 1107)

> [Sancho kissed her hands in gratitude, with his cardboard cone in his hand and his knees on the ground. The Duke ordered the cone to be taken from him and his hood to be returned and his smock to be put back on and the fiery robe taken off. Sancho begged the Duke to be allowed to keep his robe and his mitre, because he wanted to take them back home with him as keepsakes to remind him of that incredible adventure.] (Trans. Rutherford 953–954)

The narrator neither registers the audience's reaction nor mentions the *sambenito* again—until the end of *Don Quixote*, as I later analyze. When faced with such silence, how should we read Sancho's demand for his sambenito in light of the discourse analyzed earlier?

One possible interpretation is that Sancho is simply ignorant of the meaning of the sambenito, which is not as far-fetched as it may seem. Even if we tend to imagine a ubiquitous Inquisition dominating every sphere of early modern Spain, it is quite likely that many rural peasants like Sancho may not have been famil-iar with the autos de fe, which were organized in urban spaces and only infre-quently.[39] I earlier cited the inquisitorial trial in Tecamachalco in 1578 in which several witnesses claim to be ignorant of what a sambenito looks like.[40] Melchor de Santa Cruz's *Floresta española* (1574) recounts the anecdote of a deranged sol-dier who addresses an individual wearing a sambenito as if he were wearing a honorable robe: "Un soldado que se llamaba el capitán Bocanegra y estaba loco dijo a uno que traía un sambenito:—¿Qué servicios hecistes a su Majestad, que os mandó dar esa encomienda?" [A soldier who was called captain Bocanegra and was mad, said to one person wearing a sambenito: What services have you made for his Majesty, that he ordered you to be given this honorary vestment?].[41] As Santa Cruz emphasizes, there is no irony in the soldier's comment: he really thinks that the sambenito is some kind of honorary garment. Yet he frames it as if not knowing what everybody is supposed to know were a form of madness, because the efficacy of infamy is predicated on the widespread awareness of its insulting significance.

In this sense, it is telling that the narrator of *Don Quixote* feels compelled to explain that the cardboard cone named *coroza* is "al modo de las que sacan los penitenciados por el Santo Oficio" (II:69, 1103) [a cardboard cone like those worn by people condemned by the Holy Inquisition] (Trans. Rutherford 950). For any reader well versed in early modern Spanish society, the clothing on which flames are embroidered already makes abundantly clear that what Sancho wears is the kind of cardboard cone worn by those punished by the Inquisition. The fact that the narrator feels the need to explain the purpose of this headdress invites to think that he assumes that some of his readers may not know its meaning; in turn, this forces us to reconsider the traditional image of the Inquisition as an omnipresent institution in early modern Spain, an image that may have been magnified by our own historical conceptions, and to consider that many sectors in society may indeed be unaware of its symbols—or at the very least that Cer-vantes can imagine that not all his readers are aware of the details of the auto de fe ceremony.

Indeed, there is a narratological divergence in the way characters refer to the defaming headdress that indicates a divide between learned and popular per-ceptions of the Inquisition and its symbols. The narrator always refers to this cone-shaped hat with the proper term "coroza" (II:69, 1,103; II:73, 1128). Yet, when Sancho demands the sambenito and the headdress from the duke, the narrator focalizes through the peasant's speech and uses the word *mitra* (miter): "Suplicó Sancho al duque que le dejasen la ropa y mitra, que las quería llevar a su tierra, por señal y memoria de aquel nunca visto suceso" (II: 69, 1107) [Sancho begged the Duke to be allowed to keep his robe and his mitre] (Trans. Rutherford 953). Writing only a few years before the publication of the second part of *Don Quixote*, Sebastián de Covarrubias points out in his *Tesoro* (1611) that the terminological confusion between *coroza* and *mitra* was common during that time. He defines "mitra" as "el ornamento de la cabeça del obispo o arçobispo, insignia pontificial" [the headdress for bishops or archbishops, pontifical sign] and complains about its popular confusion with *coroza*: "Maravillado estoy que algunos hombres graves usen deste nombre mitra por la coroza, siendo cobertura infame y de diferente forma. . . . Pero bien se echa de ver que lo dizen sin malicia" [It surprises me that some serious men use this term mitra instead of coroza, being an infamous headdress and having a different shape. . . . But it is rather evident that they say it with no malice].[42] Arguably, the reason for the confusion is because the coroza and the miter are both elongated headdresses associated with religion. Despite their similarities, their social value could not be more antithetical, the miter being a sign of distinction for ecclesiastical authorities, whereas the coroza is one of the defaming garments imposed by the Inquisition.

It seems clear that there is a distance between the narrator, who always names this headdress "coroza," and Sancho, who uses the incorrect term "mitra"—even if his inaccurate usage reflects a common confusion in his own time. Yet the literal reading of the passage has contaminated the subsequent iconographic tradition of *Don Quixote*, at least initially. The Antwerp edition of *Don Quixote* of 1672–1673 includes an illustration by Frederik Bouttats in which Sancho is depicted wearing a miter instead of the cardboard cone he should be wearing (Fig. 4.3)—a misreading that might be ideologically motivated, because many of these illustrations are produced in the Protestant area, as I further address in the epilogue.[43]

The other interpretation is that Sancho is reclaiming the sambenito out of madness. Yet the line between ignorance, madness, and defiance is rather thin: it affects only the inscrutable intentions of a character who either misinterprets the signs of infamy by attributing them a different meaning or defiantly appropriates its insulting meaning. Yet intentions are not always clear for the external observer. This is why both Alonso de Villegas and Melchor de Santa Cruz define as mad the hypothetical protagonists in their anecdotes about the sambenito, because both the person who boasts about wearing a sambenito and the one who misinterprets it as a sign of distinction are equally disturbing for the proper functioning of infamy in articulating the social fabric. In either case, it

Figure 4.3. Frederik Bouttats, engraving depicting Sancho wearing the sambenito in II:69. In Miguel de Cervantes, *Vida y hechos del ingenioso cavallero Don Quixote de la Mancha.* Antwerp: Jerónimo and Juan Bautista Verdussen, 1672–1673, 607. BNE R/32195. Courtesy of the Biblioteca Nacional de España.

is clear that Sancho's foolishness is not idiosyncratic but rather, when read within the larger context analyzed here, is only one more literary manifestation of a recurrent foolishness in the Spanish imaginary around signs of infamy such as the sambenito, even if it establishes a particular dialogue with said context.

As we have seen, the Moriscos were often accused of not conforming to hegemonic Spanish society with their adoption of the sambenito as a sign of collective identity. Scholars have noted how Cervantes replicates the discourse of the apologists for the expulsion in the case of the Morisco Ricote; this intertextuality also applies to the sambenito episode. There is no mention of the Moriscos during the mocked auto de fe, but the connection with the Moriscos is established when the narrator yields his voice to the original author Cide Hamete Benengeli, right after Sancho demands the sambenito from the dukes: "Y dice más Cide Hamete: que tiene para sí ser tan locos los burladores como los burlados, y que no estaban los duques dos dedos de parecer tontos, pues tanto ahínco ponían en burlarse de dos tontos" (II:70, 1110) [And Cide Hamete says even more: he considers that the perpetrators of the hoax were as mad as the victims, and that the Duke and Duchess, going to such lengths to make fun of two fools, were within a hairsbreadth of looking like fools themselves] (Trans. Rutherford 966). It is striking that Cide Hamete Benengeli, who until then had refrained from openly criticizing his characters, suddenly adopts such a harsh, moralistic tone. His intervention crowns the way this episode turns upside down the logic of previous urban legends about Moriscos identifying with the sambenito. On the one hand, the character who embraces the sambenito by demanding it is Sancho, who has repeatedly identified himself as an Old Christian.[44] On the other hand, the discourse of the Christian moralists' censure of the appropriation of the sambenito is mimicked through the voice of the Morisco Cide Hamete. This chiasmus in the ideologies of representation counteracts the common cultural fantasy that the Moriscos were prone to identify as a group with the sambenito (and therefore, that their concept of honor was different from Old Christians). The entire episode deflects the inherent ethnicization that is implicit in the parallel series of anecdotes about their appropriation of the sambenito setting the Moriscos apart as a separate group by arguing that they did not belong to the community sharing the same concept of honor and shame. What this passage shows is that, quite the contrary, the possibility of failed subjectivation can happen within the Old Christian community as well and therefore it is not a particular trait of the Moriscos.

Sancho's action in this passage is limited to his individual subjectivation vis-à-vis the sambenito. Yet the cultural anxiety about how such cases may affect the whole social fabric and the efficacy of infamy surfaces at the very end of *Don Quixote*, when the text suddenly returns to this garment. As he enters his hometown for the last time, Sancho displays the sambenito again, although this time he puts it on his donkey:

Y es de saber que Sancho Panza había echado sobre el rucio y sobre el lío de
las armas, para que sirviese de repostero, la túnica de bocací pintada de llamas de fuego que le vistieron en el castillo del duque. . . . Acomodóle también
la coroza en la cabeza, que fue la más nueva transformación y adorno con que
se vio jamás jumento en el mundo. (II:73, 1128)

[It should be mentioned that Sancho Panza had draped over his dun and the
bundle of armor, as a kind of sumpter-cloth, the buckram robe with flames
painted all over it that he'd been made to wear in the Duke's castle. . . . And
he'd also put the inquisitional cardboard cone on the donkey's head, the most
original transformation and adornment ever effected on any ass in the world.]
(Trans. Rutherford 972)

William Childers makes an important point when he observes, "In this make-
shift procession, an ass is paraded through the streets dressed as a penitent,
inverting the usual practice of the penitent being paraded *on* the ass."[45] Although
Childers does not fully develop his intuition, he frames it (along with *El retablo
de las maravillas*) within his exploration of "apocalyptic satire," which, as he
notes "denotes a literary practice in which writers run the risk of undermining
their own authority and relinquishing their autonomy, in order to seek that point
of convergence with the vulnerabilities of their audience."[46] Although we read
the concept of apocalyptic satire in different ways, Childers' connection between
the switch of rider and mount and the apocalyptic horizon is formative for my
articulation of the dystopian interpretation of this passage.

The scene quickly moves from the individual to the collective when the narrator focuses on the townspeople's reaction to this figure: "los muchachos, que
son linces no escusados, divisaron la coroza del jumento y acudieron a verle, y
decían unos a otros:—Venid, muchachos, y veréis el asno de Sancho Panza más
galán que Mingo" (II:73, 1128) [the village boys—boys' lynx eyes see everything—
spotted the donkey's headgear and came to stare at it, calling to each other:
"Come here, lads, if you want to see an ass looking as spruce as a sparrow"]
(Trans. Rutherford 972). Sancho's final entrance in their town sets in motion a
thick net of perspectives and points of view. The narrator does not disclose whether
the youngsters recognize the meaning of the sambenito, in which case their use
of "galán" (gallant) would be ironic, or whether they are unaware of the real
meaning of this garment, which is not a far-fetched interpretation, because
they are probably even less aware of urban culture and the ceremony of the auto
de fe than is Sancho.

What happens afterward is a matter of speculation, because there is no further reference to Sancho's sambenito in *Don Quixote*, and Sancho's adventures,
along with those of Don Quixote, come to an end precisely with this final
entrance to their anonymous town. This episode in which the sambenito-clad
donkey is a sign of social climbing suggests the possibility of social and not

merely individual change. This open ending raises the question of what will happen next: Will ignorance about the meaning of the sambenito turn it into a fashion that will be imitated, thus triggering one of those dystopian scenarios imagined by Agustín Salucio and his contemporaries, in which the signs of infamy turn into the sign of social distinction? As happened with *El retablo de las maravillas*, the plot is interrupted right when the signs of infamy begin to take on a life on their own and spread, paradoxically, because of the abuse made of them, either because of the desire to extract economic profit from the anxiety of blood purity (as Chirinos and Chanfalla do in *El retablo de las maravillas*) or because the signs of infamy are being turned into an instrument of frivolous scorn (as the dukes do in the second part of *Don Quixote*).

Whereas Salucio's dystopian horizon was one in which conversos, Moriscos, and descendants of heretics would one day come to be the majority of the population, what we find in this passage of *Don Quixote* is that this process of identification with the signs of infamy is initiated by an Old Christian, while the Morisco author echoes the traditional moralists' defense of the early modern system of honor and infamy. Thus, this passage is an irony of the regulatory fantasies about infamy that circulated in early modern society, as it exposes cultural anxieties about the limits of infamy as a social practice and the persistent intuition that the repressive law carries with it the seeds of both individual and collective resistance to the process of subjectivation. The inversion of the man and his mount in public ceremonies of infamy, already noted by Childers, is central to the literary reconfiguration of cultural dystopias about the appropriation of insults. As the next chapter analyzes, this potential spread of infamy as a locus of collective identity is reinforced in *Don Quixote* in the segment known as "the episode of the braying mayors," which also revolves around the centrality of donkeys for the early modern system of injury and clearly presents a case of collective identification with insult, albeit a very particular one.

CHAPTER 5

"They Did Not Bray in Vain"

HISTORY, INSULT, AND COLLECTIVE IDENTITY

> *llega a dudar el oydo, si es primero el calumniar del Iudio,*
> *que el defender del Catolico*
>
> *[Our ears doubt what is first, whether the Jew's slander,*
> *or the Catholic's defense]*
> —*Pedro de Colindres*

As Charles P. Flynn points out, insults can generate cohesion and solidarity among their recipients, because "insult and ridicule of a deviant group by a dominant culture often has the ironic effect of strengthening the very behavior patterns which the dominant society condemns."[1] Although I agree with Flynn on the effect that insults can have on minority groups, it is also important to realize that hegemonic society may use this strategy for a similar purpose. The previous chapters explored how Spanish society imagines the possible heterodox responses to infamy, yet there is a parallel search for the insult of the Other. That is, hegemonic society not only fantasizes about the effect that the insult may have on its internal Others but it also uses that same mechanism to reinforce social values and thereby strengthen the in-group. At some point it realizes that it may be more effective to search for the insult of the hegemonic group by its Others than to police society by insulting marginalized groups.

Insult is a historiographical tool, in the sense that it generates a sequence of speech acts and reactions that are emplotted in a specific temporal chain. Thus, affronts can be essential elements for tales of ethnogenesis, placing a real or imagined insult as the foundational moment for the creation of a community. In some cases, it is possible to trace the process by which a specific insult has been transformed into the symbol of collective identity; consider the evolution of the figure of the shepherd in the Spanish imaginary between the fifteenth and the seventeenth centuries. In the fifteenth century, the figure of the shepherd was a derogative representation of the rustic commoner; it was used very often as a symbol of an ignorant Old Christian mob against urban *converso* elites. Thus, Lope de Barrientos aims to disparage the anti-Semitic rioters of mid-fifteenth-century Toledo by labeling them "de baja sangre pastoril" [of low shepherd stock/blood].[2] Similarly, the fifteenth-century poet Antón de Montoro responds to the accusation that he is a converso levied by Juan de Valladolid by accusing Juan of being a shepherd: "Pues con vos, don Rabadán, / ninguno non se deporta, / ni a sabios oirán, / que vuestra ciencia de can / ningún discreto conhorta; / que parecéis ovejero / destrozado con afán" [Because with you, Mr. Shepherd, no one can have a good time, nor will listen to any wisdom, because your doggy science consoles no one; since you look like a sheep herdsman, wrecked by effort].[3]

In early Castilian theater, between the end of the fifteenth century and the beginning of the sixteenth, shepherds figure prominently, very often as ignorant commoners who boast of their alleged blood purity that would make them superior to conversos. Interpreting these plays is quite difficult, because many of these playwrights may have been of converso origin themselves: it is not always clear whether the representation of shepherds on stage is intended as praise or a critique of those Old Christians who boasted of their alleged blood purity to promote their own social advancement.[4] Regardless of the intended purpose of each play—whether to mock the pretensions of social mobility of Old Christians or to locate them as the symbolic models of collective identity—both positions identified Old Christians with the figure of the shepherd. As Francisco Márquez Villanueva points out, whereas the theatrical drama of the early sixteenth century tended to cast shepherds and rustic characters in a negative light, they are dignified by the end of Philip II's reign, in parallel with the general imposition of the statutes of blood purity.[5] Although the symbolic dignification of the figure of the shepherd is influenced by the humanist recuperation of biblical and classical sources, its recasting is also the symptom of a larger search for predecessors in which the figure of the shepherd becomes the model of identity in the Spanish imaginary.[6]

The pastoral hierarchy of inclusion and exclusion becomes clear in Juan de Barrionuevo y Moya's Byzantine romance *Primera parte de la soledad entretenida* (1638).[7] Although the Spanish literary imaginary is in general reluctant to acknowledge that ethnoreligious groups other than Christians could also be shepherds, *Soledad entretenida* presents a strange symbolic hierarchy in which Christians are labeled as shepherds, Muslims are categorized as goatherds (a kind of second-rate herdsman in the cultural imaginary), and Jews are totally excluded from this symbolic system. At some point, the protagonist Calisandro encounters the only Jewish character in the entire book, Manases, who addresses Calisandro disrespectfully, "Dime pastor, o salvage" [Tell me, shepherd (or savage)].[8] The Jew Manases stands out in *Soledad entretenida* as the only character to use "shepherd" as an insult, evoking the dialectical confrontation of earlier centuries in which conversos resorted to such terminology to cast Old Christians as rustic people. In the same way that insulters negotiate their position within the community by their speech act (see chapter 1), the attribution of certain insults to some individuals may serve to characterize them as alien to the community. During the rest of his journey to his next adventure, Calisandro entertains himself by intoning all the alleged affronts Jews have committed against Christians.[9]

The compulsive search for the insult of the Other to strengthen Christian identity becomes clear in relation to the imagined figure of the Jew. Jews were often conceived as "los denostadores" (the insulters) in the European Christian imaginary, because they allegedly committed ritual acts that desecrated the symbols of Christianity.[10] Such real or imaginary acts of Jews triggered a ritual manifestation of Catholic identity in response, most usually known as "fiestas de desagravio" (reparation festivals).[11] Collective Christian identity—or at least one of its specific manifestations in early modern Spain—is articulated around that imaginary ritualized insult. The dependence on the potential insult from the Jew becomes evident in those cases in which Old Christians themselves deliberately impersonate the voice of the Jew to spread defaming libels against their own religious symbols, with the intention of galvanizing Christian society's response. The most notorious instance of this dialectical production of identity toward an external, allegedly Jewish insult took place in Granada in 1640. On Holy Thursday, a libel was posted on the door of the city council defaming the Virgin Mary and praising Judaism. In response to the libel, the Inquisition, in collaboration with the city council, published an edict offering a reward for the identification of the perpetrator. Scrutiny fell initially on the usual suspects: foreigners, passerby, and most notably Portuguese immigrants, who were often accused of being crypto-Jews.[12] Simultaneously, the city council and the Church organized a series of magnificent events to revitalize Marian devotion.[13]

On May 22, 1640, the Inquisition of Granada announced that it suspected the hermit Francisco Alejandro of posting the libel.[14] On June 25, a letter sent to Madrid stated that the author of the libel, hermit Fray Francisco Alejandro (aka Francisco de la Cruz), had confessed to his offense. He justified his act because he did it "con intento de que la ciudad acabase la obra del triunfo, y se aumentase la deboçión de la Virgen" [with the intent that the city finalized the works of the (Virgin of the) Triumph, thus increasing the devotion to the Virgin].[15] On July 9, the local inquisitors congratulate themselves about the expedient solution of the case and propose to celebrate an ad hoc *auto de fe*, anticipating that Francisco de la Cruz would undoubtedly be punished in public—although they add that it would be convenient to include other offenders from nearby inquisitorial districts to make the event even more grandiose.[16] Yet it seems that the actual auto de fe was not as spectacular as promised, as one letter succinctly notes how Francisco de la Cruz was reprimanded and condemned to row in the galleys along with five other offenders on January 16, 1641.[17]

Indeed, some consider the punishment that Francisco de la Cruz received to be insufficient. For instance, Francisco Guillén del Águila writes a pamphlet questioning the Inquisition's punishment and arguing that the hermit should have been sentenced to death as an apostate.[18] Guillén del Águila conceals Francisco de la Cruz's intention behind his thick forest of erudite references, and he only alludes in passing to madness being the extenuating circumstance that the Inquisition may have considered to spare his life.[19] But the hermit's madness is a very particular one, because it is deeply entangled with the very defense of Catholic identity shared by Guillén del Águila. Francisco de la Cruz's madness consists in reactivating the insult from the Other that is implicit in a certain defensive sense of collective identity—so that, if the expected insult does not arrive, then someone needs to fulfill its social function by impersonating it. It is clear why Guillén del Águila cannot address this important point, because doing so would render nonsensical all the ensuing celebrations in defense of the Virgin's honor, which was precisely the effect sought by Francisco de la Cruz. His decontextualization thus circumvents the issue that in this case the collective response to insult is a self-sufficient communication system in which the offender and the recipients belong to the same community.[20] In the absence of injurers, the community supplies their absent communicative function by impersonation, which ultimately reveals that the feeling of injury precedes the injurious word itself.[21]

Despite Guillén del Águila's concealment of Francisco de la Cruz's intention, his is the only printed treatise to reveal the real identity of the perpetrator, which is omitted from all subsequent accounts.[22] For instance, Luis de Paracuellos Cabeza de Vaca's *Triunfales celebraciones* (1640), which describes the reparation celebrations and compiles several literary compositions written in honor of the Virgin for that occasion, ends his work with the Inquisition's detention of the perpetrator but neither names him nor points out that he was a hermit of the same sanctuary of La Victoria, vaguely referring to him instead as "el miserable, que ciega, barbara, sacrilega, y hereticamente puso los carteles contra la Pureza de Maria Santissima" [the wretched man who in a way so blind, barbaric, sacrilegious, and heretic, posted the libel against the Purity of blessed Mary] and as "el autor" [the author].[23] Indeed, Paracuellos reproduces in *Triunfales celebraciones* texts condemning Jews, many of which were written before the identity of the perpetrator was revealed; for example, Álvaro Cubillo de Aragón's short play *El hereje*, which identifies the Jews as authors of the libel, and a poem by Gregorio Martínez de Bustos addressing the author as "Tu del impio libelo / nefando autor, aborto de la tierra / ... bibora te alimenta, / engendrada del impio Iudaismo" [You, the nefarious author of the impious libel . . . you are fed by a viper conceived by impious Judaism].[24] Paracuellos's compilation—which combines vagueness regarding the authorship of the libel with the reproduction of anti-Semitic texts written as part of the initial reactions to the libel—conveys the impression that Jews were still thought to be responsible for the sacrilege.

Many pamphlets describe the fiestas de desagravio celebrated in several cities in Andalusia. For instance, Francisco Jiménez de Santiago's *Desagravios a la virginidad en el parto de María Santíssima* (1640) transcribes a sermon delivered in Écija claiming that "agraviar los judios la lei, y a Christo, es proprio de su nacion" [Jews' insult of our religion and Christ is proper of their lineage].[25] Cipriano de Santa María's *Sermón predicado en el primer día del Octavario* (1640) transcribes a sermon delivered in Jerez de la Frontera with a similar message.[26] These pamphlets still reproduce the anti-Semitic discourse because they were issued before the news of the identity of the libel's author reached areas of Spain outside of Granada.

The most striking case of denial is that of the inquisitor Gabriel Rodríguez de Escavias's pamphlet *Exhortación al herege* (1640), which is written as a letter addressed to the hypothetical author, who is assumed to be a Jew: "Bien das a entender en los errores que publicaste que eres Hebreo, de aquel pueblo tan querido un tiempo de Dios, como aora aborrecido (estado sumamente miserable) porque vuestra ceguedad es mayor que puede ponderarse" [You well revealed in the errors that you published that you are a Hebrew, from that people once so loved by God as it is now abhorred (such a miserable state) because your blindness is beyond belief].[27] Rodríguez de Escavias's pamphlet was certainly composed before the author was identified, when rumors spread that the person was a member of the converso community. However, the license to print the work is signed by Dr. Vela de Sayoane on July 6, 1640, several weeks after the real authorship was revealed and the rumors about its Jewish origin were proven to be unfounded. Rodríguez de Escavias did not correct or at least amend his pamphlet with that piece of information, which he had to know as an inquisitor from Granada. The absence of any mention that the perpetrator was not Jewish is symptomatic of a larger state of denial.

Pedro de Colindres's *Triumpho de Christo y María* (1641) is presented as a sermon delivered in Jerez de la Frontera, yet it is unlikely that the more than one hundred folios finally published could have been a transcription of the original sermon, which was undoubtedly revised and expanded for publication many months after the authorship of the libel was revealed. Yet he still claims that the authors of the libel were Jews. Certainly, Colindres could be consciously hiding the discovery about the real authorship; yet the fact that—one year after the truth was revealed and the author was punished in an auto de fe—Colindres could publish his treatise maintaining the initial accusation of Jews shows that this piece of information had either not been widely disseminated or it reflected public opinion then.

Colindres's theological ruminations, however, gesture to the theoretical frame used in this book, when he observes that the dissemination of the news of the offenses against the Virgin was followed so quickly by praises of her that "llega a dudar el oydo, si es primero el calumniar del Iudio, que el defender del Catolico" [our ears doubt what is first, whether the Jew's slander, or the Catholic's defense].[28] Departing from the usual paradox that demonstrations against the insult actually serve to disseminate it, he develops a convoluted theological explanation about the timing of the insult and the reaction against it.[29] Although Colindres does not frame it this way, he is haunted by the intuition that insult, real or otherwise, is constitutive of the formation of collective identity, to such a degree that it can actually precede the formation of such identity.

Pulido Serrano suggests that pamphlets disseminated about the blasphemous libel deliberately ignored the discovery of the author being an Old Christian as a strategy to revitalize and spread anti-Semitic discourses.[30] Although I agree with his interpretation, I argue that such a strategy is not merely another manifestation of hatred of Jews but is also an illustrative instance of how the insistence on an insulting Other grants a sense of ontological being to the amorphous nature of religious identity. These cases show that, fanciful as any cultural archaeology of insults can be, it constitutes a narrative instance that generates a sequence of actions and reactions that emplot injuries into a historical narrative of the collective identity.[31] As Judith Butler observes, insults express a "condensed historicity" that "exceeds itself in past and future directions, an effect of prior and future invocations that constitute and escape the instance of utterance."[32] Thus, they establish a complex dialectics according to which the opposition between several stigmatized categories transforms a previous insult into the source of collective identity. Such a relational and situational approach to the foundational value that insults may have for community formation is clearly found in Cervantes's *Don Quixote* in the passage known as the episode of the braying mayors.

"They Did Not Bray in Vain": Foundational Insult as Taboo

When dealing with Cervantes's treatment of blood purity and ethnocentrism, scholarship has privileged the critique of blood purity found in his play *El retablo de las maravillas*, as well as the seemingly parodic reproduction of anti-Morisco propaganda in the representation of Moriscos in *Don Quixote* and the *Persiles*. Yet, the episode that most clearly explores the complex and at times paradoxical dynamics of insult and infamy as mechanisms of social cohesion—excluding some persons while building communities for others—is that of the braying mayors, which extends between chapters 24 and 27 of the second part of *Don Quixote*.[33]

The plot begins in chapter 24, when the two protagonists meet a man transporting some weapons. Don Quixote is curious about what promises to be a new adventure, so when the three characters arrive at an inn, the man tells them the reason for the weapons. He recounts a story in which two councilmen of his own town (whose real name is never revealed) try to recover a lost donkey. Each councilman goes along a different path to the nearby mountain while braying like a donkey to attract the animal. However, each time one of them brays, the other councilman approaches thinking that he is the lost donkey, and vice versa. After several attempts, in which the councilmen invariably confuse each other with the donkey, they finally find out that the actual donkey is dead, having been eaten by wolves (II:25, 769–771). Despite the tragic end of the animal they are looking for, the situation benefits the councilmen by enabling each to discover his ability to bray. Thus, the owner of the donkey praises his colleague by comparing him to an ass: "Ahora digo ... que de vos a un asno, compadre, no hay ninguna diferencia, en cuanto toca al rebuznar; porque en mi vida he visto ni oído cosa más propia" (II:25. 770) [I do declare ... that between you and a donkey, neighbor, there's no difference at all, as far as braying's concerned, because I've never in my life seen or heard anything more convincing] (Trans. Rutherford 655). And the other councilman replies to the accolades in kind:

> Por el Dios que me crió que podéis dar dos rebuznos de ventaja al mayor y más perito rebuznador del mundo; porque el sonido que tenéis es alto; lo sostenido de la voz, a su tiempo y compas; los dejos, muchos y apresurados, y en resolución, yo me doy por vencido y os rindo la palma y doy la bandera desta rara habilidad. (II:25; 770)

> [By the God who made me, you could give two brays' start to the best and most expert brayer in the world: the sound you produce is properly high-pitched, and you sustain the phrase with the correct tempo and rhythm, and the cadenza is fast and beautifully ornamented, and, all in all, I admit defeat, salute you and hand you the palm for this extraordinary achievement.] (Trans. Rutherford 656)

The comicality of the passage lies in both councilmen exchanging praises about their ability to bray like a donkey, using language that in any other context would constitute intolerable insults and would likely trigger a violent response. The entire scene is thus analogous to the episode in which Tomé Cecial praises Sancho's daughter with the expression "hideputa," as analyzed in chapter 1, which debated whether this expression should be understood either as a compliment or an offense depending on the context.

Yet, as the man telling this story to Don Quixote and Sancho points out, when the anecdote is retold in nearby towns, the tone of camaraderie is lost. Instead, neighbors emphasize the grotesque element and mock the inhabitants of the councilmen's town by braying at them:

> Y el diablo, que no duerme, como es amigo de sembrar y derramar rencillas y discordia por doquiera, levantando caramillos en el viento y grandes quimeras

de no nada, ordenó e hizo que las gentes de los otros pueblos, en viendo a
alguno de nuestra aldea, rebuznase, como dándoles en rostro con el rebuzno
de nuestros regidores. Dieron en ello los muchachos, que fue dar en manos
y en bocas de todos los demonios del infierno, y fue cundiendo el rebuzno de
en uno en otro pueblo, de manera que son conocidos los naturales del pueblo
del rebuzno como son conocidos y diferenciados los negros de los blancos.
(II:25, 771)

[And the devil, who never sleeps, and loves sowing discord and spreading
resentment, building squabbles in the wind and fabricating fights out of nothing, arranged for the people from other villages to bray as soon as they saw
anyone from our village, taunting us with the braying of our councillors And
then all the young boys took it up, which was as if the mouths of all the devils
in hell had taken it up, and the braying spread and spread from one village to
the next, so that by now the people from the village of the bray are as well
known and as set apart as blacks are from whites.] (Trans. Rutherford 657)

The carrier of the weapons concludes his story by explaining that this is the reason why the people from the braying town are at war with their neighbors. His
tale foregrounds some of the paradoxes that will be subsequently woven around
how insults work as a tool for collective identity.

The first paradox is one of narratological focus. The person disseminating
both the original anecdote and how it is being used to defame the inhabitants of
the braying town is a citizen of that town; yet he ought to be the one most inter-
ested in silencing the ignominious tale, based on his fellow townspeople's aggressive reaction against their neighbors. The reader, just like Don Quixote and
Sancho, learns about this story through the perspective of the man carrying the
weapons, who refers to the town not by its real place name, which is never
revealed, but precisely by the shameful name uttered to its residents: he repeatedly refers to its inhabitants as "los naturales del pueblo del rebuzno" [the natives
of the braying town] and "los de mi pueblo, que son los del rebuzno" (II:25; 771)
[the men of my village, the village of the bray] (Trans. Rutherford 657). That is,
the person who is in charge of buying and carrying the weapons to defend the
village's honor to fight against anyone who dares to remind them of the two
councilmen's story is the same person who disseminates the dishonorable story
and refers to his own village using derogatory terms.

In addition, this man explicitly compares this case with other instances of
social exclusion: "Son conocidos los naturales del pueblo del rebuzno como son
conocidos y diferenciados los negros de los blancos" (II:25, 771) [The people from
the village of the bray are as well known and as set apart as blacks are from
whites] (Trans. Rutherford 657). One wonders how the comparison is appropriate and what makes the difference between the inhabitants of the braying town
and of other towns as sizable as the difference between Blacks and whites. The

comparison seems to question the naturalization of racial difference, intuitively framing that even physiological differences between human beings are socially meaningful only when framed in a hierarchical construction of collective difference. Thus, what seemed to be a farcical tale about two people feeling pride in braying, while their fellow residents are offended when somebody brays at them, is connected to actual practices of social exclusion.[34] The question then becomes a thorny one, because it forces us to wonder what it is that exactly differentiates the inhabitants of the braying town from their neighbors. Paradoxically, as we can infer from the tale, the inhabitants of the braying town are different from those of other towns because they are precisely the ones who do not bray—or, rather, because they no longer bray.[35] On the contrary, it is the inhabitants of the nearby towns who bray constantly, as a form of mockery. The difference between this insult and the other examples analyzed in this book is that the act that is considered defaming is only practiced by the vituperators, whereas those stigmatized by it have banished that act from their community—at the same time that they use that foundational act as the source of collective identity, as the man carrying the weapons indirectly reveals and as the two protagonists will discover again a few pages later.

The story is paused when the man carrying the weapons goes on his way and leaves Don Quixote and Sancho at the inn. Two chapters and a few days later, the incongruent identity formation of the braying town reappears in the text, as Don Quixote hears the clamor of an army on the other side of a hill. When he gets closer to the source of the noise, the first thing he sees is their emblems:

> Acercóse al escuadrón, tanto, que distintamente vio las banderas, juzgó de las colores y notó las empresas que traían, especialmente una que en un estandarte o jirón de raso blanco venía, en el cual estaba pintado muy al vivo un asno como un pequeño sardesco, la cabeza levantada, la boca abierta y la lengua de fuera, en acto y postura como si estuviera rebuznando; alrededor dél estaban escritos en letras grandes estos dos versos:
> No rebuznaron en balde
> el uno y el otro alcalde. (II:27; 790)

> [He . . . approached the squadron until he could pick out the flags, distinguish the colours and read the mottoes on them, especially one on a standard or pennant of white satin, with a very realistic depiction of a small donkey with its head up, its mouth open and its tongue out, in a braying position, and round it were written these two lines in large letters:
> Our mayors twain
> Brayed not in vain.] (Trans. Rutherford 673)

As Don Quixote immediately realizes, the army belongs to the town of the bray. The encounter provides the visual evidence confirming that "los naturales del pueblo del rebuzno" are the ones who publicize the insult that motivates the military action against the neighboring towns.[36]

This episode, although relatively overlooked by the scholarly literature on *Don Quixote*, seemed to have received more attention in earlier periods, as shown in the illustration in the 1673 Antwerp edition (Fig. 5.1), which was republished in subsequent editions. By the end of the eighteenth century, there were several Spanish engravings, all of them highlighting the flag's motto (Fig. 5.2). The proliferation of iconographic renditions of this episode in the early modern period and the Enlightenment shows that it was granted more significance in the past; likely it was relegated to oblivion as inconsequential by the Romantic readings of *Don Quixote*.

When Don Quixote meets the army of the braying town, he tries to reason with them, making a speech that, even as it mistakes the true cause of the conflict, reveals a concern for the proper working of infamy:

> Hallo, según las leyes del duelo, que estáis engañados en teneros por afrentados, porque ningún particular puede afrentar a un pueblo entero . . . Siendo, pues . . . , que uno solo no puede afrentar a reino, provincia, ciudad, república ni pueblo entero, queda en limpio que no hay para qué salir a la venganza del reto de la tal afrenta, pues no lo es; porque ¡bueno sería que se matasen a cada paso los del pueblo de la Reloja con quien se lo llama, ni los cazoleros, berenjeneros, ballenatos, jaboneros, ni los de otros nombres y apellidos que andan por ahí en boca de los muchachos y de gente de poco más a menos! ¡Bueno sería, por cierto, que todos estos insignes pueblos se corriesen y vengasen, y anduviesen contino hechas las espadas sacabuches a cualquier pendencia, por pequeña que fuese! (II:27, 792)

> [I find that, according to the laws of combat, you are mistaken to consider yourselves dishonoured, for no individual can dishonor a whole community. . . . Since it is the case, then, that no one person can dishonor a whole kingdom, province, city, town or village, it is clear that there is no requirement to take up the challenge for such affront, because it is no affront at all; it would be a fine affair if the people of the town of the lady clock were fighting to the death at every turn with those who call them that, and the same goes for the stewpots, the eggplanters, the whale-calves, the soapies and others with nicknames constantly in the mouths of young boys and sundry other riff-raff.] (Trans. Rutherford 674–675)

As many scholars have pointed out, Don Quixote alludes here to what is usually known as "blasones populares" (popular blazons), the insults with which several towns are known in their surrounding area.[37] The case of the insult "berenjenero" (eggplant eaters) directed at the inhabitants of Toledo is especially pertinent for this episode in *Don Quixote* and could well constitute one of its

Figure 5.1. Frederik Bouttats, engraving depicting the episode of the braying mayors in II:27. In Miguel de Cervantes, *Vida y hechos del ingenioso cavallero Don Quixote de la Mancha*. Antwerp: Jerónimo and Juan Bautista Verdussen, 1672–1673, 243. BNE R/32195. Courtesy of the Biblioteca Nacional de España.

Figure 5.2. Francisco de Goya, *Braying Adventure* (c. 1778). Biblioteca Nacional de España.

direct sources of inspiration. In 1480, within the context of a discussion about
the preeminence of each city in the parliament of Castile, the representatives of
León ironically agreed to recognize the ambitions of Toledo, but only if Toledo
put an image of an eggplant on its flag, thus accepting the well-known insult of
their being eggplant eaters—which implied an accusation of their being recent
converts from Judaism, because eggplant eating was commonly associated with
the refusal to eat pork.[38]

Don Quixote questions the alleged affront based on a combination of chival-
ric principles and aristocratic discourses, according to which only noble individuals have honor and can find themselves in the situation of defending it,
whereas other groups, such as peasants, lack the subjective formation needed to
even be insulted. Of course, any reader immediately realizes that Don Quixote's
theoretical questioning of the insult is irrelevant in practice, because it is indeed
quite common for one individual to address an insult toward an entire community. This would thus be another instance of the chasm between Don Quixote's
theoretical knowledge and the actual social practice of how insults work.[39]

Despite its disconnection from reality, Don Quixote's speech has a momentary soothing effect on its audience, as the town dwellers listen to his words. Yet
Sancho, while trying to fraternize with the town dwellers, intervenes to claim
that braying should not be taken as an offense; he demonstrates it by braying
"tan reciamente, que todos los cercanos valles retumbaron" (II:27, 794) [with such
power that all the nearby valleys resounded] (Trans. Rutherford 676). The townspeople logically (at least within their own logic, which should have been quite
evident to the protagonists by then) interpret that Sancho is mocking them and
unleash their violence on Don Quixote and his squire by throwing stones at
them.

Although in earlier chapters we analyzed many cases of people accepting the
insults hurled at them, both in Spanish society of the time and in Don Quixote,
this case is strikingly different and more complex. The salient element in this
passage is not that "los naturales del pueblo del rebuzno" identify with the insult
raised at them but rather their schizophrenic response: they adopt simultaneously the two possible reactions to insults by responding with the utmost
violence against the alleged offense while appropriating and displaying that insult
as a way to cement their collective identity. These reactions seem to be, in principle, mutually incompatible and contradictory. Yet, as Eribon suggests about the
gamut of possible responses to insult, "Identification and disidentification can
be simultaneous."[40]

Sancho, like Don Quixote, is unable to decipher the strange dynamics of subjective formation operating in the signs of infamy occurring in this town. The
squire tries to establish some sense of solidarity with the inhabitants of the braying town by stating that he is also a good brayer and pointing out that imitating
the sound of a donkey should be considered not an affront but rather a way to

identify with the *regidores* in the foundational anecdote. What is hard to understand for Sancho (and for the readers) is that the inhabitants from the braying town do not identify with braying as a cultural practice. In fact, as we can infer, they no longer bray, because braying for them has been stigmatized as an unacceptable social act and its utterance can only trigger affront and subsequent violence. But at the same time, the braying of the *regidores* in the past constitutes the source of collective identity, as shown by the inhabitants' reference to themselves as "el pueblo del rebuzno" and their displaying a braying donkey on their flag. It is therefore a foundational braying, sacralized through interdiction and iterative transgression. Thus, the same act is simultaneously perceived as an insult in the present but as the origin and source of collective identity from the past.

We may be tempted to analyze the interdiction to bray through Freud's classic definition of taboo. Yet, the most salient feature of taboo is that the origin of the interdiction is unknown to the actors, whereas in this case, its source is blatantly acknowledged, disseminated, and displayed by them. For a taboo to be a taboo, the object has to be repressed, and the repression has to provoke a displacement in the chain of the signifier.[41] The braying is certainly repressed because, as Freud describes taboo in a different context, the real desire "lies in the risk of imitation, which would quickly lead to the dissolution of the community. If the violation were not avenged by the other members, they would become aware that they wanted to act in the same way as the transgressor."[42] This community reacts with the most extreme violence to the act of braying; the repression of the desire to bray, we should assume, is most rigorously applied to themselves, even to the mythical councilmen who once brayed in the woods and gave their current sense of collective identity to the town. These two persons are memorialized in both the story that the inhabitants disseminate and in the flag that the army carries, but they are nowhere to be seen and their titles have been transformed from *regidores* (councilmen) to *alcaldes* (sheriffs). In addition, the accuracy of the motto that "they did not bray in vain" is quite doubtful. The original purpose of the braying of the two councilmen was to find a lost donkey. Because the animal turned out to be dead, these two men did indeed bray in vain. All these modifications indicate that the historical memory of such foundational act is still in the process of being rewritten.[43] The way in which the act of braying is displayed so conspicuously probably suggests that the repressed can be concealed by placing it in plain sight.

Thus, the ultimate paradox of the town of the bray is that its people display two simultaneous but incompatible reactions against injurious interpellation. It is not a normative response to the honor code, because the inhabitants of the town of the bray place the insult at the iconographic and discursive center of collective identity—but neither is it an apocalyptic reverse (the kinds of dystopias of infamy deployed by Salucio) because these people defend their collective reputation against that very same insult, which is felt as an affront. Cervantes elaborates on previous fictions about the reversibility of infamy to craft a new model explaining the way that social dynamics work; it brings to the surface the underlying repressed logic, which is that insults can work not only to destroy social identity or to construct it but also that sometimes they perform both processes simultaneously.

As Marta Madero points out, scenes of reparation for injury are inherently theatrical, because they depend on the presence on a third gaze, in addition to those of the perpetrator and the injured.[44] In the story of the town of the bray, however, the alleged injurers are notoriously absent. The story is first known to the reader (as well as to Don Quixote and Sancho as the audience in the inn) through the man who carried the weapons, and second in the encounter with the army from the town of the bray. Yet, the injurers never show up for battle and are nowhere to be seen. The man carrying the weapons takes for granted that the anecdote of the braying councilmen is famous, yet nobody in the inn comments on the story or tries to bray when he tells it, nor is there any kind of corroboration from any other character outside the town. This absence of the injurer conveys a certain impression of loneliness and solipsistic communication, in which the town of the bray stages the collective affront on an empty stage, in a pathological ritualization of an insult that one may wonder whether it ever took place—like the reparation festivals analyzed earlier.

After Sancho and Don Quixote leave the scene, the omniscient narrator adds a comment about what happened on the battlefield: "Los del escuadrón se estuvieron allí hasta la noche, y por no haber salido a batalla sus contrarios, se volvieron a su pueblo, regocijados y alegres, y si ellos supieran la costumbre antigua de los griegos, levantaran en aquel lugar y sitio un trofeo" (II:27, 794–795) [The men in the squadron stayed where they were until nightfall when, their enemies not having come to do battle, they returned to their village, full of joy and good cheer, and if they'd known about the custom of the ancient Greeks they'd have raised a trophy on the spot] (Trans. Rutherford 676). The narratological comment reinforces the absence of interlocutors in this self-sufficient injurious communication: not only do those allegedly insulting this town never show up but also Sancho and Don Quixote have disappeared from the scene. Instead, the narrator mentions an additional hypothetical site of memory, the potential erection of a monument that is not described but that, based on the flag displayed by the army, the reader can easily imagine as a braying ass memorializing the foundational insult.

Although there is no further mention of the braying town in the second part of *Don Quixote*, it certainly has an impact on the way Sancho conceives of insults. It is right after the encounter with the brayers' town that the identification between Sancho and his ass intensifies in the text, as has been abundantly studied.[45] And it is right after the beating by the dwellers of the braying town that

Sancho again questions his chances of social climbing in the company of Don
Quixote, who responds by calling him an ass:

> ¿Ahora te vas, cuando yo venía con intención firme y valedera de hacerte señor
> de la mejor ínsula del mundo? En fin, como tú has dicho otras veces, no es la
> miel . . . , etcétera. Asno eres, y asno has de ser, y en asno has de parar cuando
> se te acabe el curso de la vida; que para mí tengo que antes llegará ella a su
> último término que tú caigas y des en la cuenta de que eres bestia. (II:28, 799)

> [You leave me now, just when I had reached the firm and resolute decision to
> make you the lord of the best island in the world? Well, after all, as you have
> so often said yourself, honey was not made . . . (for the mouths of asses). An
> ass you are, an ass you will remain and an ass you will still be when you end
> your days on this earth, and it is my belief that when you come to breathe your
> last you still will not have grasped the fact that you are an animal.] (Trans.
> Rutherford 680)[46]

Ironically, Don Quixote attacks Sancho by spouting a proverb (a linguistic device-
for which Don Quixote often criticizes Sancho), which reflects Sancho's influence
over his master. Don Quixote leaves unfinished the proverb, "no es la miel . . .
[para la boca del asno]," which indicates that he is at first reluctant to apply the
word "asno" (ass) to his squire. Yet, his initial caution turns immediately into a
heated tirade that expands on the animalizing term. Faced with such interpellation, Sancho responds by assuming the insult raised by Don Quixote: "Señor mío,
yo confieso que para ser del todo asno no me falta más de la cola; si vuestra merced
quiere ponérmela, yo la daré por bien puesta, y le serviré como jumento todos los
días que me quedan de mi vida" (II:28. 799) [Oh sir, I confess that all I need to be a
complete ass is the tail, and if you want to hang one on me to my mind I've deserved
it, and I'll serve you as a donkey for all the rest of my life] (Trans. Rutherford 681).
Certainly, this is a normative, less polemical instance regarding the assumption of
insults, because Sancho accepts the insult mainly due to the hierarchical structure
of power between him and his master. Given that this exchange follows immediately the episode of the brayers' town, it serves as its contrast: here, the assumption
of the insult is a way to avoid conflict for Sancho, whereas in the case of the braying
town, the insult's assumption was extremely belligerent.

But this assumption of the animalizing insult of the ass, although normative
in principle, triggers a curious displacement in the chain of signification, which,
as we have seen, is the main characteristic of taboo.[47] A few chapters later, in their
first encounter with the dukes in Aragon, there is an allusion to Sancho's peculiar linguistic habit of calling his ass by the word "rucio" (dun). When Sancho
asks the duchess to take care of his "dun" (rucio), she wonders what animal he
is referring to: "¿Qué rucio es este?" (II:33, 841) [What dun is this?] (Trans.
Rutherford 718). To which Sancho replies, clarifying that he has decided to use

that term to refer to his ass: "Mi asno . . . , que por no nombrarle con este nombre, le suelo llamar el rucio" (II:33, 841) [My ass . . . , and so as not to call it by a
nasty name like that I call it my dun] (Trans. Rutherford 719). We therefore witness a displacement in the chain of the signifier in Sancho's idiosyncratic speech,
which affects the entire semantic system of insults articulated around the ass.
At first, Sancho accepts with a resignation suffused with pride all the times
that Don Quixote calls him an ass. But while accepting said ass identity, he indirectly recognizes that "ass" is indeed an insult, to which he responds not by
defending himself but his own mount. This is a chiasmus of the traditional subjectivation toward the injurious word, because Sancho does not respond to
insult when he should normatively do (as when he is addressed as an "ass" by
his master), while offering a serendipitous, euphemistic response to insult when
it is not normatively necessary, given that the term "asno" applied to the animal
has a purely referential value.

Michèle Guillemont and Marie-Blanche Requejo Carrión describe the ubiquity of the donkey in Cervantes's work as forming a semantic field that they term
"asinine space."[48] The creation of this asinine semantic space becomes the master signifier around which Cervantes rearticulates the mechanics of insult. Sancho accepts the insult "ass" but consequently coins a euphemism to designate
his mount; yet he puts the sambenito and the coroza on his mount when he enters
the town, believing (or pretending to believe) that the sambenito is a luxurious
garment (as analyzed in chapter 4), thus transposing his "honorific garment" to
his donkey. Just as the term "ass" migrates from animals to men, so the sambenito is transformed from a sign of infamy into a sign of distinction and migrates
from the man to the animal. If we focus on the final entrance through Sancho,
we witness the completion of the displacement in the chain of the signifiers: we
see a dignified "rucio" wearing a dignified sambenito, carried by a man who
accepts being an "ass" and thinks that calling his daughter "hideputa" could
indeed be a compliment. Given that such a resignification of infamy is done by
a villager who boasts of being Old Christian (and who also boasts of insulting
Jews but never actually insults them), it is clear that Cervantes is using him as a
combinatoric in which to explore all the possible transformations and resignifi-
cations that could take place in the Spanish imaginary of infamy.

Although all these instances between Sancho and his donkey carefully explore
how insults affect signifying systems for their individual recipients, they also
serve as the basis for the exploration of collective identification with insults. Such
displacement in the signifying chain articulated around the word "ass" crystallizes in the text precisely when Sancho and Don Quixote encounter the town of
the bray, which indicates that the episode has left a mark on Sancho. This is quite
probably because the story of the braying town encapsulates all the paradoxes
and inconsistencies of how insults can inform collective identity and become the
kernel of potential futurities of social reversal.

Epilogue

SPANISH HISTORY AS *SAMBENITO*

La Inquisición, que tantos sambenitos colgó en las iglesias, nos ha colgado un sambenito a toda la nación.

[*The Inquisition, which hung so many sambenitos on churches' walls, has hung a sambenito on the entire nation.*]
                                                                    —Antonio Domínguez Ortiz, "*Entrevista*" 337

When exploring the use of the sambenito (most notably in chapter 4), I have focused on how the practice of hanging those garments in local churches served in early modern Spain to defame both the punished individuals and their descendants, thereby generating a series of cultural fantasies in hegemonic society about how people could contest infamy by appropriating it. In the process, this practice affected the entire community in which the sambenitos were displayed. Indeed, town councils often requested to have the sambenitos removed because their exhibition tarnished their local reputation. For instance, in 1582, after the Inquisition of Granada moved the sambenitos to the Royal Chapel in the cathedral to increase the visibility of its disciplinary actions, their placement in such a central space provoked the vehement opposition of Archbishop Pedro Guerrero and the church leaders of Granada: they felt that the Royal Chapel location memorialized an extinct Islamic past and therefore undermined their efforts to refigure Granada as an eminently Christian city. The sambenitos, however, were not moved to the church of Santiago until 1611, and even in their new, more discreet location they were still causing friction between the church of Granada and the Inquisition as late as 1639.[1] As Cécile d'Albis points out, the Inquisition's insistence on displaying the sambenitos, even though Moriscos had been deported from Granada years earlier in 1570, implied that the entire population of the city was guilty for the sins of the former Morisco inhabitants.[2] Similarly, in 1642, the council of Elorrio (Biscay) requested that the Inquisition remove the only sambenito on its church's walls because its presence diminished the reputation of the entire town.[3] Francisco Bethencourt, when comparing the inquisitorial management of infamy with similar historical practices, points out that one of the Inquisition's unique features was its interest in perpetuating the memory of the defamed as a sort of trophy that justified its mission.[4] This conception of the sambenitos as trophies collided not only with those punished with it (and their descendants) but also with the image that the local community sought to construct about itself.

These arguments about the tarnishing effects on the entire community of applying social exclusion so excessively were used not only to address specific cases; they were often part of more general debates about reforming the statutes of blood purity. In the polemical debate about implementation of blood purity statutes in the Cathedral of Toledo, held in 1547 at the instigation of Archbishop Juan Martínez de Siliceo, their opponents pointed out that the laws would encourage foreigners to perceive all Spaniards as heretics.[5] Martínez Siliceo's response suggests that such an argument implied that both Charles V and the pope, in ratifying the statutes, had acted in a premeditated manner to defame Spain, a proposition that he believed would constitute the true heresy.[6] Even though the archbishop's position prevailed in this debate, the idea that the statutes defame not only those individuals directly affected by them but also the entire kingdom that so conspicuously publicizes such forms of infamy becomes one of the talking points in subsequent criticism of the statutes. Agustín Salucio, in his *Discurso sobre los estatutos de limpieza de sangre* (c. 1599), takes up again the argument used by the critics of Siliceo's statutes: "Acerca de la reputacion del Reyno, . . . los estatutos sirven de que los estrangeros comunmente nos llamen marranos. Y que no podemos escapar de ser tenidos o por infames, o por locos. Por infames, si ay en España necessidad de inhabilitar a tanta multitud; y por locos, si nosotros mesmos nos infamamos sin necessidad" [Regarding the Kingdom's reputation, . . . the statutes are often used by foreigners to call us marranos. And that we thus cannot avoid being regarded as either infamous or fools. As infamous, if there is indeed the need to punish such a multitude of people; as fools, if we defame ourselves with no need] (*Discurso*, 6v). Later in his *Discurso*, Salucio takes up the same argument again, but this time he adds the fear of the unexpected consequences of an uncontrolled spread of infamy:

> Comunmente los estrangeros toman ocasion de nuestros estatutos para despreciar nuestra nacion, y para hazer fuertes en ella, y llamar a los Españoles marranos a boca llena. . . . Y cada dia sera peor si no se ataja el inconveniente con alguna limitacion, con la qual olvide España las raças antiguas, pues que los estrangeros entre si se olvidan de las modernas.
>
> [Foreigners often use our statutes to deprecate our nation and to position themselves against it, and they call Spaniards marranos without dissimulating. . . . And it will be worse every day if we don't remedy these inconveniences by

limiting the statutes, so that Spain forgets the old stained lineages (*raças*), since foreigners forget even about the most recent ones among them.] (45r)

Thus, in the same way that the unchecked spread of infamy threatens to increase the number of excluded and turn upside down the concepts of prestige and infamy, as analyzed in chapter 3, Salucio proposes that it also affects the collective reputation of Spain in the minds of foreigners. Furthermore, even if he does not say so explicitly, it follows that the increased awareness of Spaniards as a nation of converts may become the core of a new sense of collective identity within Spain itself.

Pedro de Valencia's *Tratado acerca de los moriscos de España* (1606) defends a similar approach to integrating the Moriscos, arguing that the discrimination against them affects the international image of Spain:

> Nos hemos querido infamar entre las demás naciones de Europa, que descendiendo ellas de no menor . . . mezcla, a los españoles solo nos valdonan Francia, y Ytalia, y tienen razón, por que la infamia es mala fama, y quitada la infamia cesa la nota y la afrenta, y ellos acerca de sí han cubierto la fama, y nosotros conservámosla, y descubrímosla con cuidado . . . como se quite lo nominal, que es la infamia, no temamos que se inficionara la sangre de los españoles con la mezcla de la de los Moros.

> [We have purposely defamed ourselves among the other nations in Europe, since they descend of no lesser . . . mixture, yet France and Italy only accuse Spain, and they are right, because infamy is bad fame, and if you lift infamy, shame and affront disappear, and they have covered up fame [infamy] while we preserve it and thoroughly expose it . . . if we remove the nominal part, which is the infamy, we should not be afraid about Spanish blood being mixed with Muslims.][7]

Thus, both Salucio and Valencia instrumentalize the international image of Spain to support their argument that the obsession with blood purity may have the unexpected consequence of tarnishing the country's reputation. When they complain that excessive zeal in the application of infamy would expose sins that were shared by other Europeans, they actually are claiming that Spaniards share the same values held by the rest of Europeans; therefore, what differed were the methods of social control and the target populations, as well as the unintended effects on the perception of collective identity in the international arena.

This tension between social control and its effects on the international image of Spain has had long-lasting effects beyond the early modern period. The epigraph captures the paradox of how methods of infamy used to target certain groups may affect the reputation of the entire society. Antonio Domínguez Ortiz synthesizes the everlasting effect that the Inquisition has exerted on the imaginary about Spain when he states, "La Inquisición, que tantos sambenitos colgó en las iglesias, nos ha colgado un sambenito a toda la nación" [The Inquisition, which hung so many sambenitos on churches' walls, has hung a sambenito on the entire nation].[8] He plays with the meaning of the proverbial expression "colgar un sambenito" (to hang a sambenito on someone), which is a linguistic fossil still used in modern Spanish to mean to harm someone's reputation. Thus, he calls attention to the paradox that the social practice of defaming individuals becomes itself the mark of infamy of the very same community that implements such a practice: the insult produced by the perpetrator is transformed into the insult against the perpetrator, as excessive zeal in the application of infamy as a tool of social control turns Spain into the epitome of repressive states in the modern imaginary and tarnished the international image of Spanish history—a historiographical concept known as the "black legend," as I will later explore.[9]

The reference to the sambenito is more than a metaphor, because the representation of this garment is indeed one of the key elements in the construction of that negative image of Spain. Several Spanish paintings represent the *auto de fe* and the sambenitos. The first extant representation of the auto de fe is the tableau by Pedro de Berruguete painted toward the end of the fifteenth century, quite likely for the Monastery of Santo Tomás in Ávila.[10] The next extant ones were produced much later during the second half of the seventeenth century as a series of paintings: one of the auto de fe in Toledo in 1656, one of Seville's in 1660, and the well-known painting by Mateo Ricci of the auto de fe in Madrid in 1680.[11] Yet the Inquisition commissioned these paintings to be placed at the office of the Suprema, and they were not intended for public display nor reflected the vitality of its action: their purpose was to memorialize their activity precisely at a time in which the public auto de fe was becoming a rare event.[12] Thus, even though sambenitos were hanging throughout Spain and Portugal, Iberians themselves seem to have had very little interest in graphically representing a cultural practice ingrained in the urban landscape of the early modern period. Furthermore, these paintings portray the entire ceremony of the auto de fe to emphasize the inquisitors' moral authority, and the penitents wearing the sambenito are just one of many elements.

Except for those few Spanish paintings intended for institutional use, most of the extant representations of the sambenito that have circulated more widely come from the Protestant world and were intended as criticism of Iberian forms of religious persecution and social exclusion. I use some of those images in chapter 4 to illustrate my analysis, but some additional commentary on the ideologies of representation is needed here. The earliest extant foreign representation of the sambenitos seems to be the engraving titled *Hispanissche Inquisition* (c. 1560), representing an auto de fe in Valladolid in 1559 (Fig. E.1).[13] This engraving was reused in several works throughout the seventeenth century to illustrate the practice of the auto de fe in general. There seems to be no new depictions for more than a century, and genuine interest in representing in detail the sambenito, often in isolated images, emerges only by the end of the seventeenth century. The

Figure E.1. Hispanissche Inquisition (1560?). Bibliothèque Nationale de France, Cabinet des Estampes, Colletion Michel Hennin, V, i, p. 46, n. 459, Paris.

1683 edition of James Salgado's *The Slaughter House* includes two engravings showing the penitents wearing sambenitos (Fig. E.2). In contrast to the impressionistic and polemical character of most of the images included in Salgado's book, these two engravings accurately portray both the sambenito and the headdress called the *coroza*. Such accuracy is lost soon after in the images included in the second edition of Charles Dellon's *Relation de l'Inquisition de Goa* in 1688 (Fig. E.3), in which the coroza is strikingly transformed into a miter.[14] These images are the basis for subsequent engravings, such as the ones that Andreas Schoonebech made for Philip Van Limborch's *Historia Inquisitionis* (1692; Fig. E.4).[15] As Francisco Bethencourt points out, interest in representing this defaming garment flourishes around the revocation of the edict of Nantes in 1685, which revoked rights previously given to French Protestants: this was a historical moment in which the Spanish Inquisition becomes a symbol of the lack of toleration and the need for reform of the penal codes, even as the Inquisition itself was starting to languish in Spain.[16]

    Although Bethencourt and Moreno have thoroughly studied the historical context in which these images were produced and subsequently disseminated, they do not address the strange distortion in the representation of the headdress of the penitents starting with the illustrations for Dellon's *Relation de l'Inquisition de Goa* in 1688. I suggest a possible interpretation for such distortion by looking again at *Don Quixote*, but this time at its illustrations. The graphic representation of the sambenito in *Don Quixote* predates by a decade the proliferation of engravings in treatises of religious polemic in the 1680s and is not usually considered along with those other images when analyzing Protestant iconography about the Inquisition. The illustrated edition of *Don Quixote* of 1672–1673 in Antwerp includes an illustration by Frederik Bouttats of Sancho wearing the sambenito (Fig. 4.3). As pointed out in chapter 4, this image seems to take the text at face value by reflecting a too literal reading of the passage in which Sancho demands the "miter" that the dukes put on him (II:69). Failing to realize that the narrator is reproducing Sancho's inaccurate speech, it thus represents Sancho

Those that are Condemned to be Burnt.

Figure E.2. James Salgado, *The Slaughter House*. London: William Marshall, 1683. Courtesy of the Newberry Library.

HOMME *qui va être Brûlé par arrest de* L'INQUISITION.

Figure E.3. "Homme qui va être brûlé par arrest de l'Inquisition." Engraving by
Bernard Picart, 1722. Courtesy of the Wellcome Collection. Based on the illustrations
for Charles Dellon's *Relation de l'Inquisition de Goa*, 1688.

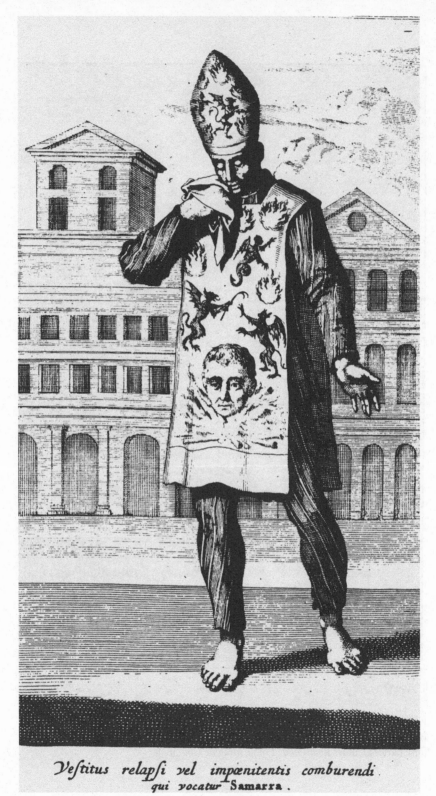

Vestitus relapsi vel impænitentis comburendi qui vocatur Samarra.

Figure E.4. Philip Van Limborch, *Historia Inquisitionis*. Amsterdam: Henricum Wetstenium, 1692, 369. BNE 2/64512. Courtesy of the Biblioteca Nacional de España.

with a miter instead of the conical coroza he should be wearing. Intentional or not, this substitution of the miter creates an incongruous representation in which several layers of interpretation overlap with each other, because it makes Sancho look like a mock bishop rather than someone who has been punished by the Inquisition. On the one hand, the image can be seen as a criticism of Catholic religious intolerance by focusing on the defamed individual, but on the other, it parodies the symbols of Catholic hierarchy by embodying them in the defamed individual as well. As a result, it reads as a twofold, dissonant iconographic strategy, which is simultaneously the mockery of Catholic symbols and a defense of those individuals defamed by the Inquisition.

This illustration became very popular throughout the seventeenth century in subsequent editions of Don Quixote printed in England, France, Holland, and Belgium.[17] Because this engraving precedes by more than a decade the first polemical images mistakenly representing those punished by the Inquisition as wearing a miter-shaped headdress—those in Charles Dellon's second edition of his Relation de l'Inquisition de Goa in 1688—we should entertain the possibility that Bouttats's engraving of Sancho may have influenced the iconography of the religious polemic: indeed, many later images reproduce the same confusion between the coroza and the miter. This interpretation would mean that a too literal reading of Cervantes's text is responsible for some of the inaccuracies in the received representations of the sambenitos that still proliferate when illustrating the Inquisition's activity. In this way, the literary dystopia, which Cervantes quite likely created to criticize the abuse of the signs of infamy in early modern Spain, has become one of the models of iconographic memorialization to conceive inquisitorial Spain as the epitome of repressive regimes.

There is symbolically another factor, even if circumstantial, that connects the illustrated versions of Don Quixote with the interest in depicting a particular Spanish use of signs of infamy. The only Spanish painter to have shown interest in depicting the sambenitos is Francisco de Goya (1746–1828), precisely at a moment when the Inquisition was increasingly perceived in Spain as an archaic institution; it was abolished shortly after his death in 1834.[18] Goya devoted one painting to the auto de fe (c. 1814–1816; Fig. E.5), as well as an entire series of drawings to depict those condemned by the Inquisition.[19] In all these compositions, like in the Protestant images, the focus is on those individuals condemned to wear the sambenito, rather than the auto de fe ceremony, emphasizing the ignominy of the performance instead of the moral authority of the inquisitors.

It is significant for the purposes of this book that Goya also depicted the episode of the braying mayors in Don Quixote (II:27; see Fig. 5.2). His drawing, engraved by José Joaquí Fabregat, was submitted in 1778 to the Real Academia Española (RAE) for inclusion in the academic edition of Don Quixote that was published in 1882 by the printer Joaquín Ibarra; however, it was not selected, and the RAE included instead the engraving by Fernando Selma. It is unclear who

Figure E.5. Francisco de Goya, *Auto de fe* (c. 1808–1812). Courtesy of Real Academia de Bellas Artes de San Fernando (Madrid), inventory number 0673.

commissioned Goya to do this drawing (when he was not yet a renowned artist) and why the RAE decided not to include Goya's composition in its edition of *Don Quixote*.[20]

Certainly, there is no direct link between Goya's drawing of the episode of the braying mayors and his depictions of penitents wearing the sambenitos at the auto de fe. They were composed in very different periods in his career and under different circumstances—the drawing for *Don Quixote* was likely commissioned and therefore does not necessarily reflect a coherent theme in Goya's artistic trajectory. Yet, even if it is only a fortuitous coincidence that the same artist illustrates the two themes analyzed in chapters 4 and 5, his artworks symbolize the connection between both instances of infamy, precisely because he created both pieces at a time when Spain—under the influence of the Enlightenment—was increasingly distancing itself from these kinds of social policing. More importantly, the juxtaposition of the two images by the same artist allows us to glimpse the evolution of the concept of the "black legend" in the Spanish imaginary.

First, we need to question whether the so-called black legend of Spain, understood as a campaign of propaganda that is sustained over time, is an accurate historiographical concept. There are certainly some historical moments in which we can trace intense propaganda activity against the Spanish Empire, such as the religious wars in Europe (of which the previous images are a good example) and during the Spanish-American War in 1898.[21] Indeed, it is not a coincidence that Emilia Pardo Bazán was allegedly the first to coin the term "black legend"

EPILOGUE   129

in a conference in Paris in 1899, just one year after the start of the U.S. propaganda campaign against Spain that accompanied the war that led to the end of
the Spanish empire. The term was later popularized by Julián Juderías's *La leyenda negra* in 1914.[22]

Yet, although criticism of Spain cannot be denied, it is debatable whether it
is a kind of propaganda that is systematic and continuous in time (as the defenders of this concept claim) or just the matter-of-course criticism that empires
naturally evoke from both competitors and people contesting their rule. What
is at issue here is the historiographical explanatory power of the black legend,
which has had a long-lasting influence on one formulation of Spanish nationalism.[23] What informs the concept of the black legend is not the criticism against
Spain in itself, but rather the Spaniards' awareness of that external perception,
the selective attention they paid to it, and how they have instrumentalized that
gaze toward all kinds of internal political and social debates, using that alleged
or real insult to articulate a sense of community.[24]

As several scholars have already pointed out, the historiographical concept
of the black legend owes its staying power not to the content and extent of the
criticism against Spain but to Spain's obsession with the external gaze. Pierre
Chaunu observes,

> La légende noire est le reflet d'un reflet, une image doublement déformée, parce
> que doublement reflétée. La "leyenda negra," c'est, si l'on veut, l'image de
> l'Espagne, au dehors, telle que l'Espagne la voit. La spécificité profonde de la
> "leyenda negra" reside moins donc dans le fait que la représentation extéri-
> eure des Espagnes a été plus importante, plus continue et plus chargée que celle
> des pays voisins, mais, plus encore, dans la mesure où cette image d'elle-même
> a affecté l'Espagne plus qu'aucune autre image de soi-même n'a affecté, dans
> le même temps, aucune autre entité nationale.

> [The black legend is a reflection of a reflection, an image doubly distorted,
> because it is doubly reflected. The black legend is, somehow, the image of Spain
> from the outside, as Spain itself sees it. The deep specificity of the black leg-
> end lies less in the fact that external representations of Spain have been impor-
> tant, more continuous and vitriolic than in nearby countries, but rather insofar
> as this image of itself has affected Spain more than any other image has
> affected, at the same time, any other national identity.][25]

Following Chaunu, Carmen Iglesias analyzed the interaction between the image
of Spain in Europe and how it was appropriated in Spain.[26] More recently, Jesús
Villanueva thoroughly traced the development of the concept of black legend as
a key element of a variety of Spanish nationalism throughout the twentieth
century, showing that, despite its being presented as a response to the international image of Spain, it has been mostly used to suppress internal dissent.

Villanueva's book, published in 2011, stops at the beginning of the twenty-first century, but his incisive analysis of the Spanish nationalist agenda underlying the concept of the black legend is still applicable to the plethora of titles published in Spain within the last decade.

Even if the concept of the black legend is a legitimate historiographical tool that can be applied to several moments in which the international image of Spain was at a low point, since the arrival of democracy in 1977 and its accession to the European Union, Spain has been devoted to branding itself in such an aggressive way that Hispanophobia seems like a relic of the past. This is precisely why it seems so surprising to witness the virulent rebirth of the concept of the black legend when no relevant actor is criticizing Spain. Yet, in the aftermath of the 2008 economic crisis, new books poured forth such as Iván Vélez's *Sobre la leyenda negra* (2014), Ricardo García Cárcel's *El demonio del Sur* (2019), and Alberto G. Ibáñez's *La leyenda negra* (2019), to name only a few; in addition, the foundational text by Julián Juderías was reissued in 2014 and 2019. The book about the black legend that has attained the most popularity and media attention is undoubtedly María Elvira Roca Barea's *Imperiofobia y leyenda negra* (2016).[27]

The black legend syndrome, like the regulatory disciplines of infamy analyzed in this book, has taken on a life of its own, growing even despite the efforts of its critics. Jesús Villanueva points out that, even if academic historiography has doubted the validity of the black legend since the publication of the 1992 first edition of García Cárcel's book *La leyenda negra: historia y opinion*, the term has nevertheless survived in historiographical practice, which has served to grant it a veneer of respectability.[28] In what seems like an ironic twist, the marketable appeal of the black legend concept also seems to engulf its rebuttals. Even Villanueva's book, which is clearly intended to counteract the black legend as a historiographical myth, places "Leyenda negra" as the most prominent part of its title and shows on its cover one of the propagandistic illustrations depicting Philip II as a monster; thus, his book is actually marketed similarly to those defending the validity of the concept.

Although it is beyond the scope of this book to analyze why there has been this explosion of interest in the concept of the black legend or to engage with the heated intellectual polemics surrounding this editorial and social phenomenon, it is important to consider the key role that the dynamics of insult and identity play in this process. The underlying logic of this concept claims that the black legend is an exceptional campaign of propaganda against Spain that has been continuously waged for centuries up to the present day. For the sake of my argument here, it does not matter whether these historical reconstructions about the negative image of Spain are accurate. What is important is that the emphasis on the historiographical concept of the black legend is based on a twofold structural contradiction inherent to the approach to the alleged insult that, rather than weakening these historical reconstructions' rhetorical force, explains the persuasiveness of their arguments; that is, they claim to be responding to an external insult (even while they are repressing internal dissent), and they represent their aim as defending Spain's legacy (while almost focusing exclusively on the negative aspect of the insult, in a strategy that is simultaneously masochistic and narcissistic).

These projects present themselves as responding to an external insult, yet they make no real attempt to engage with the alleged insulter. For instance, Roca Barea claims that the increase in the risk premium for PIGS (the derogatory acronym for Portugal, Italy, Greece, and Spain) in the aftermath of the 2008 financial crisis is the latest manifestation of the black legend; supporting this claim seems to be the explicit motivation for her book.[29] Yet it is clear that she in no way intends to rehabilitate the reputation of Spain in the international financial arena, because her book, like most books on the black legend, is written in Spanish for a domestic readership. The aftermath of the 2008 crisis also triggered a series of social protests leading to the *indignados* movement in 2011; new groups on both the left and right ends of the political have capitalized on this discontent. Some attempted to redirect social and political tensions into a resurgence of Spanish nationalism, particularly after the escalation of conflicts with Catalonia that culminated in its ill-fated referendum of independence in 2017.[30] The call to assuage old offenses diverts the emotional burden generated by socioeconomic inequality, transforming inchoate indignation about economic and political issues of the 15-M indignados protests into an artificial indignation of a nation that has been allegedly insulted from time immemorial.

Although the resurgence of nationalism is a global political phenomenon, the particular feature of Spanish nationalism is that it is largely linked to the recycling of a historical narrative of an eternally insulted nation; its main purpose seems to be to counteract the black legend. The resurgence of interest in the black legend has nothing to do with the current international image of Spain but rather with internal politics. It is an attempt to galvanize society around an insult that was allegedly uttered centuries ago and is supposed to resonate in every criticism of Spain's politics in the present; this insult is one that must be memorialized and routinely recited as a litany to structure social meaning. It is not merely that Spaniards reacted to systematic propaganda aimed at defaming their empire in the international arena, but that certain sectors of Spanish society have been particularly receptive to using any insult, real or imaginary, uttered from outside the community to reinforce their own boundaries and to serve as the foundation for the articulation of collective identity. They attribute to the insult an ontological referentiality, as confirming one's feeling of identity. The nostalgic staging of an insult that is no longer there proves useful for enabling Spaniards to feel a sense of belonging: the memorialization of the distorted image created by the Other is productive within domestic politics of identity.

Internal dissent is stigmatized as foreign and thus delegitimized by inserting it in the ghostly category of the black legend. Most of these projects have a
common internal enemy, which seems to be Catalan and Basque separatism, the
natural antagonists of Spanish nationalism. However, it is in the other variations
of that internal enemy that each of these authors reveal their own political agendas, which differ despite their superficial similarities. Each author delineates a
unique genealogy of traitors, taking as the point of departure the icons of Bartolomé de las Casas and Antonio Pérez to draw a direct line to the internal dis-
senters whom he or she identifies as unpatriotic propagators of the black legend.
Most of these books are blatantly Islamophobic, labeling leftist political parties
as traitors who are helping outsiders perpetuate the black legend.

Lastly, and more importantly for the theoretical frame of this book, despite
presenting themselves as defenders of Spain's reputation, these works devote
more attention to the negative insult than to its alleged positive aspects. They
present a long list of negative images about Spain throughout history as a starting point while promising to offer an opposing image of a grandiose and benev-
olent empire that should create a feeling of patriotism and national belonging
in the present. Yet that promise is rarely fulfilled, because most of these projects
neglect those alleged grand deeds of the Spanish Empire, to which they devote
a secondary place, providing at best only frustratingly conventional, vague, and
schematic accounts of Spanish glories that betray their intended goal. Although
the explicit object of desire is the glory of the imperial legacy, it soon proves
derivative, masked behind titles and expositions that invariably grant the alleged
affront the most prominent position. This imbalance reveals that the main objective of most of these publications is not to vindicate the grandiosity of a lost
empire, as they claim, but rather to re-create the feeling of being insulted, to
count every possible insult that may have ever been raised against Spain, to revitalize a forgotten affront so as to mobilize synergies that are fading away.[31] That
feeling of being insulted is not only exaggerated in time (all the insults are plot-
ted in an uninterrupted chain of immanent hatred toward Spain) but are also
magnified to claim that Spain is the most insulted nation of the world, which
ignores the negative stereotypes of other nations. Thus, an oft-repeated mantra
is Miguel de Unamuno's claim in his *Del sentimiento trágico de la vida* (1913) that
Spain has been "la gran calumniada de la historia" [the most defamed nation in
history].[32] This claim of Spain's exceptional position in what I call the world history of infamy has been reiterated by many authors. For instance, Rafael Sánchez Mazas claimed in the 1920s that Spain has been "la nación más injuriada"
[the most insulted nation].[33] More recent authors have made similar claims; for
example, José Antonio Vaca de Osma asserts, "Es como nuestra exclusiva, pues
país alguno de la tierra es víctima de tal persecución ideológica" [It is something
like our exclusive trait, as no other country in the world has been the target of
such ideological persecution].[34] According to this victimist line of thought, what

Spain has excelled in throughout its history is eliciting the most persistent, vile insults against itself.

The compulsive reiteration of the concept of the black legend can only mean that the absence of the insult risks rendering a certain form of collective identity irrelevant, precisely because that insult has been the constitutive element of national glorification. As we have seen throughout this book, through the narcissistic mechanics of injury and interpellation, insult can be conceived as preceding identity; therefore, if there is no insult, then it will be necessary to invent it—or at least to put it back on the pedestal from which it is allegedly missing. This defensive nationalist project reflects Wendy Brown's conception of the politics founded on historical injuries, based on "a political practice of revenge, a practice that reiterates the existence of an identity whose present past is one of insistently unredeemable injury. This past cannot be redeemed *unless* the identity ceases to be invested in it, and it cannot cease to be invested in it without giving up its identity as such, thus giving up its economy of avenging and at the same time perpetuating its hurt."[35] In this instance Brown is writing not about Spanish nationalism but about a certain trend in the discourses of social justice and minority rights—even as she is a participant in those movements. I am therefore not claiming that Spanish nationalism is exceptional in instrumentalizing historical injuries. Rather, what Spanish nationalism does by emphasizing the concept of the black legend is to mimic the language of civil rights in order to annul those rights, to structure the community around that never expiring insult, and to subsume any other historical injuries to that nationalist project—and those injuries would forever be subsumed under that frame, because the ghostly insult they have memorialized is impossible to repair. Therefore, the nationalist project is unable to break the logical circularity because the insult has become constitutive of that very same identity.

This logic produces an anxiety about the absence of the insult that is already prevalent in the foundational text of the black legend as a historiographical concept. In the prologue to the second edition of *La leyenda negra* in 1917, Julián Juderías complains, "Los momentos en que este libro se publica no pueden ser más inoportunos . . . porque al antiguo desprecio y a la injuria antigua o reciente, ha substituido la simpatía y hemos vuelto a ser el pueblo noble y caballeresco de otras veces" [the moments in which this book is published could not be more ill-timed . . . because the old affront and the old or recent injury have been replaced by fellow-feeling and we are again that noble and chivalrous people we once were].[36] Juderías reluctantly acknowledges that his book is a reaction against a ghostly insult—which is both too distant in the past (arguably the image of the Spanish Empire during the wars of religion in the early modern period) or relatively recent (quite likely the 1898 Spanish-American War or the international reaction to the *Semana trágica* in 1909)—and that image has been replaced with the more benign romantic image of Spain, which is less harmful even if equally stereotypical.[37] The second reason why Juderías believes the publication of his second edition is poorly timed is that the disaster of World War I was then dissolving the traditional importance placed on patriotism. That he decries both the disappearance of the negative image of Spain and the dilution of any sense of patriotism as ill timed (*inoportuno*) for his own project is revealing of how both injury and nationalism are deeply entangled.[38]

One hundred years later, we find a similar accounting of offenses against Spain in María Elvira Roca Barea's *Imperiofobia y leyenda negra* (2016). Her book lacks a clear focus: it is at times a defense of empire as a political form, a defense of Catholicism against accusations from Protestants, and a defense of Spain's contributions to world history. Yet it is precisely such conceptual vagueness that may explain its success, because it enables the number of alleged affronts to Spain to be inflated. By including insults that were thrown at specific historical figures (such as Philip II), general criticism of Catholicism by Protestants (even when they are not singling out Spain), or contempt toward Mediterranean identity in general (the PIGS acronym stigmatizes the southern Mediterranean, not Spain in particular), Roca Barea tends to confuse the part for the whole, thereby conflating all these categories into a foggy and encompassing rubric of Hispanophobia and magnifying the insult of the Other.[39] This compulsion to minutely monitor and record every offense ever raised against Spain (or any other concept that Spain allegedly symbolizes) is exemplified when Roca Barea, after listing all the derogatory comments against Spain that she can trace, warns her reader that "estamos todavía muy lejos de haber, no ya estudiado, sino inventariado la totalidad de esta producción" [we are far from having, not yet studied, but inventoried the totality of this production].[40] In this line of argument, keeping an exhaustive record of insults against Spain is conceived as an endless task that promises an incommensurable wealth of injury, an inexhaustible source of national masochistic pleasure with the foundational insult. The concept of the black legend has become more visible because of the historiographical corpus that has been created about it; minutely compiling all the offenses against Spain throughout centuries serves to create its own reality in its reverberation and regurgitation.

When Domínguez Ortiz claims that the Inquisition has put a sambenito on Spanish society, he certainly does not intend it as an invitation to appropriate that stigma. Yet some sectors of Spanish society are eager to embrace that figurative sambenito and to give it life in an absolute present by decontextualizing it and abstracting its historicity. They do so because they believe that it is the alleged immutability of the insult that guarantees the essentiality of the Spanish nation. Nobody would remember the concept of the black legend (or at most it would be considered as one of those erudite relics of the past) if it did not provide an opportunity for staging a theatrical affirmation of identity on an empty stage.

In this sense, the signification of the black legend in the Spanish national imaginary is reminiscent of the episode of the braying mayors in the second part of *Don Quixote* (II:27).[41] As analyzed in chapter 5, the anecdote of the two councilmen braying like donkeys as they look for a lost animal turns the inhabitants of this town into the object of their neighbors' scorn. The inhabitants of that town take up arms to restore their reputation and honor, affronted by the bray raised at them by their neighbors as a form of disrespect; yet they repeatedly refer to themselves as "the inhabitants of the braying town" and, when going into battle, fly a flag with a braying donkey, the sign of infamy against which they are supposedly fighting. Such a seemingly incongruous reaction against the external insult reveals the multifaceted nature of interpellation and subjectivation: insults can be simultaneously rejected and appropriated. In a very similar vein, the recurrent emphasis on the black legend of Spain takes as a constitutive emblem the insult its advocates pretend to be belligerently disputing. Past insults that were raised against Spain in very different historical moments and for very different reasons are collected, decontextualized, and repackaged as simply particular manifestations of an abstract and reified insult. This memorializing strategy entails a maximizing approach toward that sacralized insult that aims to keep both the cohesive value of the insult of the Other and the reputation and self-esteem that would theoretically come from belligerently contesting it. The black legend is the banner that helps deflect the difficulties of articulating a positive civic patriotism, because proclaiming it involves no real attempt to look for common values but rather a ceaseless war against a phantasmatic insult. This operation is conducted on an empty battlefield, as in *Don Quixote*'s episode, in which the inhabitants of the town of the bray are the only side to show up for battle, against an insulter who is simply not there, quite probably because that ghostly contender is but a figure of the enemy at home, a way to counteract internal dissent by projecting it into an immanent historical narrative of essentialized hatred against Spain.

Dystopias of Infamy has analyzed how early modern authors such as Cervantes explore the social fantasies of alternative communities articulated through insult. As I suggest, Cervantes creates literary formulations by taking the logic of such social fantasies to the point of absurdity, thereby exposing their inherent fetishism. Seen from our perspective, his literary creations may seem like unlikely futurities in which communities are on the brink of embracing the insult as a source of collective identity. Yet, after all, some of those seemingly unlikely dystopias from his past have indeed materialized over and over in time, cleaving to a primordial insult as a recurrent way to cement the boundaries of the community in times of uncertainty. A dystopia is not always based on a cataclysmic change in the material conditions of social structure: one could also be based on regimes of insult that structure the boundaries of communities around transformative feelings of injury.

Acknowledgments

I am very grateful for my conversations with the few colleagues with whom I have talked about this research: Natalio Ohanna, Víctor Pueyo, Enrique García Santo-Tomás, Miguel Martínez, Eric Calderwood, Manuel Olmedo Gobante, and Barbara Fuchs, as well as the graduate students at the University of Illinois with whom I shared this project. I especially want to thank Julio Baena, from whom I may have borrowed more than one idea for this book, intentionally or otherwise. I owe thanks to Linde Brocato and Marco Parodi for their careful editing of the manuscript and to the anonymous evaluators for thoroughly pointing out the flaws of my original proposal and for their constructive comments. I must thank Pamelia Dailey for shepherding me through the editorial process with Bucknell University Press, Michelle Scott and Vincent Nordhaus for conducting a thorough review of my manuscript, and Heather Dubnick for the care she used in producing the index. I am also thankful to the Research Board and the Conrad Humanities Scholar award at the University of Illinois for the funding and released time that allowed me to complete this project. And finally, I must acknowledge Pilar, who has been my main interlocutor for this project, among many other crazy ones.

Notes

INTRODUCTION

1. Fernando de Rojas, *La Celestina*, ed. Dorothy S. Severin (Madrid: Cátedra, 1993), 108.

2. All translations are mine unless otherwise noted.

3. Rojas, *La Celestina*, 109.

4. Lourdes Albuixech, "Insultos, pullas y vituperios en *Celestina*," *Celestinesca* 25, nos. 1–2 (2001): 62–63.

5. On the confusion between cuckoldry and homosexuality in a too literal reading of the marital sacrament, see Georgina Dopico Black, *Perfect Wives, Other Women: Adultery and Inquisition in Early Modern Spain* (Durham, NC: Duke University Press, 2001), 114–115.

6. See Sherry Velasco, *Lesbians in Early Modern Spain* (Nashville: Vanderbilt University Press, 2011), 1–14; and Cristian Berco, *Sexual Hierarchies, Public Status: Men, Sodomy, and Society in Spain's Golden Age* (Toronto: University of Toronto Press, 2007), 120.

7. Didier Eribon, *Insult and the Making of the Gay Self*, trans. Michael Lucey (Durham: Duke University Press, 2004), 8–9, 315–318.

8. For the analysis of insults from the point of few of formal linguistics, see Nicolas Ruwet, *Grammaire des insultes et autres études* (Paris: Éditions du Seuil, 1982), 239–314. For an informative perspective, see Juan de Dios Luque, Antonio Pamies and Francisco José Manjón, *El arte del insulto: Estudio lexicográfico* (Barcelona: Península, 1997). For the use of inappropriate forms of address, which can be interpreted as a sign of disrespect, see Françoise Maurizi, "Langue et discours: La *pulla* dans le théâtre de la fin du XVème-début du XVIème siècle," *Voces* 4 (1997): 99.

9. See, for instance, the studies on injury in Castile during the Middle Ages by Marta Madero, *Manos violentas, palabras vedadas: La injuria en Castilla y León (siglos XIII–XV)* (Madrid: Taurus, 1992); and Rafael Serra Ruiz, *Honor, honra e injuria en el derecho medieval español* (Murcia: Universidad de Murcia, 1969). There are also a wealth of local studies, such as Félix Segura Urra, "*Verba vituperosa*: El papel de la injuria en la sociedad bajomedieval," in *Aportaciones a la historia social del lenguaje: España siglos XIV–XVIII*, ed. Rocío García Bourrellier and Jesús María Usunáriz (Madrid: Iberoamericana, 2006), 149–195; Emilio Montero Cartelle, "Palabras malas e villanas (Alfonso X: Partidas): La

oralidad en las tradiciones discursivas jurídicas," in *Discurso y oralidad. Homenaje al profesor José Jesús de Bustos Tovar*, ed. Luis Cortés Rodríguez et al. (Madrid: Arco/Libros, 2007), 1:391–399; Mónica Castillo Lluch, "Del denuesto a la interjección: la historia de la expresión fijo de puta," in *Actas del VI Congreso Internacional de Historia de la lengua española*, ed. José Luis Girón Alconchel and José Jesús de Bustos Tovar (Madrid: Universidad Complutense de Madrid, 2006), 3:2697–2708; Mónica Castillo Lluch, "De verbo vedado: consideraciones sobre la agresión verbal y su expresión en castellano medieval," *Cahiers de Linguistique et Civilisation Hispaniques Médiévales* 27 (2004): 23–35; Jean Gautier-Dalche, "Remarques sur l'insulte verbale dans quelques textes juridiques leonocastillans," *Annales de la Faculté de Lettres et Sciences Humaines de Nice* 39 (1983): 117–126; and Cristina Tabernero and Jesús María Usunáriz, *Diccionario de injurias de los siglos XVI y XVII* (Kassel: Reichenberger, 2019).

10. Thomas Conley, *Toward a Rhetoric of Insult* (Chicago: University of Chicago Press, 2010).

11. See, among many others, Josiah Blackmore, "The Poets of Sodom," in *Queer Iberia: Sexualities, Cultures, and Crossing from the Middle Ages to the Renaissance*, ed. Josiah Blackmore and Gregory S. Hutcheson (Durham, NC: Duke University Press, 1999), 195–221; Kenneth R. Scholberg, *Sátira e invectiva en la España medieval* (Madrid: Gredos, 1971); Lina Rodríguez Cacho, *Pecados sociales y literatura satírica en el siglo XVI* (Madrid: Universidad Autónoma de Madrid, 1989); Mercedes Etreros, *La sátira política en el siglo XVII* (Madrid: Fundación Universitaria Española, 1983); Francisco Layna Ranz, *La disputa burlesca: Origen y trayectoria* (Toulousse: Presses Universitaires du Mirail, 1995); Ignacio Arellano and Victoriano Roncero López, eds., *Demócrito áureo: los códigos de la risa en el Siglo de Oro* (Seville: Renacimiento, 2006); Javier Huerta Calvo, Emilio Peral Vega, and Jesús Ponce Cárdenas, eds., *Tiempo de burlas: En torno a la literatura burlesca del Siglo de Oro* (Madrid: Verbum, 2001); and Carmela Pérez-Salazar, Cristina Tabernero, and Jesús M. Usunáriz, eds., *Los poderes de la palabra: El improperio en la cultura hispánica del Siglo de Oro* (New York: Peter Lang, 2013). On the *Celestina* and its sequels, see Albuixech, "Insultos"; and F. Javier Herrero Ruiz de Loizaga, "El insulto en la comedia celestinesca," in *Discurso y oralidad. Homenaje al profesor José Jesús de Bustos Tovar*, ed. Luis Cortés Rodríguez et al. (Madrid: Arco/Libros, 2007), 1:349–365. We can even find insults in religious sermons: Pedro M. Cátedra, "La modificación del discurso religioso con fines de invectiva. El sermón," *Atalaya* 5 (1994): 101–122.

12. See Víctor Infantes, "Luceros y Tizones: biografía nobiliaria y venganza política en el Siglo de Oro," *El Crotalón* 1 (1984): 115–127; and John Beusterien, "Blotted Genealogies: A Survey of the *libros verdes*," *Bulletin of Hispanic Studies* 78, no. 2 (2001): 183–197. On the circulation of libels in early modern Spain, see Antonio Castillo Gómez, "Panfletos, coplas y libelos injuriosos: Palabras silenciadas en el Siglo de Oro," in *Las Españas que (no) pudieron ser: herejías, exilios y otras conciencias (s. XVI–XX)*, ed. Manuel Peña Díaz (Huelva: Universidad de Huelva, 2009), 59–73; Antonio Castillo Gómez, "Voces, imágenes y textos. La difusión pública del insulto en la sociedad áurea," in *Los poderes de la palabra*, 59–73; Javier Ruiz Astiz, "Libelos y pasquines en la vida comunitaria: conflictividad social en Navarra (1512–1808)," in *Opinión pública y espacio urbano en la Edad Moderna*, ed. Antonio Castillo Gómez and James S. Amelang (Gijón: Trea, 2010), 399–422; Fernando Chavarría Múgica, "Pasquines escandalosos, maledicencias banderizas y desinformación irredentista: la distorsión de la comunicación política entre corte y reino después de la

anexión de Navarra a la monarquía española," in *Opinión pública*, 422–440; and Aurora Egido, "Linajes de burlas en el Siglo de Oro," in *Studia Aurea: Actas del III Congreso de la AISO*, ed. Ignacio Arellano et al. (Pamplona: GRISO-LEMSO, 1996), 1:19–50.

13. On sumptuary legislation against Jews and Muslims in medieval Castile, see José Damián González Arce, *Apariencia y poder: La legislación suntuaria castellana en los siglos XIII y XVI* (Jaén: Universidad de Jaén, 1998), 170–177; and Olivia Remie Constable, *To Live like a Moor: Christian Perceptions of Muslim Identity in Medieval and Early Modern Spain*, ed. Robin Vose (Philadelphia: University of Pennsylvania Press, 2018), 27–47. For Portugal, see Maria Filomena Lopes de Barros, "Body, Baths, and Cloth: Muslim and Christian Perceptions in Medieval Portugal," *Portuguese Studies* 21 (2005): 9–11. For the extension of this logic to the early modern period, see Javier Irigoyen-García, *Moors Dressed as Moors: Clothing, Social Distinction, and Ethnicity in Early Modern Iberia* (Toronto: University of Toronto Press, 2017), 5–12. Many of the medieval documents in Castile and Aragon were compiled by Ana Isabel Carrasco Manchado, *De la convivencia a la exclusión. Imágenes legislativas de mudéjares y moriscos. Siglos XIII–XVII* (Madrid: Sílex, 2012), 91–222.

14. Francisco J. Flores Arroyuelo, *De la aventura al teatro y la fiesta: Moros y cristianos* (Murcia: Nausícaä, 2003), 142–143; Albert A. Sicroff, *Los estatutos de limpieza de sangre. Controversias entre los siglos XV y XVII*, trans. Mauro Armiño (Madrid: Taurus, 1985), 302n171.

15. Antonio Castillo Gómez, "Letras de penitencia: Denuncia y castigo públicos en la España altomoderna," *Via Spiritus* 15 (2008): 53–74, 58–61. For a legal analysis of infamy in early modern Castile, see Aniceto Masferrer Domingo, *La pena de infamia en el derecho histórico español* (Madrid: Dykinson, 2001), 327–365.

16. See, for instance, John G. Peristiany, ed., *Honour and Shame: The Values of Mediterranean Society* (London: Weidenfeld and Nicholson, 1965); and David D. Gilmore, *Honor and Shame and the Unity of the Mediterranean* (Washington, DC: American Anthropological Association, 1987).

17. Gail Kern Paster, *The Body Embarrassed: Drama and the Disciplines of Shame in Early Modern England* (Ithaca: Cornell University Press, 1993); and Frank Henderson Stewart, *Honor* (Chicago: University of Chicago Press, 1994).

18. See, among many others, Ignacio Arellano, "Casos de honor en las primeras etapas del teatro de Lope," *Anuario Lope de Vega* 4 (1998): 7–31; Ramón Menéndez Pidal, *De Cervantes y Lope de Vega* (Buenos Aires: Espasa-Calpe, 1940), 153–184; José Antonio Maravall, "La función del honor en la sociedad tradicional," *Ideologies and Literature* 2, no. 7 (1978): 9–27; Melveena McKendrick, "Honour/Vengeance in the Spanish 'Comedia': A Case of Mimetic Transference?" *Modern Language Review* 79, no. 2 (1984): 313–335; and Antonie Adrianus Van Beysterveldt, *Répercussions du souci de la pureté de sang sur la conception de l'honneur dans la "comedia nueva" espagnole* (Leiden: Brill, 1966). Claude Chauchadis analyzes the concept of honor in Spanish moralists, *Honneur, morale et société dans l'Espagne de Philippe II* (Paris: CNRS, 1984). For more recent overviews, see Scott K. Taylor, *Honor and Violence in Golden Age Spain* (New Haven: Yale University Press, 2008), 1–16; Robert A. Lauer, "Honor/honra Revisited," in *A Companion to Early Modern Hispanic Theater*, ed. Hilaire Kallendorf (Leiden: Brill, 2014), 77–90; and Paul Michael Johnson, *Affective Geographies: Cervantes, Emotion, and the Literary Mediterranean* (Toronto: University of Toronto Press, 2020), 70–75.

19. *Manos violentas*, 28.

20. Taylor, *Honor*; and Ruth MacKay, *"Lazy, Improvident People": Myth and Reality in the Writing of Spanish History* (Ithaca: Cornell University Press, 2006), 74–89.

21. Javier Salazar Rincón, "Insulto y exclusión social: Algo más sobre la polémica entre Cervantes y Lope de Vega," *Bulletin Hispanique* 113, no. 2 (2011): 701–724, 712–713; and Ángel Iglesias Ovejero, "Nominación marginante en el picarismo literario y el folklore," *Revista de Filología Románica* 1 (1983): 137–139.

22. On this perspective, see the seminal work by René Girard, *Le Bouc émissaire* (Paris: Bernard Grasset, 1982). See also Michel Jonin, "Quand les poètes nouveaux chrétiens content leurs exploits cynégétique," in *Signes et marques du convers (Espagne XVe–XVIe siècle)*, ed. Louis Cardaillac and Haïm Vidal Sephiha (Aix-en-Provence: Université de Provence, 1993), 75; and Maurizi, "Langue," 104. From a sociological perspective, see Erving Goffman, *Stigma: Notes on the Management of Spoiled Identity* (London: Penguin, 1990); and Charles P. Flynn, *Insult and Society: Patterns of Comparative Interaction* (Port Washington: Kennikat Press, 1977).

23. Louis Althusser, *Lenin and Philosophy and Other Essays*, trans. Ben Brewster (New York: Montly Review Press, 2001), 115–120.

24. Judith Butler, *The Psychic Life of Power: Theories in Subjection* (Stanford: Stanford University Press, 1997), 95–96.

25. Butler, *Psychic Life*, 96–97.

26. Butler, *Psychic Life*, 104. Butler subsequently expanded this tack in *Excitable Speech: A Politics of the Performance* (New York: Routledge, 1997). Despite its interesting insights, this second book is oriented toward the legal practice of hate speech in the United States and is therefore less relevant here.

27. See also Eribon, *Insult*. For the specific case of "jotería" in Chicano/Latino/Mexican studies, see the contributions by Xamuel Bañales, Daniel Enrique Pérez, Vincent Cervantes, and Tijerina Revilla and Santillana in a special volume of *Aztlán* 39, no. 1 (2014).

28. Eribon, *Insult*, 66.

29. At best, we can find a passage in Cervantes's *Don Quixote* in which a woman demands to be included in a satire against women, as I analyze in chapter 2.

30. There is a rich bibliography on this topic. Just to offer a recent approach, see Susan L. Fischer and Frederick A. DeArmas, eds., *Women Warriors in Early Modern Spain: A Tribute to Bárbara Mujica* (Newark: Juan de la Cuesta, 2019). For a good overview of women's ability to contest or circumvent patriarchy in early modern Spain, see Lisa Vollendorf, *The Lives of Women: A New History of Inquisitorial Spain* (Nashville: Vanderbilt University Press, 2005).

31. Let me emphasize that I am in no way claiming that such kind of subjectivation is inaccessible to women. For an exploration of how the appropriation of insult has become an empowering tool for women in contemporary Spain, see for instance, Itziar Ziga, *Devenir perra* (Santa Cruz de Tenerife: Melusina, 2009). Ziga's approach is very indebted to Judith Butler, as is my book.

32. See Miguel Avilés, *Sueños ficticios y lucha ideológica en el Siglo de Oro* (Madrid: Nacional, 1981), 33–103; and Jean Pierre Étienvre, ed., *Las utopías en el mundo hispánico* (Madrid: Casa de Velázquez, 1990).

33. Matthew D. O'Hara, *The History of the Future in Colonial Mexico* (New Haven: Yale University Press, 2018), x. For a recent approach to the analysis of "futurities" in the Renaissance, see Charle Villaseñor Black and Mari-Tere Álvarez, eds., *Renaissance Futu-*

rities: Science, Art, Invention (Oakland: University of California Press, 2000), especially the chapters dealing with early modern Spain by Álvarez and Eamon. DeArmas ("Futurities"), also included in this collection, addresses the futurities found in *Don Quixote* in relation to Orwell's dystopia, although from a perspective different from the one I use in this book. For another recent approach applying modern apocalyptic and dystopian discourses in Hispanic literature, see David R. Castillo and Bradley J. Nelson, eds., "Writing in the End Times: Apocalyptic Imagination in the Hispanic World," *Hispanic Issues Online* 23 (2019), https://hdl.handle.net/11299/212507.

34. M. Keith Booker, *Dystopian Literature: A Theory and Research Guide* (Westport, CT: Greenwood Press, 1994), 3.

35. All quotations from *Don Quixote* come from the following edition: Miguel de Cervantes Saavedra, *Don Quijote de la Mancha*, ed. Martín de Riquer (Barcelona: Planeta, 1987). All translations come from *Don Quixote*, trans. John Rutherford (New York: Penguin, 2003).

36. Joaquín García-Medall, "El insulto desde la pragmática intercultural," in *Lengua viva: Estudios ofrecidos a César Hernández Alonso*, ed. Antonio Álvarez Tejedor (Valladolid: Universidad de Valladolid, 2008), 671. This passage of *Don Quixote* alludes to the lexical repertoire of Luis de Góngora's poetry that became a frenzied fashion at court. Despite its farcical tone, this passage suggests how Góngora's poetic project not only generated a new poetic language but could also renew the vocabulary of infamy, thus gesturing toward a reconfiguration of the community of affronters with their own lexicographical weapons. For an analysis of direct insults among the characters of *Don Quixote* and how they reflected quotidian practices, see Jesús María Usunáriz, "Un análisis de los insultos en el *Quijote* desde la historia social del lenguaje," *Anales Cervantinos* 49 (2017): 59–73.

37. Anthony Close, *Cervantes and the Comic Mind of His Age* (Oxford: Oxford University Press, 2000), 42–56, 326–339.

CHAPTER 1 — COMMUNITIES OF AFFRONTERS

1. For some of the most recent proposals about its authorship, see Juan Antonio Frago García, *El Quijote apócrifo y Pasamonte* (Madrid: Gredos, 2005); Alfonso Martín Jiménez, *Las dos segundas partes del* Quijote (Valladolid: Universidad de Valladolid, 2014); Helena Percas de Ponseti, "Un misterio dilucidado: Pasamonte fue Avellaneda," *Cervantes* 22, no. 1 (2002): 127–154; Enrique Suárez Figaredo, *Cervantes, Figueroa, y el crimen de Avellaneda* (Barcelona: Carena, 2004); and Antonio Sánchez Portero, *Cervantes y Liñán de Riaza: el autor del otro* Quijote *atribuido a Avellaneda* (Calatayud: Centro de Estudios Bilbilitanos de la Institución "Fernando el Católico," 2011). For a comprehensive overview of critical interpretations of Fernández de Avellaneda's *Don Quixote*, see Alfonso Martín Jiménez, "Ortodoxia y heterodoxia en la interpretación del *Quijote* de Avellaneda," in *Ortodoxia y heterodoxia en Cervantes*, ed. Carmen Rivero Iglesias (Alcalá de Henares: Centro de Estudios Cervantinos, 2011), 367–380.

2. Juan Diego Vila, "El *Quijote* y la sugestión conversa: silencios, elisiones y desvíos para una predicación inefable," in *Cervantes y las religiones*, ed. Ruth Fine and Santiago López Navia (Pamplona: Universidad de Navarra, 2008), 527–531.

3. On the representation of Moriscos in Cervantes's work, see, among others, Carroll B. Johnson, *Cervantes and the Material World* (Chicago: University of Illinois Press, 2000), 51–68; Francisco Márquez Villanueva, *Moros, moriscos y turcos en Cervantes* (Barcelona: Bellaterra, 2010); Steven Hutchinson, "Arbitrating the National *Oikos*," *Journal of Spanish*

Cultural Studies 2, no. 1 (2001): 69–80; Barbara Fuchs, *Passing for Spain: Cervantes and the Fictions of Identity* (Urbana: University of Illinois Press, 2003); William Childers, *Transnational Cervantes* (Toronto: University of Toronto Press, 2006), 169–193; Trevor J. Dadson, "Cervantes y los moriscos de la Mancha," in *De Cervantes y el islam*, ed. Nuria Martínez de Castilla Muñoz and Rodolfo Gil Benumeya Grimau (Madrid: Sociedad Estatal de Conmemoraciones Culturales, 2006), 135–150; Francisco Layna Ranz, *La eficacia del fracaso: Representaciones culturales en la Segunda Parte del* Quijote (Madrid: Polifemo, 2005), 293–360; and E. Michael Gerli, *Cervantes: Displacements, Inflections, and Transcendence* (Newark: Juan de la Cuesta, 2019), 142–68.

4. On this interpretation, see Márquez Villanueva, *Moros*, 310; and Carroll B. Johnson, *Transliterating a Culture: Cervantes and the Moriscos* (Newark: Juan de la Cuesta, 2009), 198. Only Rodolfo Gil Benumeya Grimau points to a potential criticism of the expulsion of the Moriscos in Fernández de Avellaneda's book; see "Residuos de morisquismo en los *Quijotes* de Cervantes y Avellaneda," in *De Cervantes y el islam*, ed. Nuria Martínez de Castilla Muñoz and Rodolfo Gil Benumeya Grimau (Madrid: Sociedad Estatal de Conmemoraciones Culturales, 2006), 208–211. Yet his interpretation is not based on an analysis of the text itself but on the possible link between the text and Philip III's confessor, Fray Luis de Aliaga, who initially opposed the expulsion. His interpretation, however, ignores the fact that Aliaga changed his position on the expulsion of the Moriscos and ended up defending it, as Emilio Callado Estela points out, "El confesor fray Luis de Aliaga y la expulsión de los moriscos," *Investigaciones Históricas* 34 (2014): 41–46. Javier Blasco identifies possible references to palace intrigues during the government of the duke of Lerma but only alludes tangentially to the expulsion of the Moriscos, "El género de las genealogías en el *Quijote* de Avellaneda," *Boletín de la Biblioteca de Menéndez Pelayo* 81 (2005): 51–79.

5. Alonso Fernández de Avellaneda, *El ingenioso hidalgo don Quijote de la Mancha*, ed. Fernando García Salinero (Madrid: Castalia, 1999), 304–305, 318. All translations come from *Don Quixote de la Mancha (Part II)*, trans. Alberta Wilson Server and John Esten Keller (Newark: Juan de la Cuesta, 2009), 223.

6. Fernández de Avellaneda, *El ingenioso hidalgo*, 135. Trans. Server and Keller, 69.

7. As I have argued elsewhere, Fernández de Avellaneda's text is quite probably a political satire criticizing the expulsion of the Moriscos, Javier Irigoyen-García, "La expulsión de los moriscos en *El ingenioso hidalgo don Quijote de la Mancha* (1614) de Alonso Fernández de Avellaneda," *MLN* 131, no. 2 (2016): 336–355.

8. Agustín Salucio, *Discurso sobre los estatutos de limpieza de sangre*, ed. facsimile Antonio Pérez y Gómez (Cieza: ". . . la fonte que mana y corre . . . ," 1975), 16r. Later on, he insists on his criticism of "los que ponen su onra en la afrenta agena" [those who put their honor on someone's else dishonor], *Discurso*, 17r.

9. Miguel de Cervantes Saavedra, *Novelas ejemplares*, ed. Harry Sieber (Madrid: Cátedra, 1995), 1:61. All translations from this work come from *Exemplary Novellas*, trans. Michael Harney (Indianapolis: Hackett, 2016), 19.

10. See Johnson, *Cervantes*, 93–114; E. Michael Gerli, *Refiguring Authority: Reading, Writing, and Rewriting in Cervantes* (Lexington: University Press of Kentucky, 1995), 24–40; and William H. Clamurro, *Cervantes's* Novelas ejemplares: *Reading their Lessons from His Time to Ours* (Lanham: Lexington, 2015), 84–91. For Gypsies in early modern Spain, see Richard J. Pym, *The Gypsies of Early Modern Spain, 1425–1783* (New York: Palgrave, 2007); and for a general overview of their representation in early modern Spanish

literature, see Bernard Leblon, *Les Gitans dans la littérature espagnole* (Toulouse: Université de Toulouse-Le Mirail, 1982).

11. Eribon, *Insult*, 15.

12. Madero, *Manos*, 21–22.

13. For a general overview, see Michèle Guillemont, "Recherches sur la violence verbale en Espagne aux XVIe et XVIIe siècles (aspects sociaux, culturels et littéraires)" (PhD diss., Paris III-Sorbonne Nouvelle, 2000); and "Images de la violence verbale en Espagne au XVIe siècle: des pêchés de langue au délit et à l'inconvenance," in *Écriture, pouvoir et société en Espagne aux XVIe et XVIIe siècles*, ed. Pierre Civil (Paris: Presses de la Sorbonne Nouvelle, 2001), 223–240. For the persecution of injury in Castile at the beginning of the seventeenth century, see Enrique Villalba Pérez, *La administración de la justicia penal en Castilla y en la corte a comienzos del siglo XVII* (Madrid: Actas, 1993), 179–185. For a study on how literary texts dealt with personal reputation, see José Carlos del Ama, *La opinión pública en la España de Cervantes* (Pamplona: Eunsa, 2013).

14. Jerónimo de Urrea, *Diálogo de la verdadera honra militar* (Venice: Joan Griso, 1566), 9r. This passage is also analyzed by Guillemont, "Recherches," 1:59–60.

15. Luis de Torres, *Veintiquatro discursos sobre los peccados de la lengua* (Burgos: Felipe de Junta, 1590), 405.

16. Madero, *Manos*, 26–27.

17. José Manuel Pedrosa, "La maledicencia venenosa frente al sabio silencio: teorías y prácticas del bien y del mal hablar en los Siglos de Oro," in *Cultura oral, visual y escrita en la España de los Siglos de Oro*, ed. Inmaculada Osuna and Eva Llergo (Madrid: Visor, 2010), 488–513.

18. Hernando de Talavera, *Breue y muy prouechosa doctrina de lo que deue saber todo Christiano* (Granada: Meinardo Ungut and Juan Pegnitzer, 1496), Ai–Bix. On this treatise, see Michèle Guillemont, "El *Tractado muy provechoso contra el común e muy continuo pecado que es detraher o murmurar y decir mal de alguno en su absencia* de Hernando de Talavera (Granada, 1496)," in *Lo converso: orden imaginario y realidad en la cultura española (siglos XIV–XVII)*, ed. Ruth Fine, Michèle Guillemont, and Juan Diego Vila (Madrid: Iberoamericana, 2013), 119–141; and Mark Johnston, "Seducing Slander: Hernando de Talavera on Eliciting Disparagement of Others," *Essays in Medieval Studies* 30 (2014): 83–95. Although we do not know the circumstances under which Talavera composed this treatise, both scholars contextualize it within the evangelization efforts in the recently conquered kingdom of Granada and the need to assimilate conversos of both Muslim and Jewish origin.

19. Talavera, *Breve y muy prouechosa doctrina*, fi–fix.

20. Michèle Estela-Guillemont, "Política y paratexto: En torno a Martín de Azpilcueta y la reedición del *Tratado de alabanza y murmuración* de 1572," in *Paratextos en la literatura española (siglos XV–XVIII)*, ed. Soledad Arredondo Sirodey, Pierre Civil, and Michel Moner (Madrid: Casa de Velázquez, 2009), 367–378.

21. Martín de Azpilcueta, *Tractado de alabança y murmuración* (Valladolid: Adrian Ghemart, 1572), 227–228.

22. Claude Chauchadis, "Virtudes y pecados de la lengua: Sebastián de Covarrubias y Martín de Azpilcueta," *Criticón* 92 (2004): 43.

23. Azpilcueta, *Tractado*, 276–77.

24. There are two extant manuscript copies, one of them at the Biblioteca Colombina in Seville, sign. 58-2-28, which is the one I consulted. Francisco Javier Escobar Borrego dates

the composition of the work between 1580 and 1590, "Dos textos desconocidos de Jerónimo de Carranza a propósito del XI Conde de Niebla y Mateo Vázquez (con unas notas sobre Hernando de Vega)," in *El duque de Medina-Sidonia: Mecenazgo y renovación artística*, ed. José Manuel Rico García and Pedro Ruiz Pérez (Huelva: Universidad de Huelva, 2015), 123. There is also a summary of this treatise in a letter addressed to Philipp II, BNE 12933/6, as well as a similar letter about honor, also addressed to Philipp II, BNE MSS/17998/4. For Jerónimo Sánchez de Carranza's work, see also Manuel Olmedo Gobante, "Del frente a la palestra: Esgrima y ejército en la carrera autorial de Jerónimo Sánchez de Carranza," in *Vidas en armas: Biografías militares en la España del Siglo de Oro*, ed. Abigaíl Castellano López and Adrián J. Sáez (Huelva: Etiópicas, 2019), 101–114. I am thankful to Manuel Olmedo Gobante for his help with Sánchez de Carranza's work.

25. On the interdiction of duels in early modern Spain, see Claude Chauchadis, *La Loi du duel: Le code du point d'honneur dans l'Espagne des XVIe–XVIIe siècles* (Toulouse: Presses Universitaires du Mirail, 1997).

26. Bartolomé Carranza de Miranda, *Comentarios sobre el catechismo christiano*, ed. José Ignacio Tellechea Idígoras (Madrid: Biblioteca de Autores Cristianos, 1972), 1:478–531.

27. José Antonio Casillas García, "La Cofradía del Nombre de Dios de los Juramentos: Apuntes sobre esta hermandad de origen burgalés," *Boletín de la Institución Fernán González* 226 (2003): 123–135; Guillemont, "Recherches," 1:92–98.

28. Johan Huizinga, *The Autumn of the Middle Ages*, trans. Rodney J. Payton and Ulrich Mammitzsch (Chicago: University of Chicago Press, 1996), 186–190; and Jean Delumeau, *La Peur en Occident, XIVe-XVIIIe siècle: Une cité assiégée* (Paris: Fayard, 1988), 400–403.

29. On blasphemy in medieval and early modern Iberia, see, among others, Gabriel Llompart, "Blasfemias y juramentos cristológicos en la baja Edad Media catalana," *Hispania Sacra* 26 (1973): 137–164; Jesús María Usunáriz, "*Verbum maledictionis*: La blasfemia y el blasfemo de los siglos XVI y XVII," in *Aportaciones a la historia social del lenguaje: España, siglos XIV-XVIII*, ed. Rocío García Bourrellier and Jesús María Usunáriz (Madrid: Iberoamericana, 2006), 197–221; Manuel Santana Molina, *El delito de blasfemia en el tribunal inquisitorial de Cuenca* (Alicante: Universidad de Alicante, 2004); Guillemont, "Recherches"; Maureen Flynn, "Betrayals of the Soul in Spanish Blasphemy," in *Religion, Body, and Gender in Early Modern Spain*, ed. Alain Saint-Saëns (San Francisco: Mellen Research University Press, 1991), 30–44; Maureen Flynn, "Blasphemy and the Play of Anger in Sixteenth-Century Spain," *Past and Present* 149 (1995): 29–56; and Cristina Tabernero Sala, "Injurias, maldiciones y juramentos en la lengua española del siglo XVII," *Revista de Lexicografía* 16 (2010): 111.

30. Domingo de Soto, *Relecciones y opúsculos:. II-1. El abuso de los juramentos: Ocultación y revelación de secretos*, ed. Antonio Osuna Fernández-Largo (Salamanca: San Esteban, 2000), 113.

31. Nicolás de Ávila, *Suma de los mandamientos y maremagnum del segundo, que enseña para el confesionario y persuade para el púlpito* (Alcalá de Henares: Juan Gracián, [1596] 1610), 484.

32. Francisco Luque Fajardo, *Fiel desengaño contra la ociosidad y los juegos*, ed. Martín de Riquer (Madrid: Real Academia Española, 1955), 264. For blasphemy during gambling, see Guillemont, "Recherches," 1:78–84; and Javier Villa-Flores, *Dangerous Speech: A Social History of Blasphemy in Colonial Mexico* (Tucson: University of Arizona Press, 2006), 77–103.

33. As William Childers points out, blasphemy "serves as a sign of horizontal solidarity," "'¡Oh hideputa, bellaco, y cómo es católico!': Sancho, Blasphemy, and the Baroque Public Sphere," in *Don Quijote: Across Four Centuries, 1605–2005*, ed. Carroll B. Johnson (Newark: Juan de la Cuesta, 2006), 73. Similarly, Javier Villa-Flores analyzes how, for the case of Colonial Mexico, blasphemy serves "as a strategy of self-affirmation and performance of masculinity," most notably for certain professions such as sailors and soldiers, *Dangerous Speech*, 38.

34. Salazar Rincón, "Insulto," 712.

35. Similarly, Marta Madero holds that "la injuria tiene la forma de una metáfora que cifra, condensado, un sistema de valores que se expresa invertido," *Manos*, 21.

36. Darío Cabanelas Rodríguez, "Fray Diego de Guadix y su 'recopilación' de arabismos," in *Antiqua et nova Romania: Estudios lingüísticos y filológicos en honor de José Mondéjar* (Granada: Universidad de Granada, 1993), 1:238–240.

37. The complete title of his lexicographical work, as shown on the cover, is *Recopilación de algunos nombres arábigos, que los moros o árabes (en España, Francia y Italia, y islas del mar Mediterráneo, y en otras muchas partes del mundo) pusieron a algunas ciudades, villas, castillos, islas, montes, torres, ríos, puentes, valles, fuentes, puertas de ciudades: con algunos vocablos y verbos arábigos y frases o maneras de hablar de árabes, de que comúnmente se usa en las lenguas latina, española y italiana.*

38. Diego de Guadix, *Recopilación de algunos nombres arábigos que los árabes pusieron a algunas ciudades y otras muchas cosas*, ed. Elena Bajo Pérez and Felipe Maíllo Salgado (Gijón: Trea, 2005), 150–151. For a contextualization of Guadix within the ambivalent status of Arabic in early modern Spain, see Mercedes García-Arenal and Fernando Rodríguez Mediano, *Un Oriente español: Los moriscos y el Sacromonte en tiempos de Contrarreforma* (Madrid: Marcial Pons, 2010), 367–371.

39. Elena Bajo Pérez and Felipe Maíllo Salgado. "Estudio introductorio," in Guadix, *Recopilación*, 95–100.

40. On the early modern Spanish racial system and terminology, see David Nirenberg, "Race and the Middle Ages: The Case of Spain and Its Jews," in *Rereading the Black Legend: The Discourses of Religious and Racial Difference in the Renaissance Empires*, ed. Margaret R. Greer, Walter D. Mignolo, and Maureen Quilligan (Chicago: University of Chicago Press, 2007), 71–87; and María Elena Martínez, *Genealogical Fictions: Limpieza de Sangre, Religion, and Gender in Colonial Mexico* (Stanford: Stanford University Press, 2008).

41. For the extensive use of the term *marrano* in medieval and early modern Spain, see Arturo Farinelli, *Marrano (storia di un vituperio)* (Geneva: Olschki, 1925).

42. Francisco del Rosal, *Diccionario etimológico: Alfabeto primero de Origen y Etimología de todos los vocablos originales de la Lengua Castellana*, ed. facsimile Enríquez Gómez Aguado (Madrid: CSIC, 1992). On Francisco del Rosal, see the introduction by Enrique Gómez Aguado to his edition of del Rosal's *Diccionario*, xiii–xxxvii. In my quotes, I follow the modern pagination inserted by the editor in the facsimile edition. I also consulted *La razón de algunos refranes: Alfabetos tercero y cuarto*, ed. B. Bussel Thompson (London: Tamesis, 1975). This work focuses on proverbs and idioms and devotes less space to injurious terms, such as the entries "Cornudo" (35), "Perros" (81), and "Gentileza" (134, in which he criticizes one-eyed people). In this section of his lexicographical project it is hard to find any systematic perspective of the value of insults in early modern Spanish society. Even less relevant here is the "Alfabeto segundo," because

this section is limited to the etymology of place names and proper names, *El origen de los nombres: Alfabeto segundo de la obra 'Origen y etimología de todos los vocablos de originales de la lengua castellana*, ed. Antonio José Mialdea Baena (Cordoba: Plurabelle, 2006).

43. In the entry "confesar," del Rosal emphasizes once again the equivalence between "converso" and "confeso," *Diccionario*, 200.

44. The misleading use of terms such as *converso* and *cristiano nuevo* reveals the underlying genealogical logic, because they were applied not only to the individuals who converted to Christianity but also to their descendants, as Lope de Barrientos complained in the middle of the fifteenth century: "quando yo pienso en mí qué razón hay para poder llamar conuersos aquellos que son hijos de nietos de conuertidos, quedo muy espantado; porque aquellos que nacieron cristianos no sauen cosa alguna de los judaicos usos" [I am horrified when I ponder the reason for naming conversos those who are great-grandsons of people who converted, because those who were born Christians know nothing about Jewish customs], *Vida y obras de Fr. Lope de Barrientos*, ed. Fray Luis G. Alonso Getino (Salamanca: Manuel Criado, 1927), 191. Yet, by the end of the sixteenth century, the memory of lineages of Jewish origin had mostly faded away.

45. Del Rosal, *Diccionario*, 418–419, 438. Yet in the entry "collación" del Rosal praises the special blood purity of the inhabitants of Cordoba, *Diccionario*, 190.

46. Del Rosal, *Diccionario*, 55, 351, 144–145, 222. In the entry "moro" [Moor] del Rosal only offers its etymology, *Diccionario*, 462.

47. Del Rosal, *Diccionario*, 118–119. In other entries, del Rosal insists on the racket characterizing commoners, such as "carambola" (172), "jubileo" (401), and "ufana" (598).

48. See, for instance, "almadrava" (69), "caçurro" (156), "çafio" (220), "civil" (240), "ganapán" (242), "gañán" (343), "vellaco" (603), "mecánicos" (448), "mezquino" (454), and "payo" (490). He also includes insults referring to intellectual disabilities, such as "bobo" (128–129), "boçal" (129), "chola" (250), and "idiota" (390), and some referring to physical disabilities, such as "gafo" (338), "gago" (338), and "gangoso" (343). There are also a few entries referring to slurs about sexuality ("buxarrón" 147; "cabra" 152; "canto" 167) and gender difference ("muger" 465).

49. Sebastián de Covarrubias y Horozco, *Tesoro de la lengua castellana o española*, ed. Martín de Riquer (Barcelona: Alta Fulla, 2003).

50. Guadix, *Recopilación*, 286.

51. Chauchadis, "Virtudes," 39–41. My own count shows thirty-six terms referring to different ways of insulting and defaming in Covarrubias's work: "afear" (45), "afrenta" (47), "apodo" (133), "baldón" (187), "befa" (203), "burla" (246–247), "calumnia" (270), "chisme" (437), "chocarrero" (437), "chufeta" (438), "denostar" (451), "desalabar" (454), "desdorar" (457), "desgayre" (459), "desonra" (461), "detrimento" (465), "disfamar" (476), "escarnecer" (537), "famoso" (583–584), "gallardetes" (625), "ignominia" (730), "infame" and "infamia" (735), "injuria" and "injuriar" (738), "insulto" (739), "libelo" (764), "mancha" (784), "mofa" (809), "mormullo" (814), "mote" (816), "murmullar" (820–821), "palabra" (845), "pasquín" (855), "pulla" (887), "sátira" and "satírico" (929–930), "tuerto" (981), and "vituperar" (1021). Marta Madero documents the different terms in medieval Castilian that refer to insults and suggests that their abundance itself reveals insults' significance as a form of social interaction, *Manos*, 25–26.

52. See, for instance, "bagasa" (184), "brizo" (236), "bruxa" (238), "celestina" (401), "çurra" (429), "estéril" (565), "fea" (587), "gallina" (622–623), "puta" (889), and "ramera" (895).

53. For the consideration of animals in early modern Spain, see Abel A. Alves, *The Animals of Spain: An Introduction to Imperial Perceptions and Human Interaction with Other Animals, 1492–1826* (Brill: Leiden, 2011); Steven Wagschal, *Minding Animals in the Old and New Worlds: A Cognitive Historical Analysis* (Toronto: University of Toronto Press, 2018); and John Beusterien, *Transoceanic Animals as Spectacle in Early Modern Spain* (Amsterdam: Amsterdam University Press, 2020).

54. Covarrubias, *Tesoro*, 864. He only points out to the insulting connotation of "perro" in the entry "canalla," *Tesoro*, 282.

55. See for instance "basta" (198–199), "bronco" (237), "canalla" (282), "cevil" (413), "ralea" (894–895), and "vellaco" (997).

56. Bajo Pérez and Maíllo Salgado, "Estudio," 116.

57. In his own entry for "behetría," which Covarrubias cites explicitly, Guadix writes, "El nombre significa comunidad o hermandad sin nobleza y sin hidalguía" [this name means community or brotherhood with no nobility nor *hidalguía*], Guadix, *Recopilación*, 395. This is one of the few terms referring to commoners for which Guadix is rather circumspect.

58. Guadix, *Recopilación*, 466.

59. Chauchadis, "Virtudes," 44.

60. Albuixech, "Insultos," 59.

61. Castillo Lluch, "De verbo vedado," 25–26. In another article, Castillo Lluch offers other examples from texts published around the time of *Don Quixote*, "Del denuesto," 2698–2702. In Fernández de Avellaneda's *Don Quixote* this expression is found three times in Sancho's speech, Castillo Lluch, "Del denuesto," 2701. This repetition suggests the possibility that, by making Sancho ignorant of this expression, Cervantes may be trying to contest the characterization that Fernández de Avellaneda had previously made of his rustic character.

62. Childers, "Oh hideputa," 82. He analyzes this passage within the context of post-Tridentine debates on how to curtail the widespread use of blasphemy, "Oh hideputa," 82–85.

63. Covarrubias, *Tesoro*, 887. On the "pullas," see Monique Joly, *La Bourle et son interpretation: Recherches sur le passage de la facétie au roman (Espagne XVIe–XVIIe siècles)* (Lille: Université de Lille, 1982), 247–267; James Pyle Wickersham Crawford, "Echarse *pullas*: A Popular Form of Tenzone," *Romanic Review* 6 (1915): 150–164; Eugenio Asensio, *Itinerario del entremés desde Lope de Rueda a Quiñones de Benavente* (Madrid: Gredos, 1971), 146–164; Salazar Rincón, "Insulto," 710–713; Lorena Núñez Pinero, "'Echar(se) pullas': Un tipo de pelea ritual en los diálogos de Minsheu (1599), Oudin (1675) y Sobrino (1708)," *Criticón* 137 (2019): 27–51; Maurizi, "Langue"; and Nicholas R. Jones, *Staging* Habla de Negros: *Radical Performances of the African Diaspora in Early Modern Spain* (University Park: Pennsylvania State University Press, 2019), 85–118. For a more general sociological perspective on this use of insults, see Charles P. Flynn, *Insult*, 82–88.

64. Rodrigo Caro, *Días geniales o lúdricos*, ed. Jean-Pierre Étienvre (Madrid: Espasa-Calpe, 1978), 2:95.

65. On the "vejamen," see Aurora Egido, "*De ludo vitando*: Gallos áulicos en la Universidad de Salamanca," *El Crotalón* 1 (1984): 609–648; Aurora Egido, "Un vejamen de 1598 en la Universidad de Granada," in *Homenaje al Profesor Antonio Gallego Morell*, ed. María Concepción Argente del Castillo Ocaña (Granada: Universidad de Granada, 1989), 1:445–460;

Francisco Layna Ranz, "Dicterio, conceptismo y frase hecha: a vueltas con el vejamen," *Nueva Revista de Filología Hispánica* 44, no. 1 (1996): 27–56; Abraham Madroñal Durán, *"De grado y de gracias": vejámenes universitarios de los Siglos de Oro* (Madrid: CSIC, 2005), 25–120; Giovanni Cara, *Il "vejamen" in Spagna: Juicio y regocijo letterario nella prima metà del XVII secolo* (Roma: Bulzoni, 2001); and María Luisa Lobato, "Vejamen de grado en Burgo de Osma (1582): Pleito y entremés inédito de *Don Pantalón de Mondapoços* (h. 1578)," in *Teatro y poder: VI y VII Jornadas de Teatro Universidad de Burgos*, ed. Aurelia Ruiza Sola (Burgos: Universidad de Burgos, 1998), 203–223. In some extreme cases, the vejamen ceremony could provoke violence from those who felt offended by it. See Madroñal Durán, who also documents the legislation to regulate the ceremony throughout the early modern period, *De grado*, 59, 65–72.

66. Layna Ranza, "Dicterio," 53–54.

67. Close, *Cervantes*, 181–326.

68. Luis Zapata, *Miscelánea o varia historia*, ed. Antonio Carrasco González (Llerena: Editores Extremeños, 1999), 98–108.

69. Zapata, *Miscelánea*, 106–107.

70. Egido, "Linajes," 25; and Maxime Chevalier, "El arte de motejar en la corte de Carlos V," *Cuadernos para Investigación de la Literatura Hispánica* 5 (1983): 61–77.

71. Maxime Chevalier notes that the reiteration of prohibiting mockery instead reveals the inefficacy of such prohibitions, *Quevedo y su tiempo: la agudeza verbal* (Barcelona: Crítica, 1992), 59. On prescriptive attempts to limit the boundaries of laughter and *motes*, see also Victoriano Roncero López, "El humor y la risa en las preceptivas de los siglos de oro," in *Demócrito áureo: los códigos de la risa en el Siglo de Oro*, ed. Ignacio Arellano and Victoriano Roncero López (Seville: Renacimiento, 2006), 285–328.

72. Zapata, *Miscelánea*, 327.

73. See Castillo Gómez, "Panfletos."

74. Layna Ranz, "Dicterio," 56.

75. Benedict Anderson, *Imagined Communities: Reflections on the Origin and Spread of Nationalism* (London: Verso, 1991), 15.

76. Close analyzes "El licenciado vidriera" as the repudiation of the *mote* tradition, *Cervantes*, 212–215.

77. The stereotype of muleteers is indeed that they were skilled "pullistas" (nicknamers), Maxime Chevalier, "Lope doctor en pullas," in *El Siglo de Oro en escena. Homenaje a Marc Vitse*, ed. Odette Gorsse and Frédéric Serralta (Toulousse: Presses Universitaires du Mirail, 2006), 219–221.

CHAPTER 2 — SELF-DEPRECATION AND FAME

1. Pedro de Valencia, *Tratado acerca de los moriscos de España*, ed. Joaquín Gil Sanjuán (Málaga: Algazara, 1997), 77.

2. Azpilcueta, *Tractado*, 292–295.

3. Fernández de Avellaneda, *El ingenioso hidalgo*, 164–165. Trans. Server and Keller, 94.

4. On this and other references to Herostratus in early modern Spanish literature, see Frederick A. DeArmas, "The Burning at Ephesus: Cervantes and Alarcón's *La verdad sospechosa*," in *Studies in Honor of Gilberto Paolini*, ed. Mercedes Vidal Tibbits (Newark: Juan de la Cuesta, 1996), 50–53.

5. Covarrubias, *Tesoro*, 282.

NOTES TO PAGES 42-47

6. On the exchanges between Cervantes and other authors, see Close, *Cervantes*, 104–107; and Salazar Rincón, "Insulto."

7. Covarrubias, *Tesoro*, 786.

8. Cervantes insists on this play on words when he later promises that the *Persiles* would be published (although it was only printed posthumously): "libro que se atreve a competir con Heliodoro, si ya por atrevido no sale con las manos en la cabeza" (1:53) [a book that dares to compete with Heliodorus, if it does not come off looking too bad by reason of its very audacity] (Trans. Harney 11). On this wordplay in Cervantes, see Jacques Lezra, *Unspeakable Subjects: The Genealogy of the Event in Early Modern Europe* (Stanford: Stanford University Press, 1997), 220–234.

9. I borrow the term from Aurora Egido, who focuses on Anastasio Pantaleón de Ribera as an author who was well known for his own "autovejámenes," "Linajes," 40.

10. Fernández de Avellaneda, *El ingenioso hidalgo*, 51–52. Trans. Server and Keller, 3. According to some scholars, Fernández de Avellaneda's attack was allegedly motivated by a previous attack of Cervantes against Lope in the prologue to the first part of *Don Quixote* in 1605, Emilio Orozco Díaz, *Cervantes y la novela del Barroco: Del* Quijote *de 1605 al* Persiles (Granada: Universidad de Granada, 1992), 89–101.

11. Salazar Rincón suggests that Cervantes could cope with insults because of his humble origins and because he was hardened by his life experiences, "Insulto," 720–722.

12. Both authors focus on physical appearances, which somehow limits the scope of insults, reducing them to a form of slander that is socially admissible. Cutting remarks about physical defects were socially acceptable in certain contexts, Salazar Rincón, "Insulto," 711; Chauchadis, "Virtudes," 43; Close, *Cervantes*, 181–212.

13. See Juan Gil, "Berenjeneros: The Aubergine Eaters," in *The Conversos and Moriscos in Late Medieval Spain and Beyond: Departures and Change*, ed. Kevin Ingram (Leiden: Brill, 2009), 121–142.

14. A similar justification of the expulsion is stated by another Morisco character in *Los trabajos de Persiles y Sigismunda*, published posthumously in 1617, Miguel de Cervantes Saavedra, *Los trabajos de Persiles y Sigismunda*, ed. Juan Bautista Avalle-Arce (Madrid: Castalia, 1969), 356.

15. Julio Baena, "Sintaxis de la ética del texto: Ricote, en el *Quijote II*, la lengua de las mariposas," *Bulletin of Spanish Studies* 83, no. 4 (2006): 507–524. Many scholars have noted that Ricote's act of self-deprecation is at the very least equivocal. See, for instance, Márquez Villanueva, *Moros*, 227–230, 415n997; Childers, *Transnational*, 174–175; and Johnson, *Affective Geographies*, 120–123.

16. Pedro de León comments about the *almadrabas* of Zahara that "es tanta la golosina que algunos tienen de esta vida picaresca, que algunas veces se van a ella algunos mozos, hijos de gente principal" [there is so much fancy for this picaresque life, that sometimes young men who are the sons of notable people choose it]; to support his assertion, he refers to the conversation he had with one of those *pícaros*, who was the son of a count, *Grandeza y miseria en Andalucía: Testimonio de una encrucijada histórica (1578–1616)*, ed. Pedro Herrera Puga (Granada: Facultad de Teología, 1981), 76–77. On the hybridization of literary genres in this novella, see Edwin Williamson, "Challenging the Hierarchies: The Interplay of Romance and the Picaresque in *La ilustre fregona*," *Bulletin of Spanish Studies* 81, no. 4–5 (2004): 655–674; and Jorge Checa, "El *romance* y su sombra: hibridación genérica en *La ilustre fregona*," *Revista de Estudios Hispánicos* 25, no. 1 (1999): 29–48.

17. Katherine L. Brown reads this episode as the central passage of the novella, because it indicates the fragmentation of identity and the impossibilities of a unified reading, "Invento del 'quinto cuarto': La conciencia dividida, la fragmentación textual y la paradoja de la lectura en 'La ilustre fregona,'" *Cervantes* 36, no. 2 (2016): 145-168.

18. Monique Joly, "Erotismo y marginación social en la novela cervantina," *Cervantes* 12, no. 2 (1992): 18.

19. On the reading of Costanza as a bargaining chip between men, see Carroll B. Johnson, "Observaciones sobre el orden patriarcal en *La ilustre fregona*," in *Siglos Dorados: Homenaje a Augustin Redondo*, ed. Pierre Civil (Madrid: Castalia, 2004), 1:653-666; Eric Kartchner, *Unhappily ever After: Deceptive Idealism in Cervantes's Marriage Tales* (Newark: Juan de la Cuesta, 2005), 93-95; Theresa Ann Sears, *A Marriage of Convenience: Ideal and Ideology in the* Novelas ejemplares (New York: Peter Lang, 1993), 199; and Javier Irigoyen-García, "'Si no es adivinando la mitad del pergamino': Discurso y realidad en *La ilustre fregona*," in *Novelas ejemplares: Las grietas de la ejemplaridad*, ed. Julio Baena (Newark: Juan de la Cuesta, 2008), 227-249.

20. As Eribon frames it, "Individual subjectivity is always 'collective,' we might say, because an individual is always socialized—socialized within a social realm traversed by hierarchies and division," *Insult*, xvii.

21. Covarrubias, *Tesoro*, 257, 378-382.

22. Covarrubias, *Tesoro*, 360.

23. *Lazarillo de Tormes*, ed. Francisco Rico (Madrid: Cátedra, 1995), 10.

24. On the circulation of lists of persons accused of bigamy and adultery, see Castillo Gómez, "Letras de penitencia," 58-60. On consenting cuckoldry as a legal category in the Middle Ages and the early modern period, see Madero, *Manos*, 110-111; and Segura Urra, "*Verba vituperosa*," 173. On the prosecution of bigamy by the Inquisition, see Enrique Gacto, "El delito de bigamia y la Inquisición española," in *Sexo barroco y otras transgresiones modernas* (Madrid: Alianza, 1990), 127-152.

25. On the interpretation that Lázaro is a cynic, see George A. Shipley, "The Critic as Witness for the Prosecution: Making the Case against Lázaro de Tormes," *PMLA* 97, no. 2 (1982): 179-194; and Stephen Gilman, "The Death of Lazarillo de Tormes," *PMLA* 81, no. 3 (1966): 149-166. On the interpretation that Lázaro sacrifices his honor, see Georgina Sabat de Rivers, "La moral que Lázaro nos propone," *MLN* 95, no. 2 (1980): 242-244.

26. Close, *Cervantes*, 286.

27. Butler, *Psychic Life*, 104.

28. Shipley, "Critic," 186.

29. Butler, *Psychic Life*, 115-116.

30. Butler, *Psychic Life*, 118.

31. Gilman, "Death," 154.

32. Julio Baena, "Lazarillo de Tormes y el Levítico: la piedra de escándalo de la utopía infame," *Dissidences: Hispanic Journal of Theory and Criticism* 1, no. 1 (2005): 1-28.

33. On Juan de Luna's Protestantism, see Eduard Boehmer, "Juan de Luna," *Zeifschrift für vergleichende Literaturgeschichte* 14 (1904): 423-430; Joseph L. Laurenti, "El nuevo mundo social de la *Segunda Parte de la vida de Lazarillo de Tormes* . . . de Juan de Luna," *Boletín de la biblioteca nacional de Menéndez Pelayo* 47 (1971): 151-190; Robert S. Rudders, "Nueva luz sobre Juan de Luna," in *La picaresca: Orígenes, textos y estructuras*, ed. Manuel Criado del Val (Madrid: Fundación Universitaria Española, 1979), 485-491; Judith A. Whitenack, "'Cronista y no autor': Juan de Luna's *Lazarillo*," *Hispanic Journal* 15, no. 1 (1994): 45-62;

Gustavo Alfaro, "Los *Lazarillos* y la Inquisición," *Hispanófila* 26, no. 3 (1983): 11–19; and Alan Francis, "La estrategia satírica en el *Lazarillo* de Juan de Luna," *Nueva Revista de Filología Hispánica* 25 (1976): 363–373. On this work, see also Marina Scordilis Brownlee, "Generic Expansion and Generic Subversion: The Two Continuations of *Lazarillo de Tormes*," *Philological Quarterly* 61 (1982): 317–327; Judith A. Whitenack, "Juan de Luna's *Lazarillo*: Continuation or Subversion?" *Philological Quarterly* 67, no. 2 (1988): 177–194; and Marcel Bataillon, *Novedad y fecundidad del* Lazarillo de Tormes (Madrid: Anaya, 1986).

34. Although it is certainly interesting for other reasons, I do not consider the 1555 *Segunda parte* because it barely touches on the subject of this book.

35. Juan de Luna, *Segunda parte del Lazarillo*, ed. Pedro M. Piñero (Madrid: Cátedra, 1988), 290.

36. This is a Mediterranean legend about men who looked like fish and could live under water, which in its most common version in Spain was known as the Peje Nicolao. On this figure, see Julio Caro Baroja, "El 'Pesce Cola' o el 'Peje Nicolao,'" *Revista de dialectología y tradiciones populares* 39 (1984): 7–16; María del Río Parra, *Una era de monstruos: Representaciones de lo deforme en el Siglo de Oro español* (Madrid: Iberoamericana, 2003); Robert S. Rudders, "Lazarillo de Tormes y los peces: la continuación homónima de 1555," *Explicación de textos literarios* 2 (1974): 257–266; Víctor Pueyo, *Cuerpos plegables: anatomías de la excepción en España y en América Latina (Siglos XVI–XVIII)* (Woodbridge: Tamesis, 2016), 61–67; Giuseppe Cavarra, *La leggenda di colapesce* (Messina: Intilla, 1998); and Alberto Salamanca Ballesteros, *Monstruos, ostentos y hermafroditas* (Granada: Universidad de Granada, 2007), 72–75.

37. Alfaro already notices the similarity between the mechanism and the instruments of torture used by the Inquisition, "Los *Lazarillos*," 17. For the use of gags by the Inquisition, see Consuelo Maqueda Abreu, *El auto de fe* (Madrid: Istmo, 1992), 238–240.

38. This passage also shows how interpellation works both ways. Not only does Lázaro begin to interiorize his identity as a fish-man, but even the fishermen believe that the conditions of his confinement will eventually turn him into a monster: "Crecía la codicia a la medida de la ganancia, la cual les hizo dudar de mi salud. Para conservarla entraron en bureo si sería bueno sacarme las noches del agua, por temer que la mucha humedad y frialdad no me acortasen la vida. . . . Determinaron estuviese siempre en ella, creyendo que la costumbre se tornaría en naturaleza" [Greed grew with profits, which made them concern about my health. To preserve it, they debated whether it would be convenient to take me out of the water at night, fearing that too much humidity and cold would shorten my life. . . . They decided to keep me permanently in the water, believing that habit would turn into nature] (Luna, *Segunda parte*, 297).

39. Harry Vélez-Quiñones, *Monstrous Displays: Representation and Perversion in Spanish Literature* (New Orleans: University Press of the South, 1999), ix–x.

40. See for instance Gutierre de Cetina's paradox defending the honorability of cuckoldry, which is but a literary exercise to play the devil's advocate, *Paradoja: Trata que no solamente no es cosa mala, dañosa ni vergonzosa ser un hombre cornudo, mas que los cuernos son buenos y provechosos*, ed. Gonzalo Santonja (Valladolid: Maxtor, 2016). On the figure of the cuckold in early modern Spanish literature, see Félix Cantizano Pérez, *El erotismo en la poesía de adúlteros y cornudos en el Siglo de Oro* (Madrid: Editorial Complutense, 2007).

41. Francisco de Quevedo, *Poesía completa*, ed. José Manuel Blecua (Barcelona: Planeta, 1999), 639. My translation cannot convey the play on words with "cuantía." The *caballeros*

de cuantía were a social category that, although not entirely recognized as *hidalgos* and therefore as nobles, were considered as close to them in prestige, based on the premise that they had to own arms and a horse, Domingo Centenero de Arce, *De repúblicas urbanas a ciudades nobles: Un análisis de la evolución y desarrollo del republicanismo castellano (1550–1621)* (Madrid: Biblioteca Nueva, 2012), 61–66. The only arms displayed by this hypothetical cuckold would be, of course, his horns.

42. Quevedo, *Poesía*, 643.

43. Francisco de Quevedo, *Prosa festiva completa*, ed. Celsa Carmen García-Valdés (Madrid: Cátedra, 1993), 312, 315.

CHAPTER 3 — DYSTOPIAS OF INFAMY

1. David Nirenberg, *Communities of Violence: Persecution of Minorities in the Middle Ages* (Princeton: Princeton University Press, 1996), 18–19.

2. For the development of the statutes of blood purity, see Albert A. Sicroff, *Los estatutos de limpieza de sangre: Controversias entre los siglos XV y XVII*, trans. Mauro Armiño (Madrid: Taurus, 1985); Juan Hernández Franco, *Sangre limpia, sangre española: El debate de los estatutos de limpieza (siglos XV–XVII)* (Madrid: Cátedra, 2011); and Martínez, *Genealogical Fictions*.

3. Jean-Pierre Dedieu, *L'Administration de la foi: l'Inquisition de Tolède, XVIe–XVIIIe siècle* (Madrid: Casa de Velázquez, 1989), 341–342.

4. Bernardo J. López Belinchón, "La memoria de la infamia," in *Felipe II (1527–1598): Europa y la Monarquía Católica*, ed. José Martínez Millán (Madrid: Parteluz, 1998), 3:271–274. There were some lists of converso families, such as the one produced in Segovia in 1510 to ensure their religious instruction, Marcel Bataillon, "Les nouveaux-chrétiens de Ségovie en 1510," *Bulletin Hispanique* 58 (1956): 207–231; or in Cordoba in 1521, Augustin Redondo, "Le discours d'exclusion des 'deviants' tenu par l'Inquisition à l'époque de Charles V," in *Les problèmes de l'exclusion en Espagne (XVIe–XVIIe siècles)*, ed. Augustin Redondo (Paris: Publications de la Sorbonne, 1983), 31. In the wake of the expulsion of the Moriscos, several voices called for the expulsion of all the conversos of Jewish origin, regardless of whether they had been condemned by the Inquisition or not, Juan Ignacio Pulido Serrano, "La expulsión frustrada: Proyectos para la erradicación de la herejía judaica en la Monarquía Hispana," in *VIIa Reunión Científica de la Fundación Española de Historia Moderna*, ed. Francisco José Aranda Pérez (Ciudad Real: Universidad de Castilla-La Mancha, 2004), 1:891–904. Yet those listings of Jewish genealogies were never promoted by the Inquisition or the monarchy and were rarely considered for legally determining who was an Old Christian or not.

5. For instance, Nirenberg analyzes how in the Middle Ages many of the laws against Jews and Muslims had the goal of obtaining economic compensation from these two communities in exchange for not applying them, *Communities*, 163. See also Ángel Galán Sánchez for how special taxation of the Moriscos during the sixteenth century was actually a way to mark them as a separate religious minority, "El dinero del rey y la 'ley de la comunidad': Pacto político y contrato fiscal en el Reino de Granada tras la conquista," in *Avant le contrat social: Le contrat politique dans l'Occident médiéval, XIIIe–XVe siècle*, ed. François Foronda (Paris: Publications de la Sorbonne, 2011), 653–683; and "'Herejes consentidos': La justificación de una fiscalidad diferencial en el Reino de Granada," *Historia. Instituciones. Documentos* 33 (2006): 173–209.

6. López Belinchón, "La memoria," 274–275.

7. Beusterien, "Blotted Genealogies," 190–191; Infantes, "Luceros," 115–127.

8. See Antonio Domínguez Ortiz, *Los judeoconversos en España y américa* (Madrid: Istmo, 1978), 200–202; Christiane Stallaert, *Ni una gota de sangre impura: La España inquisitorial y la Alemania nazi cara a cara* (Barcelona: Galaxia Gutenberg, 2006), 252–255; Ruth Pike, *Linajudos and Conversos in Seville: Greed and Prejudice in Sixteenth- and Seventeenth-Century Spain* (New York: Peter Lang, 2000); and Enrique Soria Mesa, "Los linajudos: Honor y conflicto social en la Granada del Siglo de Oro," in *Violencia y conflictividad en el universo barroco*, ed. Julián J. Lozano Navarro and Juan Luis Castellano (Granada: Comares, 2010), 401–427. For the literary parodies of apocryphal genealogies, see also Egido, "Linajes." The anxiety of social reputation as an opportunity for economic extortion is illustrated in Cervantes's novella *Rinconete y Cortadillo*" in which a band of crooks read their assignments, which consist of posting signs of infamy for several people in Seville (*Novelas ejemplares*, 1:236–237).

9. This is also the main point of the anonymous treatise (also attributed to Salucio), "Del origen de los villanos que llaman christianos viejos" [Of the Origin of the Peasants Named Old Christians], which claims that all who pretended to be Old Christians were indeed the descendants of Muslims, Jews, or debased *mozárabes* (the Christians who stayed under Muslim rule and those of low origin who have no memory of their lineages, Francisco López Estrada, ed., "Dos tratados de los siglos XVI y XVII sobre los mozárabes," *Al-Andalus* 16, no. 1 (1951): 336–345. Antonio Domínguez Ortiz, who disputes the attribution of this treatise to Salucio, suggests that its goal may have been "infamar... a toda España, para demostrar que la distinción entre cristianos viejos y nuevos era ilusoria" [to defame... all Spain, in order to demonstrate that the distinction between Old and New Christians was an illusion], *La clase social de los conversos en Castilla en la edad moderna* (Granada: Universidad de Granada, 1991), 217.

10. Hernández Franco, *Sangre limpia*, 162–192.

11. Later on, Salucio alludes again to the Moriscos by reproducing the common stereotype of their fertility rates (24v–25r). However, the overarching idea in his treatise is that the "reproduction" of the "stain" is not the product of some groups being more fertile than others but in the way perception of the "stain" permeates the entire social fabric.

12. Quoted in Domínguez Ortiz, *La clase social*, 251.

13. Quoted in Domínguez Ortiz, *La clase social*, 230.

14. Butler, *Psychic Life*, 81.

15. This case has been studied in detail by Jaime Contreras, *Sotos contra Riquelmes: Regidores, inquisidores y criptojudíos* (Madrid: Siglo XXI, 2013).

16. Contreras, *Sotos contra Riquelmes*, 290–295.

17. Miquel Forteza, *Els descendents dels jueus conversos de Mallorca* (Palma de Mallorca: Moll, 1972), 14–15.

18. Stallaert, *Ni una gota*, 148–149.

19. Beusterien, "Blotted Genealogies," 191.

20. Beusterien, "Blotted Genealogies," 193.

21. On the Moriscos who stayed in Spain after the expulsion, see Trevor J. Dadson, "Official Rhetoric versus Local Reality: Propaganda and the Expulsion of the Moriscos," in *Rhetoric and Reality in Early Modern Spain*, ed. Richard J. Pym (London: Tamesis, 2006), 1–24; and Enrique Soria Mesa, *Los últimos moriscos. Pervivencias de la población de origen islámico en el reino de Granada (siglos XVII–XVIII)* (Valencia: Universitat de València, 2014).

22. Quoted in Henri Lapeyre, *Geografía de la España morisca*, trans. Luis C. Rodríguez García (Valencia: Diputación Provincial de Valencia, 1986), 329.

23. Stallaert, *Ni una gota*, 258.

24. Valencia, *Tratado*, 131.

25. See Henry Méchoulan, *El honor de Dios*, trans. Enrique Sordo (Barcelona: Argos Vergara, 1981), 196; Stallaert, *Ni una gota*, 284; James B. Tueller, *Good and Faithful Christians: Moriscos and Catholicism in Early Modern Spain* (New Orleans: University Press of the South, 2002), 101; and Lapeyre, *Geografía*, 28–36, 116–119, 150–158, 180–183.

26. Pedro Aznar Cardona, *Expulsión justificada de los Moriscos Españoles* (Huesca: Pedro Cabarte, 1612), 2:127v.

27. Pedro Fernández de Navarrete, *Conservación de monarquías y discursos políticos*, in *Obras de don Diego de Saavedra Fajardo y del licenciado Pedro Fernández de Navarrete* (Madrid: Atlas, 1947), 466b.

28. For a detailed study of the different versions of the tale and the folkloric and literary sources available to Cervantes, see Maurice Molho, *Cervantes: raíces folklóricas* (Madrid: Gredos, 1976), 46–214. For a recent analysis of the ideological implications of each version, see Julio Baena, "The Emperor's Old—and Perennial—Clothes: Two Spanish Fine-Tunings to Andersen's Received Wisdom," *International Journal of Žižek Studies* 9, no. 2 (2015): 1–14.

29. Don Juan Manuel, *El conde Lucanor*, ed. Alfonso I. Sotelo (Madrid: Cátedra, 1991), 215.

30. Don Juan Manuel, *El conde Lucanor*, 218.

31. Baena, "The Emperor's," 10–12.

32. Even though the title and the characters refer to it as a "retablo" (tableau), they also use the word "manta" (blanket), which is probably some sort of screen on which the alleged images are supposed to be projected.

33. I have modified here Patterson's translation to better reflect the obsession with blood purity.

34. On the interpretation that Cervantes criticizes the doctrine of blood purity in this play, see William Rozenblat, "Cervantes y los conversos (algunas reflexiones acerca del *Retablo de las maravillas*)," *Anales Cervantinos* 17 (1978): 99–110; Bruce W. Wardropper, "The Butt of the Satire in *El retablo de las maravillas*," *Cervantes* 4, no. 1 (1984): 32–33; Ryan Prendergast, *Reading, Writing, and Errant Subjects in Inquisitorial Spain* (Burlington: Ashgate, 2011), 101–106; Christina H. Lee, *The Anxiety of Sameness in Early Modern Spain* (Manchester: Manchester University Press, 2016), 143–145; and Enrique Martínez López, "Mezclar berzas con capachos: armonía y guerra de castas en el *Entremés del retablo de las maravillas* de Cervantes," *Boletín de la Real Academia Española* 72, no. 255 (1992): 67–171. On the contrary, some attribute those beliefs to Cervantes himself as a defender of blood purity; for instance, Jaime Contreras, "Conflicto social y estatutos de limpieza en la obra de Cervantes," *Torre de los Lujanes* 56 (2005): 101. John Beusterien suggests that the play deconstructs the creation of whiteness in opposition to increasing African slavery, *An Eye on Race: Perspectives from Theater in Imperial Spain* (Lewisburg: Bucknell University Press, 2006), 141–171. From a different angle, José R. Cartagena Calderón analyzes Cervantes's parody of manhood, *Masculinidades en obras: El drama de la hombría en el teatro imperial* (Newark: Juan de la Cuesta, 2008), 234–253.

35. Molho, *Cervantes*, 108–117; William Childers, "'Ese tan borrado sobrescrito': The Deconstruction of Lope's Religious Theater in *El retablo de las maravillas* and *El rufián dichoso*," *Bulletin of the Comediantes* 56 no. 2 (2004): 248–250; David R. Castillo and William Egginton, *Medialogies: Reading Reality in the Age of Inflationary Media* (New York: Bloomsbury, 2017), 31–33; and Gerli, *Refiguring*, 95–109.

36. Martínez López assumes that the town dwellers are indeed not Old Christians, despite the lack of explicit textual evidence supporting this interpretation, "Mezclar," 74, 95–97, 107–135.

37. Martínez Lopez, "Mezclar," 96–97.

38. For Martínez López, this is the only positive moment in the play, gesturing toward the potential understanding between Old and New Christians, "Mezclar," 155–157.

39. Ruth Fine, "El entrecruzamiento de lo hebreo y lo converso en la obra de Cervantes: Un encuentro singular," in *Cervantes y las religiones*, ed. Ruth Fine and Santiago López Navia (Pamplona: Universidad de Navarra, 2008), 437–439.

40. Julio Baena, *Discordancias cervantinas* (Newark: Juan de la Cuesta, 2003), 190.

41. For a general application of Girard's argument to discrimination against ethnic minorities in early modern Spain, see Louis Cardaillac, "Vision simplificatrice des groupes marginaux par le groupe dominant dans l'Espagne des XVIe et XVIIe siècles," in *Les problèmes de l'exclusion en Espagne (XVIe–XVIIe siècles)*, ed. Augustin Redondo (Paris: Publications de la Sorbonne, 1983), 19–21.

42. I have modified Patterson's translation of this passage, which reflects a different interpretation from the one I am following here.

43. Baena, "The Emperor's," 12.

CHAPTER 4 — FANCY *SAMBENITOS*

1. As Marta Madero points out, injury can be provoked by all sorts of actions and omissions, including body language, *Manos*, 26.

2. On the ceremony of the auto de fe, see Joseph Pérez, *Breve historia de la Inquisición en España*, trans. María Pons Irazazábal (Barcelona: Crítica, 2009), 140–153; Francisco Bethencourt, "The Auto da Fé: Ritual and Imagery," *Journal of the Warburg and Courtauld Institutes* 55 (1992): 155–168; Doris Moreno Martínez, "Cirios, trompetas y altares: El auto de fe como fiesta," *Espacio, Tiempo y Forma: Serie IV. Historia Moderna* 10 (1997): 148–164; Doris Moreno Martínez, "Una apacible idea de la gloria: El auto de fe barroco y sus escenarios simbólicos," *Manuscrits* 17 (1999): 159–177; Jaime Contreras, "Fiesta y auto de fe: un espacio sagrado y profano," in *Las relaciones de sucesos en España (1500–1750)*, ed. Henry Ettinghausen et al. (Alcalá de Henares: Universidad de Alcalá, 1996), 79–90; Maqueda Abreu, *El auto de fe*; Miguel Jiménez Monteserín, "El auto de fe," in *L'Inquisition espagnole et la construction de la monarchie confessionelle (1478–1561)*, ed. Raphaël Carrasco (Paris: Ellipses, 2002), 140–152; and Ana María Cuadro García, "Las sogas, las sedas y las burlas: El mundo nuevo del auto de fe," in *Poder y cultura festiva en la Andalucía moderna*, ed. Raúl Molina Recio and Manuel Peña Díaz (Cordoba: Universidad de Córdoba, 2006), 115–140.

3. On the sambenitos, see Pérez, *Breve historia*, 146–147; Bartolomé Bennassar, "La Inquisición o la pedagogía del miedo," in *Inquisición española: poder político y control social*, ed. Bartolomé Bennassar, trans. Javier Alfaya (Barcelona: Crítica, 1981), 116–120; Francisco Bethencourt, *La Inquisición en la época moderna. España, Portugal, Italia, Siglos XV–XIX* (Madrid: Akal, 1997), 328–334; Julio Caro Baroja, *Los judíos en la España*

moderna y contemporánea (Madrid: Istmo, 2000), 1:346–353; Maqueda Abreu, *El auto de fe*, 235–254; and Castillo Gómez, "Letras de penitencia," 63–68. Castillo Gómez reproduces in his appendix some of the few extant sambenitos. The etymology of the term "sambenito" is uncertain. Early modern authors considered it a distortion of "saco bendito" (sacred frock), Covarrubias, *Tesoro*, 925. Américo Castro has refuted this interpretation, suggesting instead that the term takes its origin from some kind of scapular originally identified with Benedictine monks, "Sambenito," *Revista de Filología Española* 15 (1928): 180. At the beginning of the seventeenth century, Francisco del Rosal proposes an alternative, far-fetched etymology based on "sábana" (sheet), *Diccionario*, 554–555.

4. López Belinchón, "La memoria," 273; Dedieu, *L'Administration*, 283; Juan Blázquez Miguel, *La Inquisición en Castilla-La Mancha* (Madrid: Universidad de Córdoba, 1986), 91–92; and Juan Blázquez Miguel, *El tribunal de la Inquisición en Murcia* (Murcia: Academia Alfonso X el Sabio, 1986), 30–31. In the case of Valencia, the Inquisition allowed him to pay a fine, instead of hanging the sambenitos, Ricardo García Cárcel, *Herejía y sociedad en el siglo XVI: La Inquisición en Valencia 1530–1609* (Barcelona: Península, 1980), 164–165.

5. The extant sambenitos of Tui are reproduced in Jesús Casás Otero, *Los sambenitos del Museo Diocesano de Tui* (Tui: Museo Diocesano, 2004), 91–92. There is also a copy of several sambenitos in Cordoba in Rafael Gracia Boix, *Colección de documentos para la historia de la Inquisición de Córdoba* (Cordoba: Monte de Piedad y Caja de Ahorros de Córdoba, 1982), 248–253.

6. Luis R. Corteguera, *Death by Effigy: A Case from the Mexican Inquisition* (Philadelphia: University of Pennsylvania Press, 2012), 35, 72, 74.

7. José María García Fuentes, *La Inquisición en Granada en el siglo XVI: Fuentes para su estudio* (Granada: Universidad de Granada, 1981), 247–249.

8. García Fuentes, *La Inquisición*, 260–261.

9. García Fuentes, *La Inquisición*, 260.

10. Pedro Malón de Chaide, *La conversión de la Magdalena*, ed. P. Félix García (Madrid: Espasa-Calpe, 1930–1947), 1:221.

11. Alonso de Villegas, *Fructus Sanctorum y quinta parte del Flos Sanctorum* (Cuenca: Juan Masselin, 1594), 56v. There is an error in the foliation, which restarts after folio 438. This should be fol. 494v instead of fol. 56v.

12. Andrés Núñez de Andrada, *Primera parte del Vergel de la Escritura divina* (Cordoba: Andrés Barrera, 1600), 153r.

13. In one application to the Order of Calatrava in 1637, one of the witnesses against the applicant claims that, when one of his ancestors tried to participate in an aristocratic equestrian performance in Seville, his father took the family to see their sambenito to remind them of their origin and to behave humbly, Pike, *Linajudos*, 125. Although I have not been able to locate the exact passage of Pike's source at the Archivo Histórico Nacional, her paraphrase of this anecdote sounds very similar to that of Núñez de Andrada, which suggests that it crystallized as an urban legend that could be used in real legal cases.

14. Covarrubias, *Tesoro*, 925.

15. Alonso de Castillo Solórzano, *Jornadas alegres*, ed. Julia Barella and Mita Valvassori (Madrid: Sial 2019), 193.

16. Peter N. Dunn holds that the moral criticism focuses on pride, *Castillo Solórzano and the Decline of the Spanish Novel* (Oxford: Basil Blackwell, 1952), 83–84. This is certainly one of the main themes, but to sustain his interpretation Dunn simply disregards the many other options proposed by the narrator and the tale itself.

17. On the differential taxation of the Moriscos, see Galán Sánchez, "'Herejes consentidos'"; "El dinero del rey."

18. Morisco studies is an ever-growing field across various languages and disciplines. Some of the most recent books in English are L. P. Harvey, *Muslims of Spain, 1500 to 1614* (Chicago: University of Chicago Press, 2005); Mary Elizabeth Perry, *The Handless Maiden: Moriscos and the Politics of Religion in Early Modern Spain* (Princeton: Princeton University Press, 2005); Matthew Carr, *Blood and Faith: The Purging of Muslim Spain* (New York: New Press, 2009); and James B. Tueller, *Good and Faithful Christians* (New Orleans, University Press of the South, 2002). In Spanish, see García-Arenal and Rodríguez Mediano, *Un Oriente español*; Rafael Carrasco, *Deportados en nombre de Dios. La expulsión de los moriscos: cuarto centenario de una ignominia* (Barcelona: Destino, 2009); and Antonio Moliner Prada, ed., *La expulsión de los moriscos* (Barcelona: Nabla, 2009).

19. Augustin Redondo, *Revisitando las culturas del Siglo de Oro* (Salamanca: Universidad de Salamanca, 2007), 39.

20. Martín González de Cellorigo, *Memorial* [Valladolid, 1597], 6v. I cite the copy held at the Biblioteca Nacional de España R/13027.

21. Pascual Boronat y Barrachina, *Los moriscos españoles y su expulsión* (Valencia: Francisco Vives y Mora, 1901), 1:296.

22. Juan de Pineda, *Tercera parte de la Monarchia Ecclesiastica* (Salamanca: Juan Fernández, 1588), 219v.

23. Salucio, *Discurso*, 22v.

24. Valencia, *Tratado*, 131. On the myth of the inassimilable Morisco, see José María Perceval, *Todos son uno; Arquetipos, xenofobia y racismo: La imagen del morisco en la Monarquía Española durante los siglos XVI y XVII* (Almería: Instituto de Estudios Almerienses, 1997).

25. Fermín Mayorga, *Los moriscos de Hornachos crucificados y coronados de espinas* (Madrid: Cultiva, 2009), 67–68.

26. Jaime Bleda, *Corónica de los moros de España* (Valencia: Felipe Mey, 1618), 883a.

27. Damián Fonseca, *Justa expulsión de los Moriscos de España* (Roma: Jacomo Mascardo, 1612), 125–126.

28. Henry Charles Lea, *Los moriscos españoles: Su conversión y expulsión*, trans. Jaime Lorenzo Miralles (Alicante: Aguaclara, 1990), 164–165.

29. Carrasco, *Deportados*, 217–218. See also Jean-Pierre Dedieu and Bernard Vincent, "Face à l'Inquisition: Jugements et attitudes des morisques à l'égard du tribunal," in *Les morisques et l'Inquisition*, ed. Louis Cardaillac (Paris: Publisud, 1990), 82. Trying to determine whether Moriscos had a concept of social honor similar to Old Christians is beyond the scope of this book. Yet it is telling that an anonymous Morisco exiled in Tunis conceives the resilience of the Morisco community as anchored in their Islamic faith against the Inquisition and anyone who "ynjustamente nos quiera ofender" [unfairly wants to offend us], *Tratado de los dos caminos, por un morisco refugiado en Túnez*, ed. Álvaro Galmés de Fuentes and Juan Carlos Villaverde Amieva (Madrid:

160   NOTES TO PAGES 92–95

Instituto Universitario Seminario Menéndez Pidal, 2005), 207. This author does not
make any allusion to Moriscos adopting as a source of pride those signs of infamy
imposed on them by the Inquisition. On the opinions about the Inquisition among Jews,
Moriscos, and Spanish Protestants, see Ricardo García Cárcel and Doris Moreno Martínez, "La opinión de las víctimas de la Inquisición en la España de los siglos XVI y
XVII," in *Estudios en homenaje al profesor Teófanes Egido*, ed. María de los Ángeles
Sobaler Seco and Máximo García Fernández (Valladolid: Junta de Castilla y León,
2004), 2:87–103.

30. I have not found analogous anecdotes about conversos of Jewish origin. At most,
Jerónimo de la Cruz claims that in 1631 that he witnessed in Valladolid a Portuguese
Judaizer wearing his sambenito with so much defiant pride that it created a scandal in
the city, *Defensa de los estatutos y noblezas españolas* (Zaragoza: Pedro Escuer, 1637),
106–107.

31. Mercedes García-Arenal, *Inquisición y moriscos: Los procesos del tribunal de
Cuenca* (Madrid: Siglo XXI, 1983), 99.

32. For a study of the mockeries endured by Don Quixote and Sancho at the dukes'
palace, see, among others, Bryant Creel, "The Palace of the Apes: The Ducal Chateau and
Cervantes's Repudiation of Satiric Malice," in *Don Quijote across Four Centuries: 1605–
2005*, ed. Carroll B. Johnson (Newark: Juan de la Cuesta, 2006), 87–105. For a recent
analysis of this and other shaming punishments in Cervantes's oeuvre, see Johnson,
Affective Geographies, 80–88.

33. Moreno Martínez, "Una apacible idea," 162. For José Antonio Escudero López
there is no criticism of the Inquisition in this episode but only a veiled festive irony, "El
Quijote y la Inquisición," in *El derecho en la época del Quijote*, ed. Bruno Aguilera Barchet (Cizur Menor: Aranzadi, 2006), 79. Meanwhile, other scholars read it as a direct
attack on the Holy Office, Ludovik Osterc Berlán, *El Quijote, la iglesia y la Inquisición*
(México: UNAM, 1972), 23–42; and Prendergast, *Reading*, 92–97. James Iffland suggests
that Cervantes's irreverence serves simultaneously to alleviate the social terror of the
Inquisition and to counteract the dukes' mockery, *De fiestas y aguafiestas: Risa, locura e
ideología en Cervantes y Avellaneda* (Madrid: Iberoamericana, 1999), 502, 508–10.

34. See, among many others, Stephen Gilman, "Los inquisidores literarios de Cervantes," in *Actas del III congreso internacional de hispanistas*, ed. Carlos H. Magis
(México: El Colegio de México, 1970), 3–25; and Georgina Dopico Black, "Canons Afire:
Libraries, Books, and Bodies in Don Quixote's Spain," in *Cervantes' Don Quixote: A Casebook*, ed. Roberto González Echevarría (Oxford: Oxford University Press, 2005), 95–123.

35. François Géal, *Figures de la bibliothèque dans l'imaginaire espagnol du Siècle
d'Or* (Paris: Champion, 1999), 233.

36. On the few censored passages in the first editions of Don Quixote, see Adolfo García García, "Inquisición y censura en la época de Cervantes," in *Escrituras silenciadas en
la época de Cervantes*, ed. Manuel Casado Arboniés et al. (Alcalá de Henares: Universidad de Alcalá, 2006), 143–144; Ángel Alcalá, *Literatura y ciencia antes la Inquisición
española* (Madrid: Ediciones del Laberinto, 2001), 114–117; and Osterc Berlán, *El Quijote*, 32–42.

37. Corteguera, *Death*, 3–6.

38. Corteguera, *Death*, 30. On how the Inquisition prosecuted impersonators who
appropriated its symbols, see also, for a later period, Michèle Escamilla-Colin, *Crimes
et châtiments dans l'Espagne inquisitoriale* (Paris: Berg, 1992), 2:231–237. In his *Compen-*

dio, Pedro de León refers to the story of a false inquisitor who was very active around the area of Seville between the end of the sixteenth and the beginning of the seventeenth century and who was then prosecuted by the Inquisition, *Grandeza*, 354–355. On a parodic play about inquisitorial trials in Aragon by the end of the fifteenth century and the Inquisition's response, see José Antonio Mateos Royo, "Entre bromas y veras: una parodia en Daroca sobre el Santo Oficio o el proceso de Jaime de Santa Cruz," *Studium: Revista de Humanidades* 4 (1997): 185–186. In Cervantes's novella *Rinconete y Cortadillo* we find a group of crooks who are paid to post signs of infamy (among them sambenitos) to defame several people in Seville (*Novelas ejemplares*, 1:236–237).

39. Henry Kamen, *The Spanish Inquisition: A Historical Revision* (New Haven: Yale University Press, 1997), 315.

40. Corteguera, *Death*, 35, 72, 74.

41. Melchor de Santa Cruz, *Floresta española*, ed. María Pilar Cuartero and Maxime Chevalier (Barcelona: Crítica, 1997), 167.

42. Covarrubias, *Tesoro*, 808. See also his lexicographical entry for "coroça" (361). Diego de Guadix defines "coroça" using "mitra" as a quasi-synonym: "Llaman en España a una suerte de mitra afrentosa con que la justicia suele afrentar y castigar a aquellos cuyos delictos sean tan feos, que merecen ser grauemente punigdos" [In Spain they use this name for some kind of infamant miter with which justice usually ashame and punish those whose crimes are so abhorrent, that they deserve to be severely punished], *Recopilación*, 558.

43. This is not the only detail in which the iconographic tradition of *Don Quixote* has not accurately represented the text. The sambenito seems to correspond to the one used in the autos de fe, which was yellow (or purple in the case of Barcelona), with black being reserved only for the worst offenders. On the color of the sambenitos, see Moreno Martínez, "Cirios," 157. This detail is elided in most iconographic representations of *Don Quixote*, which invariably represent Sancho wearing the traditional white or yellow sambenito, instead of the black one that he wears in the text.

44. He boasts of being Old Christian at least four times, Escudero López, "El Quijote," 73–74.

45. William Childers, "Not These Bones: Apocalyptic Satire in Baroque Spain and the Cold War United States," in Castillo and Nelson, *Writing in the End Times*, 132.

46. Childers, "Not These Bones," 153.

CHAPTER 5 — "THEY DID NOT BRAY IN VAIN"

1. Flynn, *Insult*, 63.

2. Barrientos, *Vida y obras*, 184. Although the Spanish adjective "pastoril" later acquired a more positive connotation to refer to pastoral romances, it had a derogatory connotation at least until the sixteenth century, as opposed to the learned word "pastoral."

3. Antón de Montoro, *Cancionero de Antón de Montoro*, ed. Emilio Cotarelo y Mori (Madrid: José Perales y Martínez, 1900), 273.

4. Alfredo Hermenegildo, "Sobre la dimensión social del teatro primitivo español," *Prohemio* 2 (1975): 25–50; David Gitlitz, "Lucas Fernández y Pierre Menard: El auto de la pasión," in *Encuentros and Desencuentros: Spanish Jewish Cultural Interaction throughout History*, ed. Carlos Carrete Parrondo et al. (Tel Aviv: University Publishing Projects, 2000), 504; Yvonne Yarbro-Bejarano, "Juan del Encina and Lucas Fernández: Conflicting Attitudes towards the Passion," *Bulletin of the Comediantes* 36, no. 1 (1984): 5–21;

Elaine C. Wertheimer, *Honor, Love, and Religion in the Theater before Lope de Vega* (Newark: Juan de la Cuesta, 2003); Ronald Surtz, "Pastores judíos y reyes magos gentiles: Teatro franciscano y milenarismo en Nueva España," *Nueva Revista de Filología Hispánica* 36, no. 1 (1998): 334–337; and Ronald Surtz, "Cardinal Juan Martínez Silíceo in an Allegorical *entremés* of 1556," in *Essays on Hispanic Literature in Honor of Edmund L. King*, ed. Silvia Molloy and Luis Fernández Cifuentes (London: Tamesis, 1983), 230–232.

5. Francisco Márquez Villanueva, *Fuentes literarias cervantinas* (Madrid: Gredos, 1973), 69–83.

6. For a more detailed analysis of the evolution of the figure of the shepherd in early modern Spain, see Javier Irigoyen-García, *The Spanish Arcadia: Sheep Herding, Pastoral Discourse, and Ethnicity in Early Modern Spain* (Toronto: University of Toronto Press, 2013), 79–94.

7. On this baroque romance, see Begoña Souviron López, *La mujer en la ficción arcádica: aproximación a la novela pastoril española* (Frankfurt: Vervuert, 1997), 179; Irigoyen-García, *The Spanish Arcadia*, 209–218; Mercedes Alcalá Galán, "La mora y/o morisca en la imaginación literaria de los Siglos de Oro: *La soledad entretenida* de Barrionuevo y Moya y las trampas de la maurofilia," in *Actas XIII Simposio Internacional de Mudejarismo* (Teruel: Centro de Estudios Mudéjares, 2017), 261–668; and Christine Marguet, "Literatura e historia local: escribir los pasados histórico-míticos en la novela de frontera *Soledad entretenida* (1638–1644) de Juan de Barrionuevo y Moya," *E-Spania* (February 2016), doi.org/10.4000/e-spania.25276.

8. Juan de Barrionuevo y Moya, *Primera parte de la soledad entretenida* (Écija: Luis Estupiñán, 1638), 29r.

9. Barrionuevo y Moya, 29v.

10. Madero, *Manos*, 119–121.

11. For these kinds of events in seventeenth-century Madrid, see Juan Ignacio Pulido Serrano, *Injurias a Cristo: Religión, política y antijudaísmo en el siglo XVII (Análisis de las corrientes antijudías durante la Edad Moderna)* (Alcalá de Henares: Universidad de Alcalá, 2002).

12. AHN, Inquisición, leg. 2628, exp. 26. This document includes a transcription of the infamous libel and the printed edict published by the Inquisition in Granada requesting help to identify the perpetrator.

13. This case has been amply studied yet from perspectives different from the one explored in this book. Juan Ignacio Pulido Serrano analyzes it within the context of anti-Semitic discourses in early modern Spain, "La fe desatada en devoción: Proyección pública de la Inquisición en Granada (1640)," *Torre de los Lujanes* 40 (1999): 95–108. Castillo Gómez focuses on the material circulation of libels, "Panfletos," 63–65; "Delinquir escribiendo," 289–295. Cécile d'Albis deals with this case within the larger context of the festival culture of early modern Granada, "Les fêtes cívico-religieuses à Grenade aux XVIe et XVIIe siècles" (PhD diss., École des Hautes Études en Sciences Sociales/ Universidad de Granada, 2008), 738–765. Francisco Domínguez Matito focuses on the literary compositions produced for this event, "Introducción," in Cubillo de Aragón, *El hereje*, 36–46. For a detailed summary of the festivals organized in Granada in honor of the Virgin, see Francisco Henríquez de Jorquera, *Anales de Granada*, ed. Antonio Marín Ocete (Granada: Publicaciones de la Facultad de Letras, 1934), 2:846–875.

14. AHN, Inquisición, leg. 2628, exp. 33. Unfortunately, this file was empty when I consulted it, and therefore the information proving Francisco de la Cruz's responsibility

is missing. Domínguez Matito seems to be referring to this file when he explains that the hermit was discovered because he inadvertently revealed some details of the sacrilegious libel that were not public knowledge, "Introducción," 42.

15. AHN, Inquisición, leg. 2628, exp. 55. See also Henríquez de Jorquera, *Anales*, 2:862.

16. AHN, Inquisición, leg. 2628, exp. 66. On October 30, the Inquisition sent the trial to the Court, AHN, Inquisición, leg. 2628, exp. 97 (when I consulted it, there was only the cover letter, with no actual trial on it).

17. AHN, Inquisición, leg. 2628, exp. 113. Henríquez de Jorquera writes that this auto de fe occurred on December 16, 1640, *Anales*, 2:879. Pulido Serrano also considers that the actual auto de fe was rather discreet, "La fe desatada," 101.

18. Francisco Guillén del Águila, *Libelo difamatorio de la religión católica que un sedicioso depositó en las casas del cabildo de Granada* (n.p., 1640). According to him, Juan Pérez de Lara also published a pamphlet in Latin defending the same harsh sentencing, *Libelo*, 15r.

19. Guillén del Águila, *Libelo*, 6r.

20. Guillén del Águila reveals that the Inquisition breached its own protocols when rushing to announce that it had identified the perpetrator, *Libelo*, 14r–v. Such action, although it served to promote the Inquisition's efficiency, threatened to undermine the entire purpose of the vindication ceremonies once the perpetrator turned out to be one of the members of the community.

21. For Pulido Serrano, Guillén del Águila's pamphlet is full of anti-Semitic propaganda, "La fe desatada," 101. Although Pulido Serrano does not say it explicitly, he seems to imply that Guillén del Águila downplays the hermit's intention so he can reproduce the customary anti-Jewish propaganda. Although the pamphlet certainly contains anti-Semitic discourses, this is not its main structuring argument. Guillén del Águila even fantasizes that, if a Jew encountered the hermit rowing in the galleys, he would be surprised by the Inquisition's leniency, *Libelo*, 5v.

22. Other than in Guillén del Aguila's work, the real identity of the perpetrator and the intention behind his act are only revealed in the Inquisition's private correspondence. Henríquez de Jorquera's *Anales de Granada* (c. 1646) also reveals the name of the author, *Anales*, 2:862. Yet this work, important as it has become for historians of Granada, remained in manuscript form until the twentieth century and did not achieve the same circulation as the other pamphlets analyzed here.

23. Álvaro Cubillo de Aragón, *El hereje*, ed. Francisco Domínguez Matito (Vigo: Academia del Hispanismo, 2008), 74–75; Luis Paracuellos Cabeza de Vaca, *Triunfales celebraciones*, ed. facsimile Miguel Luis López-Guadalupe Muñoz (Granada: Universidad de Granada, 2004), 130v, 133r.

24. Paracuellos Cabeza de Vaca, *Triunfales celebraciones*, 120r.

25. Francisco Jiménez de Santiago, *Desagravios a la virginidad en el parto de María Santíssima* (Écija: Luis Estupiñán, 1640), 2v.

26. Cipriano de Santa María, *Sermón predicado en el primer día del Octavario que celebró la nobleza de la ciudad de Xerez de la Frontera, en desagravio de nuestra santa Fe* (Jerez de la Frontera, 1640).

27. Gabriel Rodríguez de Escavias, *Exhortación al herege que puso en la ciudad de Granada jueves santo en la noche cinco de abril del año de mil y seiscientos y quarenta un papel contra nuestra Santa Fe Católica* (Granada: Francisco García de Velasco, 1640), 117v. I cite the copy of the pamphlet included in an inquisitorial document, AHN, Inq, libro 1252, fol. 115r–126r. This pamphlet is already cited by Castillo Gómez, "Panfletos," 64n22.

28. Pedro de Colindres, *Triumpho de Christo y María, consagrado a los desagravios de los ultrajes, que contra su Ley, Original, y Virginal pureza publicó horrendamente sacrílego el cartel que se fixó en Granada* (Écija: Luis de Estupiñán, 1641), 17r.

29. Colindres, *Triumpho*, 16v–33r.

30. Pulido Serrano, "La fe desatada," 101.

31. I rely here on Hayden White's concept of the narrative emplotment of historical narratives, *Tropics of Discourse: Essays in Cultural Criticism* (Baltimore: Johns Hopkins University Press, 1990), 81–100.

32. Butler, *Excitable Speech*, 3. Yet, as she also warns, "the past and future of the utterance cannot be narrated with any certainty," *Excitable Speech*, 3.

33. Given the farcical tone of the episode, it has usually been analyzed as a carnivalesque literary manifestation of popular folklore, or reading it as a fable has favored the study of its literary, folkloric, biblical, and iconographic sources. See Laura J. Gorfkle, *Discovering the Comic in* Don Quixote (Chapel Hill: University of North Carolina, 1993), 46–47; Iffland, *De fiestas*, 431–437; Karl-Ludwig Selig, "*Don Quijote*, II, XXIV–XXVIII: La aventura del rebuzno," *Teaching Language through Literature* 22 (1983): 27–29; Alberto Rodríguez, "Del episodio del rebuzno al gobierno de Sancho: la evolución simbólica de la imagen del burro," in *Peregrinamente peregrinos: Actas del V Congreso Internacional de la Asociación de Cervantistas*, ed. Alicia Villar Lecumberri (Palma de Mallorca: Asociación de Cervantistas, 2004), 2:1676–1679; Márquez Villanueva, *Fuentes*, 54–55; Giuseppe Di Stefano, "'Venid, mochachos, y veréis el asno de Sancho Panza,'" *Nueva Revista de Filología Hispánica* 38, no. 2 (1990): 887–899; Julia D'Onofrio, "De las orejas a la cola: Deleite, parodia y autoconocimiento en las representaciones simbólicas del asno y el mono en el *Quijote* (II, 24–28)," *Anales Cervantinos* 50 (2018): 105–135; Santiago Ausín Olmos, "Ecos de la Biblia en el *Quijote*: Abrahán y don Quijote. La burra de Balaam y el relato del rebuzno," in *La Biblia en la literatura del Siglo de Oro*, ed. Ignacio Arellano Ayuso and Ruth Fine (Pamplona: Universidad de Navarra, 2010), 45–48; Bruce R. Burningham, *Radical Theatricality: Jongleuresque Performance on the Early Spanish Stage* (West Lafayette, IN: Purdue University Press, 2007), 124–125; and Wagschal, *Minding Animals*, 214–215. Because the chapters dealing with the town of the bray frame the return of Ginés de Pasamonte as the puppeteer Maese Pedro, several scholars have suggested that they were part of the critique against Jerónimo de Pasamonte, one of the alleged authors of the apocryphal *Quixote* of 1614, Martín Jiménez, *Las dos segundas partes*, 209–218; and Nadine Ly, "La agudeza de Sancho: del rebuzno a la cuestión de la imitación creadora," *Criticón* 127 (2016): 105–128.

34. Some scholars have pointed out, in passing, to a possible relationship between these two episodes and the doctrine of blood purity, suggesting some sort of comparison with *El retablo de las maravillas*. See Enrique Martínez López, "Duelos y quebrantos: Rebuznos de casta en un menú cervantino; Sobre los que con desazón comen 'duelos y quebrantos los sábados' y los motejados de 'cazoleros' o 'berenjeneros,'" *Casa del Tiempo* 83–84 (2005–2006): 89; and José Luis Abellán, "Una denuncia de la irracionalidad: la aventura del rebuzno," *Torre de los Lujanes* 58 (2006): 110.

35. Romà Rofes Herrera provided me with the best answer to this question in a graduate seminar. I am grateful for his permission to use his intuition, which has proven instrumental to my analysis of this passage.

36. Gonzalo Correas registers the proverb "Rebuznaron en balde, el uno y el otro alcalde" [The mayors twain brayed in vain] in his *Vocabulario de refranes y frases prover-*

biales (1627), ed. Louis Combet, Robert Jammes, and Maïte Mir-Andreu (Madrid: Castalia, 2000), 706. It is unclear whether Correas takes it from Cervantes or whether both authors borrow it from popular wisdom.

37. On the identification of these insults, see José Esteban, *¡Judas!... ¡Hi... de puta! Insultos y animadversión entre españoles* (Sevilla: Renacimiento, 2003); Ángel Iglesias Ovejero, "El relato oral en la época clásica y en el folklore moderno: El caso del blasón popular," in *La edición de textos: Actas del I Congreso Internacional de Hispanistas del Siglo de Oro*, ed. Pablo Jauralde, Dolores Noguera, and Alfonso Rey (London: Tamesis, 1990), 245–252; Chevalier, "Lope," 221–223; and Miguel A. Moreta-Lara, *La imagen del moro y otros ensayos marruecos* (Málaga: Aljaima, 2005), 147–155. For the insults that each town aim at each other, see also Antonia Morel d'Arleux, "Algunos aspectos del blasón popular de los extremeños en el Siglo de Oro," *Paremia* 2 (1993): 117–124; Antonio Domínguez Ortiz, *Estudios de historia social y económica de España* (Granada: Universidad de Granada, 1987), 357–369; Juan Gil, "Berenjeneros," 123–125; Miguel Ángel Teijeiro Fuentes, "Galicia y los gallegos en la literatura española del Siglo de Oro," *Scriptura* 11 (1996): 203–246; Andrés de Mañaricua, *Polémica sobre Vizcaya en el siglo XVII: El Búho Gallego y El Tordo Vizcaíno* (Bilbao: Gran Enciclopedia Vasca, 1976); and Noël Salomon, *Lo villano en el teatro del Siglo de Oro*, trans. Beatriz Chenot (Madrid: Castalia, 1985), 368–371.

38. Juan Gil, "Berenjeneros," 123–125.

39. Stanislav Zimic reads this episode as a pacifist critique, *Los cuentos y las novelas del* Quijote (Pamplona: Universidad de Navarra, 2003), 261–265. In a similar vein, Eduardo Olid Guerrero analyzes political discourses justifying war that Cervantes might be reflecting, "'En servicio de su rey en la guerra justa': la segunda parte del *Quijote* leída a través de las ideas de Nicolás Maquiavelo y Francisco Vitoria," *eHumanista/Cervantes* 4 (2015): 371–374.

40. Eribon, *Insult*, 140.

41. Sigmund Freud, *Totem and Taboo*, trans. James Strachey (New York: W. W. Norton, 1989), 35–39.

42. Freud, *Totem*, 43.

43. Rutherford translates "alcaldes" as "mayors," as most scholarship does, quite probably because that is the meaning of the word in modern Spanish and is more in line with the original title of "regidores" (councilmen). However, in early modern Spanish, the title "alcalde" does not refer to a local government position but to an office that combined both juridical and police enforcement functions. The main reason for the change in title is obviously stylistic, because "alcalde" rhymes with "en balde."

44. Madero, *Manos*, 46.

45. See Márquez Villanueva, *Fuentes*, 63–64. In Castilian theater, the commoner is frequently animalized as an ass, Salomon, *Lo villano*, 25–27.

46. Rutherford resolves the ellipsis in his translation. I put it in brackets to indicate that the second part of the proverb is elided in the original in Spanish.

47. Freud, *Totem*, 35–39.

48. Guillemont and Requejo Carrió coin the term "espacio asinino" to suggest that Cervantes's use of the ass symbology opposes the social determinism of Mateo Alemán's *Guzmán de Alfarache*, "De asnos y rebuznos: Ambigüedad y modernidad de un diálogo," *Criticón* 101 (2007): 69–70. Such "espacio asinino" would also be an intermittent one, because there is a textual problem with Sancho's donkey, which is sometimes referred to

as missing while in other instances Sancho suddenly rides it with no explanation; Cervantes himself made fun of this plot slippage in the second part, Baena, *Discordancias cervantinas*, 120-130. The evocatory force of "ass" as an insult proves also to be as intermittent as the actual animal, because it depends on highly codified social norms that are rarely verbalized.

EPILOGUE: SPANISH HISTORY AS *SAMBENITO*

1. Antonio Domínguez Ortiz, "Los sambenitos de la catedral de Granada," *Miscelánea de Estudios árabes y Hebraicos* 26-28, no. 2 (1977-1979): 315-318; Rafael Marín López, "Notas sobre la canonjía inquisitorial en la catedral de Granada," in *Estudios sobre iglesia y sociedad en Andalucía en la edad moderna*, ed. Miguel Luis López-Guadalupe Muñoz and Antonio Luis Cortés Peña (Granada: Universidad de Granada, 1999), 61; and d'Albis, "Les fêtes," 417-223.

2. D'albis, "Les fêtes," 419.

3. Bethencourt, *La Inquisición*, 330n93. For similar cases, see also Kamen, *The Spanish Inquisition*, 243.

4. Bethencourt, *La Inquisición*, 333.

5. Sicroff, *Los estatutos*, 162-163.

6. Sicroff, *Los estatutos*, 163.

7. Valencia, *Tratado*, 140.

8. Antonio Domínguez Ortiz, "Entrevista con Antonio Domínguez Ortiz," *Revista de la Asociación Española de Neuropsiquiatría* 18, no. 66 (1998): 337.

9. Among the abundant scholarship about the black legend of Spain in the early modern period, see Sverker Arnoldsson, *La leyenda negra: Estudios sobre sus orígenes* (Göteborg: Göteborgs Universitet, 1960); Jocelyn N. Hillgarth, *The Mirror of Spain, 1500-1700: The Formation of a Myth* (Ann Arbor: University of Michigan Press, 2003); Ricardo García Cárcel, *La leyenda negra: historia y opinión* (Madrid: Alianza, [1992] 1998); Joseph Pérez, *La leyenda negra* (Madrid: Gadir, 2009); Antonio Sánchez Jiménez, *Leyenda negra: la batalla sobre la imagen de España en tiempos de Lope de Vega* (Madrid: Cátedra, 2016); and Yolanda Rodríguez Pérez, Antonio Sánchez Jiménez, and Harm den Boer, eds., *España ante sus críticos: las claves de la Leyenda Negra* (Madrid: Iberoamericana, 2015). Although "black legend" is often capitalized, I intentionally write it in lowercase letters, as a way to play down the alleged historiographical validity of this concept.

10. Bethencourt, *La Inquisición*, 469.

11. María Victoria Caballero Gómez, "El auto de fe de 1680: Un lienzo para Francisco Rizi," *Revista de la Inquisición* 3 (1994): 69-70; María Victoria González de Caldas, "Nuevas imágenes del Santo Oficio en Sevilla: El auto de fe," in *Inquisición española y mentalidad inquisitorial*, ed. Ángel Alcalá (Barcelona: Ariel, 1984), 245-255.

12. Bethencourt, *La Inquisición*, 471-472.

13. For a thorough analysis of this engraving, see Pierre Civil, "Leyenda negra y represión antiprotestante: *Hispanissche Inquisition*, una estampa polémica del Auto de Fe de Valladolid de 1559," in *Reforma y disidencia religiosa: La recepción de las doctrinas reformadas en la Península Ibérica en el siglo XVI*, ed. Michel Boeglin, Ignasi Fernández Terricabras, and David Kahn (Madrid: Casa de Velázquez, 2018), 351-363.

14. Charles Dellon, *L'Inquisition de Goa: La relation de Charles Dellon (1687)*, ed. Charles Amiel and Anne Lima (Paris: Chandeigne, 1997), 201-202.

15. On the subsequent reworking of the engravings included in Dellon's *Relation*, see the observations by Amiel and Lima in their edition of the text (32–35).

16. Bethencourt, "The Auto da Fé," 160–168.

17. As shown by a search in the *Cervantes Project* database at Texas A&M University, http://cervantes.dh.tamu.edu/V2/CPI/. The 1780 edition by Ibarra also represents Sancho wearing a miter, arguably because he is obviously reusing the same plate, but the equivalent engraving of a 1797 edition in Madrid corrects this detail by replacing the miter with the conical coroza. On the iconographic tradition of the illustrated editions of the *Quixote*, see José Manuel Lucía Megías, *Leer el* Quijote *en imágenes: Hacia una teoría de los modelos iconográficos* (Madrid: Calambur, 2006).

18. Bethencourt, *La Inquisición*, 480.

19. This series is accessible at www.museodelprado.es.

20. See Isabel Escandell Proust, "Goya, autor de dos imágenes de *Don Quijote*," in *Volver a Cervantes: Actas del IV Congreso Internacional de la Asociación de Cervantistas, Lepanto 1–8 de octubre de 2000*, ed. Antonio Pablo Bernat Vistarini (Palma: Universitat de les Illes Balears, 2001), 1:419–422; and Javier Blas and José Manuel Matilla, "Imprenta e ideología: El *Quijote* de la Academia, 1773–1780," in *Imágenes del* Quijote: *Modelos de representación en las ediciones de los siglos XVII al XIX*, ed. Patrick Lenaghan (Madrid: Hispanic Society of America and Museo Nacional del Prado, 2003), 84.

21. On the stereotyping of Spain during the the Spanish-American War of 1898, see María DeGuzmán, *Spain's Long Shadow: The Black Legend, Off-Whiteness, and Anglo-American Empire* (Minneapolis: University of Minnesota Press, 2005).

22. Jesús Villanueva has extensively documented how the term was amply disseminated but also contested during the period between 1898 and the publication of Juderías's seminal book, *Leyenda negra: Una polémica nacionalista en la España del siglo XX* (Madrid: Catarata, 2011), 46–78.

23. See García Cárcel, *La leyenda negra*, 14, 250; and Villanueva, *Leyenda negra*.

24. A quite different use of the black legend is found in the United States, in which it is mainly deployed to promote Hispanism and the Hispanic cultural heritage, Barbara Fuchs, "The Black Legend and the Golden Age Dramatic Canon," in *La Leyenda Negra en el crisol de la comedia: el teatro del Siglo de Oro frente a los estereotipos antihispánicos*, ed. Yolanda Rodríguez Pérez and Antonio Sánchez Jiménez (Madrid: Iberoamericana, 2016), 219–236.

25. Pierre Chaunu, "La légende noire antihispanique," *Revue de Psychologie des Peuples* 19 (1964): 196.

26. Carmen Iglesias, "España desde fuera," in *España. Reflexiones sobre el ser de España*, ed. Eloy Benito Ruano (Madrid: Real Academia de la Historia, 1997), 377–383.

27. María Elvira Roca Barea, *Imperiofobia y leyenda negra: Roma, Rusia, Estados Unidos y el Imperio español* (Madrid: Siruela, [2016] 2017). For a critique of Roca Barea's book, see, among others, José Luis Villacañas, *Imperiofilia y el populismo nacional-católico* (Madrid: Lengua de Trapo, 2019); Miguel Martínez, "El imperio del extremo centro," CTXT, https://ctxt.es/es/20171220/Politica/16846/imperio-colonialismo-roca-barea-imperiofobia-c%27s.htm (accessed June 7, 2020); and Richard L. Kagan, "¿Por qué la leyenda negra? ¿Por qué ahora?" *Cuadernos de Historia Moderna* 43, no. 1 (2018): 279–283.

28. Villanueva, *Leyenda negra*, 165–166. Even though I disagree with his conclusion, José Antonio Vaca de Osma is probably correct when he points out the inconsistency of García Cárcel's seminal work, which begins by claiming that the black legend is a spurious

historiographical concept but still keeps it in its title and devotes more than 300 pages to minutely documenting international criticism of Spain, *El imperio y la leyenda negra* (Madrid: Rialp, 2004), 147–148. In a similar vein, Español Bouché sarcastically claims that García Gárcel's work is like writing about theology without being a believer, *Leyendas negras: vida y obra de Julián Juderías* (Salamanca: Junta de Castilla y León, 2007), 192.

29. Roca Barea, *Imperiofobia*, 457–471.

30. Villacañas infers that Roca Barea is writing against Catalonian nationalism, even though she never explicitly refers to it, *Imperiofilia*, 330.

31. Although I focus here on the way Spanish nationalism engages with the perceived insult from the outside, I am not claiming that this approach to insult is unique to a specific element of the conservative political spectrum in Spain, although it is most commonly embraced by conservative parties.

32. Miguel de Unamuno, *Del sentimiento trágico de la vida* (Madrid: Espasa-Calpe, 1980), 255. This is an opinion Unamuno recanted later, as Villanueva points out, *La leyenda negra*, 66–67, 83–85.

33. Quoted in Villanueva, *La leyenda negra*, 99.

34. Vaca de Osma, *El imperio*, 147.

35. Wendy Brown, *States of Injury: Power and Freedom in Late Modernity* (Princeton: Princeton University Press, 1995), 73.

36. Julián Juderías, *La leyenda negra: Estudios acerca del concepto de España en el extranjero* (Zaragoza: Servando Gotor, 2019), 22.

37. On the romantic image of Spain, see Jesús Torrecilla, *España exótica: La formación de la imagen española moderna* (Boulder, CO: Society of Spanish and Spanish-American Studies, 2004). Later on, Juderías acknowledges again that the image of Spain has improved in his own time, but he regards such change with suspicion: "Pero, dirán algunos, ¿no se ha producido últimamente una reacción favorable a España? ¿No hablan ya de nosotros elogiándonos y ponderando nuestra cultura, nuestro carácter y hasta nuestro pasado? Corramos también un velo sobre estos novísimos elogios. El tiempo se encargará de decirnos lo que valen y lo que significan" [But, some may say, isn't there a favorable reaction to Spain? Isn't it true that they talk about us praising us and lauding our culture, our personality and even our past? Let's throw a heavy veil over these very recent praises. Time will tell us how much they are worth and what they really mean], *La leyenda negra*, 285.

38. Even though Juderías does not mention it, his insistence throughout the book on the "unity" of Spain from times immemorial seems to be responding to growing Catalan nationalism during the years of World War I, Villanueva, *La leyenda negra*. For a recent biography of Juderías, see Español Bouché, *Leyendas negras*.

39. García Cárcel labels this kind of thought as a conception of national identity that is both narcissistic and masochistic, *La leyenda negra*, 17. Villacañas labels it as a compensatory megalomania, *Imperiofilia*, 109, 218. For similar comments about this concept throughout the twentieth century, see Villanueva, *La leyenda negra*, 84–85, 110, 146.

40. Roca Barea, *Imperiofobia*, 166.

41. As much as I disagree with such a position, let me state clearly that my analogy between the emphasis on the black legend and this episode in *Don Quixote* is not intended to disqualify this line of thought as braying—the Spanish verb "rebuznar" has the connotation of speaking loudly and insultingly, making nonsense, which is not what my comparison seeks to underline.

Bibliography

Abellán, José Luis. "Una denuncia de la irracionalidad: la aventura del rebuzno." *Torre de los Lujanes* 58 (2006): 103–110.

Albuixech, Lourdes. "Insultos, pullas y vituperios en *Celestina*." *Celestinesca* 25, no. 1–2 (2001): 57–68.

Alcalá, Ángel. *Literatura y ciencia antes la Inquisición española*. Madrid: Ediciones del Laberinto, 2001.

Alcalá Galán, Mercedes. "La mora y/o morisca en la imaginación literaria de los Siglos de Oro: *La soledad entretenida* de Barrionuevo y Moya y las trampas de la maurofilia." In *Actas XIII Simposio Internacional de Mudejarismo*, 261–268. Teruel: Centro de Estudios Mudéjares, 2017.

Alfaro, Gustavo. "Los *Lazarillos* y la Inquisición." *Hispanófila* 26, no. 3 (1983): 11–19.

Althusser, Louis. *Lenin and Philosophy and Other Essays*. Translated by Ben Brewster. New York: Monthly Review Press, 2001.

Álvarez, Mari-Tere. "Moon Shot: From Renaissance Imagination to Modern Reality." In Villaseñor Black and Álvarez, 9–18.

Alves, Abel A. *The Animals of Spain: An Introduction to Imperial Perceptions and Human Interaction with Other Animals, 1492–1826*. Brill: Leiden, 2011.

Anderson, Benedict. *Imagined Communities: Reflections on the Origin and Spread of Nationalism*. London: Verso, 1991.

Arellano, Ignacio. "Casos de honor en las primeras etapas del teatro de Lope." *Anuario Lope de Vega* 4 (1998): 7–31.

Arellano, Ignacio, and Victoriano Roncero López. *Demócrito áureo: los códigos de la risa en el Siglo de Oro*. Seville: Renacimiento, 2006.

Arnoldsson, Sverker. *La leyenda negra. Estudios sobre sus orígenes*. Göteborg: Göteborg University, 1960.

Asensio, Eugenio. *Itinerario del entremés desde Lope de Rueda a Quiñones de Benavente*. Madrid: Gredos, 1971.

Ausín Olmos, Santiago. "Ecos de la Biblia en el *Quijote*: Abrahán y don Quijote: La burra de Balaam y el relato del rebuzno." In *La Biblia en la literatura del Siglo de Oro,* edited by Ignacio Arellano Ayuso and Ruth Fine, 29–49. Pamplona: Universidad de Navarra, 2010.

Ávila, Nicolás de. *Suma de los mandamientos y maremagnum del segundo, que enseña para el confesionario y persuade para el púlpito.* Alcalá de Henares: Juan Gracián, 1610. First published 1596.

Avilés, Miguel. *Sueños ficticios y lucha ideológica en el Siglo de Oro.* Madrid: Nacional, 1981.

Aznar Cardona, Pedro. *Expulsión justificada de los Moriscos Españoles.* Huesca: Pedro Cabarte, 1612.

Azpilcueta, Martín de. *Tractado de alabança y murmuración.* Valladolid: Adrian Ghemart, 1572.

Baena, Julio. *Discordancias cervantinas.* Newark: Juan de la Cuesta, 2003.

———. "The Emperor's Old—and Perennial—Clothes: Two Spanish Fine-Tunings to Andersen's Received Wisdom." *International Journal of Žižek Studies* 9, no. 2 (2015): 1–14.

———. "Lazarillo de Tormes y el Levítico: la piedra de escándalo de la utopía infame." *Dissidences: Hispanic Journal of Theory and Criticism* 1, no. 1 (2005): 1–28.

———. "Sintaxis de la ética del texto: Ricote, en el *Quijote II*, la lengua de las mariposas." *Bulletin of Spanish Studies* 83, no. 4 (2006): 507–524.

Bajo Pérez, Elena, and Felipe Maíllo Salgado. "Estudio introductorio." In Guadix, *Recopilación* 13–131.

Bañales, Xamuel. "Jotería: A Decolonizing Political Project." *Aztlán* 39, no. 1 (2014): 155–165.

Barrientos, Lope de. *Vida y obras de Fr. Lope de Barrientos.* Edited by Fray Luis G. Alonso Getino. Salamanca: Manuel Criado, 1927.

Barrionuevo y Moya, Juan de. *Primera parte de la soledad entretenida.* Écija: Luis Estupiñán, 1638.

Bataillon, Marcel. "Les nouveaux-chrétiens de Ségovie en 1510." *Bulletin Hispanique* 58 (1956): 207–231.

———. *Novedad y fecundidad del* Lazarillo de Tormes. Madrid: Anaya, 1986.

Bennassar, Bartolomé. "La Inquisición o la pedagogía del miedo." In *Inquisición española: poder político y control social,* edited by Bartolomé Bennassar, 94–125. Translated by Javier Alfaya. Barcelona: Crítica, 1981.

Berco, Cristian. *Sexual Hierarchies, Public Status: Men, Sodomy, and Society in Spain's Golden Age.* Toronto: University of Toronto Press, 2007.

Bethencourt, Francisco. "The Auto da Fé: Ritual and Imagery." *Journal of the Warburg and Courtauld Institutes* 55 (1992): 155–168.

———. *La Inquisición en la época moderna. España, Portugal, Italia, siglos XV–XIX.* Madrid: Akal, 1997.

Beusterien, John. "Blotted Genealogies: A Survey of the *libros verdes.*" *Bulletin of Hispanic Studies* 78, no. 2 (2001): 183–197.

———. *An Eye on Race: Perspectives from Theater in Imperial Spain.* Lewisburg: Bucknell University Press, 2006.

———. *Transoceanic Animals as Spectacle in Early Modern Spain.* Amsterdam: Amsterdam University Press, 2020.

Blackmore, Josiah. "The Poets of Sodom." In *Queer Iberia: Sexualities, Cultures, and Crossing from the Middle Ages to the Renaissance,* edited by Josiah Blackmore and Gregory S. Hutcheson, 195–221. Durham, NC: Duke University Press, 1999.

Blas, Javier, and José Manuel Matilla. "Imprenta e ideología: El *Quijote* de la Academia, 1773–1780." In *Imágenes del Quijote: Modelos de representación en las ediciones de los siglos XVII al XIX*, edited by Patrick Lenaghan, 73–117. Madrid: Hispanic Society of America and Museo Nacional del Prado, 2003.

Blasco, Javier. "El género de las genealogías en el *Quijote* de Avellaneda." *Boletín de la Biblioteca de Menéndez Pelayo* 81 (2005): 51–79.

Blázquez Miguel, Juan. *La Inquisición en Castilla-La Mancha*. Madrid: Universidad de Córdoba, 1986.

———. *El tribunal de la Inquisición en Murcia*. Murcia: Academia Alfonso X el Sabio, 1986.

Bleda, Jaime. *Corónica de los moros de España*. Valencia: Felipe Mey, 1618.

Boehmer, Eduard. "Juan de Luna." *Zeifschrift für vergleichende Literaturgeschichte* 14 (1904): 423–430.

Boronat y Barrachina, Pascual. *Los moriscos españoles y su expulsión*. 2 vols. Valencia: Francisco Vives y Mora, 1901.

Booker, M. Keith. *Dystopian Literature: A Theory and Research Guide*. Westport, CT: Greenwood Press, 1994.

Brown, Katherine L. "Invento del 'quinto cuarto': La conciencia dividida, la fragment- ación textual y la paradoja de la lectura en 'La ilustre fregona.'" *Cervantes* 36, no. 2 (2016): 145–168.

Brown, Wendy. *States of Injury: Power and Freedom in Late Modernity*. Princeton: Princeton University Press, 1995.

Brownlee, Marina Scordilis. "Generic Expansion and Generic Subversion: The Two Continuations of *Lazarillo de Tormes*." *Philological Quarterly* 61 (1982): 317–327.

Burningham, Bruce R. *Radical Theatricality: Jongleuresque Performance on the Early Spanish Stage*. West Lafayette, IN: Purdue University Press, 2007.

Butler, Judith. *Excitable Speech: A Politics of the Performance*. New York: Routledge, 1997.

———. *The Psychic Life of Power: Theories in Subjection*. Stanford: Stanford University Press, 1997.

Caballero Gómez, María Victoria. "El auto de fe de 1680: Un lienzo para Francisco Rizi." *Revista de la Inquisición* 3 (1994): 69–140.

Cabanelas Rodríguez, Darío. "Fray Diego de Guadix y su 'recopilación' de arabismos." In *Antiqua et nova Romania: Estudios lingüísticos y filológicos en honor de José Mon- déjar*, 1:235–246. 2 vols. Granada: Universidad de Granada, 1993.

Callado Estela, Emilio. "El confesor fray Luis de Aliaga y la expulsión de los moriscos." *Investigaciones Históricas* 34 (2014): 27–46.

Cantizano Pérez, Félix. *El erotismo en la poesía de adúlteros y cornudos en el Siglo de Oro*. Madrid: Editorial Complutense, 2007.

Cara, Giovanni. *Il "vejamen" in Spagna: Juicio y regocijo letterario nella prima metà del XVII secolo*. Rome: Bulzoni, 2001.

Cardaillac, Louis. "Vision simplificatrice des groupes marginaux par le groupe domi- nant dans l'Espagne des XVIe et XVIIe siècles." In *Les problèmes de l'exclusion en Espagne (XVIe–XVIIe siècles)*, edited by Augustin Redondo, 11–22. Paris: Publications de la Sorbonne, 1983.

Caro, Rodrigo. *Días geniales o lúdricos*. Edited by Jean-Pierre Étienvre. 2 vols. Madrid: Espasa-Calpe, 1978.

Caro Baroja, Julio. *Los judíos en la España moderna y contemporánea*. 2 vols. Madrid: Istmo, 2000.

———. "El 'Pesce Cola' o el 'Peje Nicolao.'" *Revista de dialectología y tradiciones populares* 39 (1984): 7–16.

Carr, Matthew. *Blood and Faith: The Purging of Muslim Spain*. New York: New Press, 2009.

Carranza de Miranda, Bartolomé. *Comentarios sobre el catechismo christiano*. Edited by José Ignacio Tellechea Idígoras. 2 vols. Madrid: Biblioteca de Autores Cristianos, 1972.

Carrasco, Rafael. *Deportados en nombre de Dios. La expulsión de los moriscos: cuarto centenario de una ignominia*. Barcelona: Destino, 2009.

Carrasco Manchado, Ana Isabel. *De la convivencia a la exclusión: Imágenes legislativas de mudéjares y moriscos. Siglos XIII–XVII*. Madrid: Sílex, 2012.

Cartagena Calderón, José R. *Masculinidades en obras: El drama de la hombría en el teatro imperial*. Newark: Juan de la Cuesta, 2008.

Casás Otero, Jesús. *Los sambenitos del Museo Diocesano de Tui*. Tui: Museo Diocesano, 2004.

Casillas García, José Antonio. "La Cofradía del Nombre de Dios de los Juramentos: Apuntes sobre esta hermandad de origen burgalés." *Boletín de la Institución Fernán González* 226 (2003): 123–135.

Castillo, David R., and William Egginton. *Medialogies: Reading Reality in the Age of Inflationary Media*. New York: Bloomsbury, 2017.

Castillo, David R., and Bradley J. Nelson, eds. "Writing in the End Times: Apocalyptic Imagination in the Hispanic World." *Hispanic Issues Online* 23 (2019). https://hdl.handle.net/11299/212507.

Castillo Gómez, Antonio. "Delinquir escribiendo: Escrituras infamantes y represión inquisitorial en los Siglos de Oro." In *Escrituras silenciadas en la época de Cervantes*, edited by Manuel Casado Arboniés, Antonio Castillo Gómez, Paulina Numhauser, and Emilio Solá, 283–296. Alcalá de Henares: Universidad de Alcalá, 2006.

———. "Letras de penitencia: Denuncia y castigo públicos en la España altomoderna." *Via Spiritus* 15 (2008): 53–74.

———. "Panfletos, coplas y libelos injuriosos: Palabras silenciadas en el Siglo de Oro." In *Las Españas que (no) pudieron ser: herejías, exilios y otras conciencias (s. XVI–XX)*, edited by Manuel Peña Díaz, 59–73. Huelva: Universidad de Huelva, 2009.

———. "Voces, imágenes y textos: La difusión pública del insulto en la sociedad áurea." In Pérez-Salazar, Tabernero, and Usunáriz, 59–73.

Castillo Lluch, Mónica. "Del denuesto a la interjección: la historia de la expresión fijo de puta." In *Actas del VI Congreso Internacional de Historia de la lengua española*, edited by José Luis Girón Alconchel and José Jesús de Bustos Tovar, 3:2697–2708. 3 vols. Madrid: Universidad Complutense de Madrid, 2006.

———. "De verbo vedado: consideraciones sobre la agresión verbal y su expresión en castellano medieval." *Cahiers de Linguistique et Civilisation Hispaniques Médiévales* 27 (2004): 23–35.

Castillo Solórzano, Alonso de. *Jornadas alegres*. Edited by Julia Barella and Mita Valvassori. Madrid: Sial 2019.

Castro, Américo. "Sambenito." *Revista de Filología Española* 15 (1928): 179–181.

Cátedra, Pedro M. "La modificación del discurso religioso con fines de invectiva. El sermón." *Atalaya* 5 (1994): 101–122.

Cavarra, Giuseppe. *La leggenda di colapesce*. Messina: Intilla, 1998.

Centenero de Arce, Domingo. *De repúblicas urbanas a ciudades nobles: Un análisis de la evolución y desarrollo del republicanismo castellano (1550-1621)*. Madrid: Biblioteca Nueva, 2012.

Cervantes Saavedra, Miguel de. *Teatro completo*. Edited by Florencio Sevilla Arroyo and Antonio Rey Hazas. Barcelona: Planeta, 1987.

———. *Cervantes' Eight Interludes*. Translated by Charles Patterson. Milwaukee: Applause, 2015.

———. *Don Quijote de la Mancha*. Edited by Martín de Riquer. Barcelona: Planeta, 1987.

———. *Don Quixote*. Translated by John Rutherford. New York: Penguin, 2003.

———. *Exemplary Novellas*. Translated by Michael Harney. Indianapolis: Hackett, 2016.

———. *Novelas ejemplares*. Edited by Harry Sieber. 2 vols. Madrid: Cátedra, 1995.

———. *Los trabajos de Persiles y Sigismunda*. Edited by Juan Bautista Avalle-Arce. Madrid: Castalia, 1969.

Cervantes, Vincent [Xiomara]. "Traces of Transgressive Traditions: Shifting Liberation Theologies through Jotería Studies." *Aztlán* 39, no. 1 (2014): 195-206.

Cetina, Gutierre de. *Paradoja: Trata que no solamente no es cosa mala, dañosa ni vergonzosa ser un hombre cornudo, mas que los cuernos son buenos y provechosos*. Edited by Gonzalo Santonja. Valladolid: Maxtor, 2016.

Chauchadis, Claude. *Honneur, morale et société dans l'Espagne de Philippe II*. Paris: CNRS, 1984.

———. *La Loi du duel: Le code du point d'honneur dans l'Espagne des XVIe-XVIIe siècles*. Toulouse: Presses Universitaires du Mirail, 1997.

———. "Virtudes y pecados de la lengua: Sebastián de Covarrubias y Martín de Azpilcueta." *Criticón* 92 (2004): 39-45.

Chaunu, Pierre. "La légende noire antihispanique." *Revue de Psychologie des Peuples* 19 (1964): 188-223.

Chavarría Múgica, Fernando. "Pasquines escandalosos, maledicencias banderizas y desinformación irredentista: la distorsión de la comunicación política entre corte y reino después de la anexión de Navarra a la monarquía española." In *Opinión pública y espacio urbano en la Edad Moderna*, edited by Antonio Castillo Gómez and James S. Amelang, 422-440. Gijón: Trea, 2010.

Checa, Jorge. "El *romance* y su sombra: hibridación genérica en *La ilustre fregona*." *Revista de Estudios Hispánicos* 25, no. 1 (1999): 29-48.

Chevalier, Maxime. "El arte de motejar en la corte de Carlos V." *Cuadernos para Investigación de la Literatura Hispánica* 5 (1983): 61-77.

———. "Lope doctor en pullas." In *El Siglo de Oro en escena. Homenaje a Marc Vitse*, edited by Odette Gorsse and Frédéric Serralta, 217-225. Toulouse: Presses Universitaires du Mirail, 2006.

———. *Quevedo y su tiempo: la agudeza verbal*. Barcelona: Crítica, 1992.

Childers, William. "'Ese tan borrado sobrescrito': The Deconstruction of Lope's Religious Theater in *El retablo de las maravillas* and *El rufián dichoso*." *Bulletin of the Comediantes* 56, no. 2 (2004): 241-268.

———. "Not These Bones: Apocalyptic Satire in Baroque Spain and the Cold War United States." In Castillo and Nelson, "Writing in the End Times," 125-164.

———. "'¡Oh hideputa, bellaco, y cómo es católico!': Sancho, Blasphemy, and the Baroque Public Sphere." In *Don Quijote: Across Four Centuries, 1605–2005*, edited by Carroll B. Johnson, 71–86. Newark: Juan de la Cuesta, 2006.

———. *Transnational Cervantes*. Toronto: University of Toronto Press, 2006.

Civil, Pierre. "Leyenda negra y represión antiprotestante: *Hispanissche Inquisition*, una estampa polémica del Auto de Fe de Valladolid de 1559." In *Reforma y disidencia religiosa: La recepción de las doctrinas reformadas en la Península Ibérica en el siglo XVI*, edited by Michel Boeglin, Ignasi Fernández Terricabras, and David Kahn, 351–363. Madrid: Casa de Velázquez, 2018.

Clamurro, William H. *Cervantes's* Novelas ejemplares: *Reading their Lessons from His Time to Ours*. Lanham, MD: Lexington, 2015.

Close, Anthony. *Cervantes and the Comic Mind of His Age*. Oxford: Oxford University Press, 2000.

Colindres, Pedro de. *Triumpho de Christo y María, consagrado a los desagravios de los ultrajes, que contra su Ley, Original, y Virginal pureza publicó horrendamente sacrílego el cartel que se fixó en Granada*. Écija: Luis de Estupiñán, 1641.

Conley, Thomas. *Toward a Rhetoric of Insult*. Chicago: University of Chicago Press, 2010.

Constable, Olivia Remie. *To Live like a Moor: Christian Perceptions of Muslim Identity in Medieval and Early Modern Spain*. Edited by Robin Vose. Philadelphia: University of Pennsylvania Press, 2018.

Contreras, Jaime. "Conflicto social y estatutos de limpieza en la obra de Cervantes." *Torre de los Lujanes* 56 (2005): 87–103.

———. "Fiesta y auto de fe: un espacio sagrado y profano." In *Las relaciones de sucesos en España (1500–1750)*, edited by Henry Ettinghausen, Víctor Infantes de Miguel, Augustin Redondo, and María Cruz García de Enterría, 79–90. Alcalá de Henares: Universidad de Alcalá, 1996.

———. *Sotos contra Riquelmes: Regidores, inquisidores y criptojudíos*. Madrid: Siglo XXI, 2013.

Correas, Gonzalo. *Vocabulario de refranes y frases proverbiales (1627)*, edited by Louis Combet, Robert Jammes, and Maïte Mir-Andreu. Madrid: Castalia, 2000.

Corteguera, Luis R. *Death by Effigy: A Case from the Mexican Inquisition*. Philadelphia: University of Pennsylvania Press, 2012.

Covarrubias y Horozco, Sebastián de. *Tesoro de la lengua castellana o española*. Edited by Martín de Riquer. Barcelona: Alta Fulla, 2003.

Crawford, James Pyle Wickersham. "Echarse *pullas*: A Popular Form of Tenzone." *Romanic Review* 6 (1915): 150–164.

Creel, Bryant. "The Palace of the Apes: The Ducal Chateau and Cervantes's Repudiation of Satiric Malice." In *Don Quijote across Four Centuries: 1605–2005*, edited by Carroll B. Johnson, 87–105. Newark: Juan de la Cuesta, 2006.

Cuadro García, Ana María. "Las sogas, las sedas y las burlas: El mundo nuevo del auto de fe." In *Poder y cultura festiva en la Andalucía moderna*, edited by Raúl Molina Recio and Manuel Peña Díaz, 115–140. Cordoba: Universidad de Córdoba, 2006.

Cubillo de Aragón, Álvaro. *El hereje*. Edited by Francisco Domínguez Matito. Vigo: Academia del Hispanismo, 2008.

Dadson, Trevor J. "Cervantes y los moriscos de la Mancha." In *De Cervantes y el islam*, edited by Nuria Martínez de Castilla Muñoz and Rodolfo Gil Benumeya Grimau, 135–150. Madrid: Sociedad Estatal de Conmemoraciones Culturales, 2006.

———. "Official Rhetoric versus Local Reality: Propaganda and the Expulsion of the Moriscos." In *Rhetoric and Reality in Early Modern Spain*, edited by Richard J. Pym, 1–24. London: Tamesis, 2006.

d'Albis, Cécile. "Les fêtes cívico-religieuses à Grenade aux XVIe et XVIIe siècles." PhD diss., École des Hautes Études en Sciences Sociales/Universidad de Granada, 2008.

DeArmas, Frederick A. "The Burning at Ephesus: Cervantes and Alarcón's *La verdad sospechosa*." In *Studies in Honor of Gilberto Paolini*, edited by Mercedes Vidal Tibbits, 41–56. Newark: Juan de la Cuesta, 1996.

———. "Futurities, Empire, and Censorship: Cervantes in Conversation with Ovid and Orwell." In Villaseñor Black and Álvarez, 65–82.

Dedieu, Jean-Pierre. *L'Administration de la foi: l'Inquisition de Tolède, XVIe–XVIIIe siècle*. Madrid: Casa de Velázquez, 1989.

Dedieu, Jean-Pierre, and Bernard Vincent. "Face à l'Inquisition: Jugements et attitudes des morisques à l'égard du tribunal." In *Les morisques et l'Inquisition*, edited by Louis Cardaillac, 81–93. Paris: Publisud, 1990.

DeGuzmán, María. *Spain's Long Shadow: The Black Legend, Off-Whiteness, and Anglo-American Empire*. Minneapolis: University of Minnesota Press, 2005.

de la Cruz, Jerónimo. *Defensa de los estatutos y noblezas españolas*. Zaragoza: Pedro Escuer, 1637.

Del Ama, José Carlos. *La opinión pública en la España de Cervantes*. Pamplona: Eunsa, 2013.

Dellon, Charles. *L'Inquisition de Goa: La relation de Charles Dellon (1687)*. Edited by Charles Amiel and Anne Lima. Paris: Chandeigne, 1997.

Del Río Parra, María. *Una era de monstruos: Representaciones de lo deforme en el Siglo de Oro español*. Madrid: Iberoamericana, 2003.

Del Rosal, Francisco. *Diccionario etimológico. Alfabeto primero de Origen y Etimología de todos los vocablos originales de la Lengua Castellana*. Ed. facsimile Enríquez Gómez Aguado. Madrid: CSIC, 1992.

———. *El origen de los nombres: Alfabeto segundo de la obra 'Origen y etimología de todos los vocablos de originales de la lengua castellana*. Edited by Antonio José Mialdea Baena. Cordoba: Plurabelle, 2006.

———. *La razón de algunos refranes: Alfabetos tercero y cuarto*. Edited by B. Bussel Thompson. London: Tamesis, 1975.

Delumeau, Jean. *La Peur en Occident, XIVe–XVIIIe siècle: Une cité assiégée*. Paris: Fayard, 1988.

Di Stefano, Giuseppe. "'Venid, mochachos, y veréis el asno de Sancho Panza.'" *Nueva Revista de Filología Hispánica* 38, no. 2 (1990): 887–899.

Domínguez Matito, Francisco. "Introducción." In Cubillo de Aragón, *El hereje*, 13–63.

Domínguez Ortiz, Antonio. *La clase social de los conversos en Castilla en la edad moderna*. Granada: Universidad de Granada, 1991.

———. "Entrevista con Antonio Domínguez Ortiz." *Revista de la Asociación Española de Neuropsiquiatría* 18, no. 66 (1998): 325–342.

———. *Estudios de historia social y económica de España*. Granada: Universidad de Granada, 1987.

———. *Los judeoconversos en España y américa*. Madrid: Istmo, 1978.

———. "Los sambenitos de la catedral de Granada." *Miscelánea de Estudios árabes y Hebraicos* 26–28, no. 2 (1977–1979): 315–318.

Domínguez Ortiz, Antonio, and Bernard Vincent. *Historia de los moriscos: Vida y tragedia de una minoría*. Madrid: Revista de Occidente, 1978.

D'Onofrio, Julia. "De las orejas a la cola: Deleite, parodia y autoconocimiento en las representaciones simbólicas del asno y el mono en el *Quijote* (II, 24–28)." *Anales Cervantinos* 50 (2018): 105–135.

Dopico Black, Georgina. "Canons Afire: Libraries, Books, and Bodies in *Don Quixote*'s Spain." In *Cervantes' Don Quixote: A Casebook*, edited by Roberto González Echevarría, 95–123. Oxford: Oxford University Press, 2005.

———. *Perfect Wives, Other Women: Adultery and Inquisition in Early Modern Spain*. Durham, NC: Duke University Press, 2001.

Dunn, Peter N. *Castillo Solórzano and the Decline of the Spanish Novel*. Oxford: Basil Blackwell, 1952.

Eamon, William. "Medicine as Hunt: Searching for the Secrets of the New World." In Villaseñor Black and Álvarez, 100–117.

Egido, Aurora. "Linajes de burlas en el Siglo de Oro." In *Studia Aurea: Actas del III Congreso de la AISO*, edited by Ignacio Arellano, María del Carmen Pinillos, Frédéric Serralta, and Marc Vitse, 1:19–50. 3 vols. Pamplona: GRISO-LEMSO, 1996.

———. "*De ludo vitando*: Gallos áulicos en la Universidad de Salamanca." *El Crotalón* 1 (1984): 609–648.

———. "Un vejamen de 1598 en la Universidad de Granada." In *Homenaje al Profesor Antonio Gallego Morell*, edited by María Concepción Argente del Castillo Ocaña, 1:445–460. 3 vols. Granada: Universidad de Granada, 1989.

Eribon, Didier. *Insult and the Making of the Gay Self*. Translated by Michael Lucey. Durham, NC: Duke University Press, 2004.

Escamilla-Colin, Michèle. *Crimes et châtiments dans l'Espagne inquisitoriale*. 2 vols. Paris: Berg, 1992.

Escandell Proust, Isabel. "Goya, autor de dos imágenes de *Don Quijote*." In *Volver a Cervantes: Actas del IV Congreso Internacional de la Asociación de Cervantistas, Lepanto 1–8 de octubre de 2000*, edited by Antonio Pablo Bernat Vistarini, 1:415–438. Palma: Universitat de les Illes Balears, 2001.

Escobar Borrego, Francisco Javier. "Dos textos desconocidos de Jerónimo de Carranza a propósito del XI Conde de Niebla y Mateo Vázquez (con unas notas sobre Hernando de Vega)." In *El duque de Medina-Sidonia: Mecenazgo y renovación artística*, edited by José Manuel Rico García and Pedro Ruiz Pérez, 119–141. Huelva: Universidad de Huelva, 2015.

Escudero López, José Antonio. "El *Quijote* y la Inquisición." In *El derecho en la época del Quijote*, edited by Bruno Aguilera Barchet, 65–79. Cizur Menor: Aranzadi, 2006.

Español Bouché, Luis. *Leyendas negras: vida y obra de Julián Juderías*. Salamanca: Junta de Castilla y León, 2007.

Esteban, José. *¡Judas!... ¡Hi... de puta! Insultos y animadversión entre españoles*. Seville: Renacimiento, 2003.

Estela-Guillemont, Michèle. "Política y paratexto: En torno a Martín de Azpilcueta y la reedición del *Tratado de alabanza y murmuración* de 1572." In *Paratextos en la literatura española (siglos XV–XVIII)*, edited by Soledad Arredondo Sirodey, Pierre Civil, and Michel Moner, 367–378. Madrid: Casa de Velázquez, 2009.

Étienvre, Jean Pierre, ed. *Las utopías en el mundo hispánico*. Madrid: Casa de Velázquez, 1990.

Etreros, Mercedes. *La sátira política en el siglo XVII*. Madrid: Fundación Universitaria Española, 1983.

Farinelli, Arturo. *Marrano (storia di un vituperio)*. Geneva: Olschki, 1925.

Fernández de Avellaneda, Alonso. *Don Quixote de la Mancha (Part II)*. Translated by Alberta Wilson Server and John Esten Keller. Newark: Juan de la Cuesta, 2009.

——. *El ingenioso hidalgo don Quijote de la Mancha*. Edited by Fernando García Salinero. Madrid: Castalia, 1999.

Fernández de Navarrete, Pedro. *Conservación de monarquías y discursos políticos*. In *Obras de don Diego de Saavedra Fajardo y del licenciado Pedro Fernández de Navarrete*, 448–557. Madrid: Atlas, 1947.

Fine, Ruth. "El entrecruzamiento de lo hebreo y lo converso en la obra de Cervantes: Un encuentro singular." In *Cervantes y las religiones*, edited by Ruth Fine and Santiago López Navia, 435–451. Pamplona: Universidad de Navarra, 2008.

Fischer, Susan L., and Frederick A. DeArmas, eds. *Women Warriors in Early Modern Spain: A Tribute to Bárbara Mujica*. Newark: Juan de la Cuesta, 2019.

Flores Arroyuelo, Francisco J. *De la aventura al teatro y la fiesta. Moros y cristianos*. Murcia: Nausícaä, 2003.

Flynn, Charles P. *Insult and Society: Patterns of Comparative Interaction*. Port Washington, NY: Kennikat, 1977.

Flynn, Maureen. "Betrayals of the Soul in Spanish Blasphemy." In *Religion, Body, and Gender in Early Modern Spain*, edited by Alain Saint-Saëns, 30–44. San Francisco: Mellen Research University Press, 1991.

——. "Blasphemy and the Play of Anger in Sixteenth-Century Spain." *Past and Present* 149 (1995): 29–56.

Fonseca, Damián. *Justa expulsión de los Moriscos de España*. Roma: Jacomo Mascardo, 1612.

Forteza, Miquel. *Els descendents dels jueus conversos de Mallorca*. Palma de Mallorca: Moll, 1972.

Frago García, Juan Antonio. *El Quijote apócrifo y Pasamonte*. Madrid: Gredos, 2005.

Francis, Alan. "La estrategia satírica en el *Lazarillo* de Juan de Luna." *Nueva Revista de Filología Hispánica* 25 (1976): 363–373.

Freud, Sigmund. *Totem and Taboo*. Translated by James Strachey. New York: W. W. Norton, 1989.

Fuchs, Barbara. "The Black Legend and the Golden Age Dramatic Canon." In *La Leyenda Negra en el crisol de la comedia: el teatro del Siglo de Oro frente a los estereotipos antihispánicos*, edited by Yolanda Rodríguez Pérez and Antonio Sánchez Jiménez, 219–236. Madrid: Iberoamericana, 2016.

——. *Passing for Spain: Cervantes and the Fictions of Identity*. Urbana: University of Illinois Press, 2003.

Gacto, Enrique. "El delito de bigamia y la Inquisición española." In *Sexo barroco y otras transgresiones modernas*, 127–152. Madrid: Alianza, 1990.

Galán Sánchez, Ángel. "El dinero del rey y la 'ley de la comunidad': Pacto político y contrato fiscal en el Reino de Granada tras la conquista." In *Avant le contrat social: Le contrat politique dans l'Occident médiéval, XIIIe–XVe siècle*, edited by François Foronda, 653–683. Paris: Publications de la Sorbonne, 2011.

——. "'Herejes consentidos': La justificación de una fiscalidad diferencial en el Reino de Granada." *Historia: Instituciones. Documentos* 33 (2006): 173–209.

García-Arenal, Mercedes. *Inquisición y moriscos: Los procesos del tribunal de Cuenca*. Madrid: Siglo XXI, 1983.

García-Arenal, Mercedes, and Fernando Rodríguez Mediano. *Un Oriente español: Los moriscos y el Sacromonte en tiempos de Contrarreforma*. Madrid: Marcial Pons, 2010.

García Cárcel, Ricardo. *El demonio del Sur: La Leyenda Negra de Felipe II*. Madrid: Cátedra, 2017.

———. *Herejía y sociedad en el siglo XVI: La Inquisición en Valencia 1530-1609*. Barcelona: Península, 1980.

———. *La leyenda negra: historia y opinión*. Madrid: Alianza, 1998. First published 1992.

García Cárcel, Ricardo, and Doris Moreno Martínez. "La opinión de las víctimas de la Inquisición en la España de los siglos XVI y XVII." In *Estudios en homenaje al profesor Teófanes Egido*, edited by María de los Ángeles Sobaler Seco and Máximo García Fernández, 2:87-103. 2 vols. Valladolid: Junta de Castilla y León, 2004.

García Fuentes, José María. *La Inquisición en Granada en el siglo XVI: Fuentes para su estudio*. Granada: Universidad de Granada, 1981.

García García, Adolfo. "Inquisición y censura en la época de Cervantes." In *Escrituras silenciadas en la época de Cervantes*, edited by Manuel Casado Arboniés, Antonio Castillo Gómez, Paulina Numhauser, and Emilio Sola, 133-146. Alcalá de Henares: Universidad de Alcalá, 2006.

García-Medall, Joaquín. "El insulto desde la pragmática intercultural." In *Lengua viva: Estudios ofrecidos a César Hernández Alonso*, edited by Antonio Álvarez Tejedor, 667-680. Valladolid: Universidad de Valladolid, 2008.

Gautier-Dalche, Jean. "Remarques sur l'insulte verbale dans quelques textes juridiques leono-castillans." *Annales de la Faculté de Lettres et Sciences Humaines de Nice* 39 (1983): 117-126.

Géal, François. *Figures de la bibliothèque dans l'imaginaire espagnol du Siècle d'Or*. Paris: Champion, 1999.

Gerli, E. Michael. *Cervantes: Displacements, Inflections, and Transcendence*. Newark: Juan de la Cuesta, 2019.

———. *Refiguring Authority: Reading, Writing, and Rewriting in Cervantes*. Lexington: University Press of Kentucky, 1995.

Gil, Juan. "Berenjeneros: The Aubergine Eaters." In *The Conversos and Moriscos in Late Medieval Spain and Beyond: Departures and Change*, edited by Kevin Ingram, 121-142. Leiden: Brill, 2009.

Gil Benumeya Grimau, Rodolfo. "Residuos de morisquismo en los *Quijotes* de Cervantes y Avellaneda." In *De Cervantes y el islam*, edited by Nuria Martínez de Castilla Muñoz and Rodolfo Gil Benumeya Grimau, 197-211. Madrid: Sociedad Estatal de Conmemoraciones Culturales, 2006.

Gilman, Stephen. "The Death of Lazarillo de Tormes." *PMLA* 81, no. 3 (1966): 149-166.

———. "Los inquisidores literarios de Cervantes." In *Actas del III congreso internacional de hispanistas*, edited by Carlos H. Magis, 3-25. México: El Colegio de México, 1970.

Gilmore, David D., ed. *Honor and Shame and the Unity of the Mediterranean*. Washington, DC: American Anthropological Association, 1987.

Girard, René. *Le Bouc émissaire*. Paris: Bernard Grasset, 1982.

Gitlitz, David. "Lucas Fernández y Pierre Menard: El auto de la pasión." In *Encuentros and Desencuentros: Spanish Jewish Cultural Interaction throughout History*, edited by

Carlos Carrete Parrondo, Marcelo Dascal, Francisco Márquez Villanueva, and Ángel Sáenz Badillos, 503–515. Tel Aviv: University Publishing Projects, 2000.

Goffman, Erving. *Stigma: Notes on the Management of Spoiled Identity*. London: Penguin, 1990.

González Arce, José Damián. *Apariencia y poder: La legislación suntuaria castellana en los siglos XIII y XVI*. Jaén: Universidad de Jaén, 1998.

González de Caldas, María Victoria. "Nuevas imágenes del Santo Oficio en Sevilla: El auto de fe." In *Inquisición española y mentalidad inquisitorial*, edited by Ángel Alcalá, 237–265. Barcelona: Ariel, 1984.

González de Cellorigo, Martín. *Memorial* [Valladolid, 1597]. Biblioteca Nacional de España R/13027.

Gorfkle, Laura J. *Discovering the Comic in* Don Quixote. Chapel Hill: University of North Carolina, 1993.

Gracia Boix, Rafael. *Colección de documentos para la historia de la Inquisición de Córdoba*. Cordoba: Monte de Piedad y Caja de Ahorros de Córdoba, 1982.

Guadix, Diego de. *Recopilación de algunos nombres arábigos que los árabes pusieron a algunas ciudades y otras muchas cosas*. Edited by Elena Bajo Pérez and Felipe Maíllo Salgado. Gijón: Trea, 2005.

Guillemont, Michèle. "Images de la violence verbale en Espagne au XVIe siècle: des pêchés de langue au délit et à l'inconvenance." In *Écriture, pouvoir et société en Espagne aux XVIe et XVIIe siècles*, edited by Pierre Civil, 223–240. Paris: Presses de la Sorbonne Nouvelle, 2001.

———. "El *Tractado muy provechoso contra el común e muy continuo pecado que es detraher o murmurar y decir mal de alguno en su absencia* de Hernando de Talavera (Granada, 1496)." In *Lo converso: orden imaginario y realidad en la cultura española (siglos XIV–XVII)*, edited by Ruth Fine, Michèle Guillemont, and Juan Diego Vila, 119–141. Madrid: Iberoamericana, 2013.

———. "Recherches sur la violence verbale en Espagne aux XVIe et XVIIe siècles (aspects sociaux, culturels et littéraires)." 2 vols. PhD diss, Paris III-Sorbonne Nouvelle, 2000.

Guillemont, Michèle, and Marie-Blanche Requejo Carrió. "De asnos y rebuznos: Ambigüedad y modernidad de un diálogo." *Criticón* 101 (2007): 57–87.

Guillén del Águila, Francisco. *Libelo difamatorio de la religión católica que un sedicioso depositó en las casas del cabildo de Granada*. N.p., 1640.

Harvey, L. P. *Muslims of Spain, 1500 to 1614*. Chicago: University of Chicago Press, 2005.

Henríquez de Jorquera, Francisco. *Anales de Granada*. Edited by Antonio Marín Ocete. 2 vols. Granada: Publicaciones de la Facultad de Letras, 1934.

Hermenegildo, Alfredo. "Sobre la dimensión social del teatro primitivo español." *Prohemio* 2 (1975): 25–50.

———. "En torno a la burla de los linajes." *La palabra y el hombre* 23 (1977): 55–65.

Hernández Franco, Juan. *Sangre limpia, sangre española: El debate de los estatutos de limpieza (siglos XV–XVII)*. Madrid: Cátedra, 2011.

Herrero Ruiz de Loizaga, F. Javier. "El insulto en la comedia celestinesca." In *Discurso y oralidad: Homenaje al profesor José Jesús de Bustos Tovar*, edited by Luis Cortés Rodríguez, Antonio Miguel Bañón Hernández, María del Mar Espejo Muriel, and José Luis Muñío Valverde, 1:349–365. Madrid: Arco/Libros, 2007.

Hillgarth, Jocelyn N. *The Mirror of Spain, 1500–1700: The Formation of a Myth.* Ann Arbor: University of Michigan Press, 2003.

Huerta Calvo, Javier, Emilio Peral Vega, and Jesús Ponce Cárdenas, eds. *Tiempo de burlas: En torno a la literatura burlesca del Siglo de Oro.* Madrid: Verbum, 2001.

Huizinga, Johan. *The Autumn of the Middle Ages.* Translated by Rodney J. Payton and Ulrich Mammitzsch. Chicago: University of Chicago Press, 1996.

Hutchinson, Steven. "Arbitrating the National *Oikos.*" *Journal of Spanish Cultural Studies* 2, no. 1 (2001): 69–80.

Ibáñez, Alberto G. *La leyenda negra: Historia del odio a España.* Cordoba: Almuzara, 2019.

Iffland, James. *De fiestas y aguafiestas: Risa, locura e ideología en Cervantes y Avellaneda.* Madrid: Iberoamericana, 1999.

Iglesias, Carmen. "España desde fuera." In *España. Reflexiones sobre el ser de España,* edited by Eloy Benito Ruano, 377–428. Madrid: Real Academia de la Historia, 1997.

Iglesias Ovejero, Ángel. "Nominación marginante en el picarismo literario y el folklore." *Revista de Filología Románica* 1 (1983): 137–181.

———. "El relato oral en la época clásica y en el folklore moderno: El caso del blasón popular." In *La edición de textos: Actas del I Congreso Internacional de Hispanistas del Siglo de Oro,* edited by Pablo Jauralde, Dolores Noguera, and Alfonso Rey, 245–252. London: Tamesis, 1990.

Infantes, Víctor. "Luceros y Tizones: biografía nobiliaria y venganza política en el Siglo de Oro." *El Crotalón* 1 (1984): 115–127.

Irigoyen-García, Javier. "La expulsión de los moriscos en *El ingenioso hidalgo don Quijote de la Mancha* (1614) de Alonso Fernández de Avellaneda." *MLN* 131, no. 2 (2016): 336–355.

———. *Moors Dressed as Moors: Clothing, Social Distinction, and Ethnicity in Early Modern Iberia.* Toronto: University of Toronto Press, 2017.

———. "'Si no es adivinando la mitad del pergamino': Discurso y realidad en *La ilustre fregona.*" In *Novelas ejemplares: Las grietas de la ejemplaridad,* edited by Julio Baena, 227–249. Newark: Juan de la Cuesta, 2008.

———. *The Spanish Arcadia: Sheep Herding, Pastoral Discourse, and Ethnicity in Early Modern Spain.* Toronto: University of Toronto Press, 2013.

Jiménez de Santiago, Francisco. *Desagravios a la virginidad en el parto de María Santíssima.* Écija: Luis Estupiñán, 1640.

Jiménez Monteserín, Miguel. "El auto de fe." In *L'Inquisition espagnole et la construction de la monarchie confessionelle (1478–1561),* edited by Raphaël Carrasco, 140–152. Paris: Ellipses, 2002.

Johnson, Carroll B. *Cervantes and the Material World.* Chicago: University of Illinois Press, 2000.

———. "Observaciones sobre el orden patriarcal en *La ilustre fregona.*" In *Siglos Dorados: Homenaje a Augustin Redondo,* edited by Pierre Civil, 1:653–666. Madrid: Castalia, 2004.

———. *Transliterating a Culture: Cervantes and the Moriscos.* Newark: Juan de la Cuesta, 2009.

Johnson, Paul Michael. *Affective Geographies: Cervantes, Emotion, and the Literary Mediterranean.* Toronto: University of Toronto Press, 2020.

Johnston, Mark. "Seducing Slander: Hernando de Talavera on Eliciting Disparagement of Others." *Essays in Medieval Studies* 30 (2014): 83–95.

Joly, Monique. *La Bourle et son interpretation: Recherches sur le passage de la facétie au roman (Espagne XVIe–XVIIe siècles)*. Lille: Université de Lille, 1982.

———. "Erotismo y marginación social en la novela cervantina." *Cervantes* 12, no. 2 (1992): 7–19.

Jones, Nicholas R. *Staging* Habla de Negros: *Radical Performances of the African Diaspora in Early Modern Spain*. University Park: Pennsylvania State University Press, 2019.

Jonin, Michel. "Quand les poètes nouveaux chrétiens content leurs exploits cynégétique." In *Signes et marques du convers (Espagne XVe–XVIe siècle)*, edited by Louis Cardaillac and Haïm Vidal Sephiha, 63–82. Aix-en-Provence: Université de Provence, 1993.

Juderías, Julián. *La leyenda negra: Estudios acerca del concepto de España en el extranjero*. Zaragoza: Servando Gotor, 2019. First published 1914.

Juan Manuel, Don. *El conde Lucanor*. Edited by Alfonso I. Sotelo. Madrid: Cátedra, 1991.

Kagan, Richard L. "¿Por qué la leyenda negra? ¿Por qué ahora?" *Cuadernos de Historia Moderna* 43, no. 1 (2018): 279–283.

Kamen, Henry. *The Spanish Inquisition: A Historical Revision*. New Haven: Yale University Press, 1997.

Kartchner, Eric. *Unhappily ever After: Deceptive Idealism in Cervantes's Marriage Tales*. Newark: Juan de la Cuesta, 2005.

Lapeyre, Henri. *Geografía de la España morisca*. Translated by Luis C. Rodríguez García. Valencia: Diputación Provincial de Valencia, 1986.

Lauer, Robert A. "Honor/honra Revisited." In *A Companion to Early Modern Hispanic Theater*, edited by Hilaire Kallendorf, 77–90. Leiden: Brill, 2014.

Laurenti, Joseph L. "El nuevo mundo social de la *Segunda Parte de la vida de Lazarillo de Tormes* . . . de Juan de Luna." *Boletín de la biblioteca nacional de Menéndez Pelayo* 47 (1971): 151–190.

Layna Ranz, Francisco. "Dicterio, conceptismo y frase hecha: a vueltas con el vejamen." *Nueva Revista de Filología Hispánica* 44, no. 1 (1996): 27–56.

———. *La disputa burlesca: Origen y trayectoria*. Toulouse: Presses Universitaires du Mirail, 1995.

———. *La eficacia del fracaso: Representaciones culturales en la Segunda Parte del Quijote*. Madrid: Polifemo, 2005.

Lazarillo de Tormes. Edited by Francisco Rico. Madrid: Cátedra, 1995.

Lea, Henry Charles. *Los moriscos españoles: Su conversión y expulsión*. Translated by Jaime Lorenzo Miralles. Alicante: Aguaclara, 1990.

Leblon, Bernard. *Les Gitans dans la littérature espagnole*. Toulouse: Université de Toulouse-Le Mirail, 1982.

Lee, Christina H. *The Anxiety of Sameness in Early Modern Spain*. Manchester: Manchester University Press, 2016.

León, Pedro de. *Grandeza y miseria en Andalucía: Testimonio de una encrucijada histórica (1578–1616)*. Edited by Pedro Herrera Puga. Granada: Facultad de Teología, 1981.

Lezra, Jacques. *Unspeakable Subjects: The Genealogy of the Event in Early Modern Europe*. Stanford: Stanford University Press, 1997.

Llompart, Gabriel. "Blasfemias y juramentos cristológicos en la baja Edad Media catalana." *Hispania Sacra* 26 (1973): 137–164.

Lobato, María Luisa. "Vejamen de grado en Burgo de Osma (1582): Pleito y entremés inédito de *Don Pantalón de Mondapoços* (h. 1578)." In *Teatro y poder: VI y VII Jornadas de Teatro Universidad de Burgos*, edited by Aurelia Ruiza Sola, 203–223. Burgos: Universidad de Burgos, 1998.

Lopes de Barros, Maria Filomena. "Body, Baths, and Cloth: Muslim and Christian Perceptions in Medieval Portugal." *Portuguese Studies* 21 (2005): 1–12.

López Belinchón, Bernardo J. "La memoria de la infamia." In *Felipe II (1527–1598): Europa y la Monarquía Católica*, edited by José Martínez Millán, 3:271–289. Madrid: Parteluz, 1998.

López Estrada, Francisco, ed. "Dos tratados de los siglos XVI y XVII sobre los mozárabes." *Al-Andalus* 16, no. 1 (1951): 331–361.

Lucía Megías, José Manuel. *Leer el* Quijote *en imágenes: Hacia una teoría de los modelos iconográficos*. Madrid: Calambur, 2006.

Luna, Juan de. *Segunda Parte del Lazarillo*. Edited by Pedro M. Piñero. Madrid: Cátedra, 1988.

Luque, Juan de Dios, Antonio Pamies, and Francisco José Manjón. *El arte del insulto: Estudio lexicográfico*. Barcelona: Península, 1997.

Luque Fajardo, Francisco. *Fiel desengaño contra la ociosidad y los juegos*. Edited by Martín de Riquer. Madrid: Real Academia Española, 1955.

Ly, Nadine. "La agudeza de Sancho: del rebuzno a la cuestión de la imitación creadora." *Criticón* 127 (2016): 105–128.

MacKay, Ruth. *"Lazy, Improvident People": Myth and Reality in the Writing of Spanish History*. Ithaca: Cornell University Press, 2006.

Madero, Marta. *Manos violentas, palabras vedadas: La injuria en Castilla y León (siglos XIII–XV)*. Madrid: Taurus, 1992.

Madroñal Durán, Abraham. *"De grado y de gracias": vejámenes universitarios de los Siglos de Oro*. Madrid: CSIC, 2005.

Malón de Chaide, Pedro. *La conversión de la Magdalena*. Edited by P. Félix García. 3 vols. Madrid: Espasa-Calpe, 1930–1947.

Mañaricua, Andrés de. *Polémica sobre Vizcaya en el siglo XVII: El Búho Gallego y El Tordo Vizcaíno*. Bilbao: Gran Enciclopedia Vasca, 1976.

Maqueda Abreu, Consuelo. *El auto de fe*. Madrid: Istmo, 1992.

Maravall, José Antonio. "La función del honor en la sociedad tradicional." *Ideologies and Literature* 2, no. 7 (1978): 9–27.

Marín López, Rafael. "Notas sobre la canonjía inquisitorial en la catedral de Granada." In *Estudios sobre iglesia y sociedad en Andalucía en la edad moderna*, edited by Miguel Luis López-Guadalupe Muñoz and Antonio Luis Cortés Peña, 59–74. Granada: Universidad de Granada, 1999.

Marguet, Christine. "Literatura e historia local: escribir los pasados histórico-míticos en la novela de frontera *Soledad entretenida* (1638–1644) de Juan de Barrionuevo y Moya." *E-Spania* (February 2016). doi.org/10.4000/e-spania.25276.

Márquez, Antonio. *Literatura e Inquisición en España, 1478–1834*. Madrid: Taurus, 1980.

Márquez Villanueva, Francisco. *Fuentes literarias cervantinas*. Madrid: Gredos, 1973.

——. *Moros, moriscos y turcos en Cervantes*. Barcelona: Bellaterra, 2010.

Martín Jiménez, Alfonso. *Las dos segundas partes del* Quijote. Valladolid: Universidad de Valladolid, 2014.

——. "Ortodoxia y heterodoxia en la interpretación del *Quijote* de Avellaneda." In *Ortodoxia y heterodoxia en Cervantes*, edited by Carmen Rivero Iglesias, 367–380. Alcalá de Henares: Centro de Estudios Cervantinos, 2011.

Martínez, María Elena. *Genealogical Fictions: Limpieza de Sangre, Religion, and Gender in Colonial Mexico*. Stanford: Stanford University Press, 2008.

Martínez, Miguel. "El imperio del extremo centro." CTXT. https://ctxt.es/es/20171220/Politica/16846/imperio-colonialismo-roca-barea-imperiofobia-c%27s.htm (accessed June 7, 2020).

Martínez López, Enrique. "Duelos y quebrantos: Rebuznos de casta en un menú cervantino. Sobre los que con desazón comen 'duelos y quebrantos los sábados' y los motejados de 'cazoleros' o 'berenjeneros.'" *Casa del Tiempo* 83–84 (2005–2006): 84–93.

——. "Mezclar berzas con capachos: armonía y guerra de castas en el *Entremés del retablo de las maravillas* de Cervantes." *Boletín de la Real Academia Española* 72, no. 255 (1992): 67–171.

Masferrer Domingo, Aniceto. *La pena de infamia en el derecho histórico español*. Madrid: Dykinson, 2001.

Mateos Royo, José Antonio. "Entre bromas y veras: una parodia en Daroca sobre el Santo Oficio o el proceso de Jaime de Santa Cruz." *Studium: Revista de Humanidades* 4 (1997): 175–191.

Maurizi, Françoise. "Langue et discours: La *pulla* dans le théâtre de la fin du XVème-début du XVIème siècle." *Voces* 4 (1997): 97–105.

Mayorga, Fermín. *Los moriscos de Hornachos crucificados y coronados de espinas*. Madrid: Cultiva, 2009.

McKendrick, Melveena. "Honour/Vengeance in the Spanish 'Comedia': A Case of Mimetic Transference?" *Modern Language Review* 79, no. 2 (1984): 313–335.

Méchoulan, Henry. *El honor de Dios*. Translated by Enrique Sordo. Barcelona: Argos Vergara, 1981.

Menéndez Pidal, Ramón. *De Cervantes y Lope de Vega*. Buenos Aires: Espasa-Calpe, 1940.

Meneses, Felipe de. *Tratado de juramentos del Presentado Philippe de Meneses, regente en el Colegio de S. Gregorio de Valladolid*. In Domingo de Soto, *Contra el abuso de los juramentos*, 266–455. Anvers: Juan Stelsio, 1569.

Molho, Maurice. *Cervantes: raíces folklóricas*. Madrid: Gredos, 1976.

Moliner Prada, Antonio, ed. *La expulsión de los moriscos*. Barcelona: Nabla, 2009.

Montero Cartelle, Emilio. "Palabras malas e villanas (Alfonso X: Partidas): La oralidad en las tradiciones discursivas jurídicas." In *Discurso y oralidad. Homenaje al profesor José Jesús de Bustos Tovar*, edited by Luis Cortés Rodríguez, Antonio Miguel Bañón Hernández, María del Mar Espejo Muriel, and José Luis Muñío Valverde, 1:391–399. Madrid: Arco/Libros, 2007.

Montoro, Antón de. *Cancionero de Antón de Montoro*. Edited by Emilio Cotarelo y Mori. Madrid: José Perales y Martínez, 1900.

Morel d'Arleux, Antonia. "Algunos aspectos del blasón popular de los extremeños en el Siglo de Oro." *Paremia* 2 (1993): 117–124.

Moreno Martínez, Doris. "Cirios, trompetas y altares: El auto de fe como fiesta." *Espacio, Tiempo y Forma. Serie IV. Historia Moderna* 10 (1997): 143–171.

———. "Una apacible idea de la gloria: El auto de fe barroco y sus escenarios simbólicos." *Manuscrits* 17 (1999): 159–177.

Moreta-Lara, Miguel A. *La imagen del moro y otros ensayos marruecos.* Málaga: Aljaima, 2005.

Nirenberg, David. *Communities of Violence: Persecution of Minorities in the Middle Ages.* Princeton: Princeton University Press, 1996.

———. "Race and the Middle Ages: The Case of Spain and Its Jews." In *Rereading the Black Legend: The Discourses of Religious and Racial Difference in the Renaissance Empires,* edited by Margaret R. Greer, Walter D. Mignolo, and Maureen Quilligan, 71–87. Chicago: University of Chicago Press, 2007.

Núñez de Andrada, Andrés. *Primera parte del Vergel de la Escritura divina.* Cordoba: Andrés Barrera, 1600.

Núñez Pinero, Lorena. "'Echar(se) pullas': Un tipo de pelea ritual en los diálogos de Minsheu (1599), Oudin (1675) y Sobrino (1708)." *Criticón* 137 (2019): 27–51.

O'Hara, Matthew D. *The History of the Future in Colonial Mexico.* New Haven: Yale University Press, 2018.

Ojea, Diego de. *Breve instrucción de la devoción, Cofradía e indulgencias y milagros del Rosario de nuestra señora: Y otra de la Cofradía de los juramentos.* Madrid: Querinos Gerardo, 1589.

Olid Guerrero, Eduardo. "'En servicio de su rey en la guerra justa': la segunda parte del *Quijote* leída a través de las ideas de Nicolás Maquiavelo y Francisco Vitoria." *eHumanista/Cervantes* 4 (2015): 356–386.

Olmedo Gobante, Manuel. "Del frente a la palestra: Esgrima y ejército en la carrera autorial de Jerónimo Sánchez de Carranza." In *Vidas en armas: Biografías militares en la España del Siglo de Oro,* edited by Abigaíl Castellano López and Adrián J. Sáez, 101–114. Huelva: Etiópicas, 2019.

Orozco Díaz, Emilio. *Cervantes y la novela del Barroco: Del* Quijote *de 1605 al Persiles.* Granada: Universidad de Granada, 1992.

Osterc Berlán, Ludovik. *El Quijote, la iglesia y la Inquisición.* México: UNAM, 1972.

Paracuellos Cabeza de Vaca, Luis de. *Triunfales celebraciones.* Ed. facsimile Miguel Luis López-Guadalupe Muñoz. Granada: Universidad de Granada, 2004.

Paster, Gail Kern. *The Body Embarrassed: Drama and the Disciplines of Shame in Early Modern England.* Ithaca: Cornell University Press, 1993.

Pedrosa, José Manuel. "La maledicencia venenosa frente al sabio silencio: teorías y prácticas del bien y del mal hablar en los Siglos de Oro." In *Cultura oral, visual y escrita en la España de los Siglos de Oro,* edited by Inmaculada Osuna and Eva Llergo, 488–513. Madrid: Visor, 2010. 488–513.

Percas de Ponseti, Helena. "Un misterio dilucidado: Pasamonte fue Avellaneda." *Cervantes* 22, no. 1 (2002): 127–154.

Perceval, José María. *Todos son uno, Arquetipos, xenofobia y racismo: La imagen del morisco en la Monarquía Española durante los siglos XVI y XVII.* Almería: Instituto de Estudios Almerienses, 1997.

Pérez, Daniel Enrique. "Jotería Epystemologies: Mapping a Research Agenda, Unearthing a Lost Heritage, and Building 'Queer Aztlán.'" *Aztlán* 39, no. 1 (2014): 143–154.

Pérez, Joseph. *Breve historia de la Inquisición en España*. Translated by María Pons Ira-zazábal. Barcelona: Crítica, 2009.

———. *La leyenda negra*. Madrid: Gadir, 2009.

Pérez-Salazar, Carmela, Cristina Tabernero, and Jesús M. Usunáriz, eds. *Los poderes de la palabra: El improperio en la cultura hispánica del Siglo de Oro*. New York: Peter Lang, 2013.

Peristiany, John G., ed. *Honour and Shame: The Values of Mediterranean Society*. London: Weidenfeld and Nicholson, 1965.

Perry, Mary Elizabeth. *The Handless Maiden: Moriscos and the Politics of Religion in Early Modern Spain*. Princeton: Princeton University Press, 2005.

Pike, Ruth. *Linajudos and Conversos in Seville: Greed and Prejudice in Sixteenth- and Seventeenth-Century Spain*. New York: Peter Lang, 2000.

Pineda, Juan de. *Tercera parte de la Monarchia Ecclesiastica*. Salamanca: Juan Fernández, 1588.

Prendergast, Ryan. *Reading, Writing, and Errant Subjects in Inquisitorial Spain*. Burlington: Ashgate, 2011.

Pueyo, Víctor. *Cuerpos plegables: anatomías de la excepción en España y en América Latina (Siglos XVI–XVIII)*. Woodbridge: Tamesis, 2016.

Pulido Serrano, Juan Ignacio. "La expulsión frustrada: Proyectos para la erradicación de la herejía judaica en la Monarquía Hispana." In *VIIa Reunión Científica de la Fundación Española de Historia Moderna*, edited by Francisco José Aranda Pérez, 1:891–904. Ciudad Real: Universidad de Castilla-La Mancha, 2004.

———. "La fe desatada en devoción: Proyección pública de la Inquisición en Granada (1640)." *Torre de los Lujanes* 40 (1999): 95–108.

———. *Injurias a Cristo: Religión, política y antijudaísmo en el siglo XVII (Análisis de las corrientes antijudías durante la Edad Moderna)*. Alcalá de Henares: Universidad de Alcalá, 2002.

Pym, Richard J. *The Gypsies of Early Modern Spain, 1425–1783*. New York: Palgrave, 2007.

Quevedo, Francisco de. *Poesía completa*. Edited by José Manuel Blecua. Barcelona: Planeta, 1999.

———. *Prosa festiva completa*. Edited by Celsa Carmen García-Valdés. Madrid: Cátedra, 1993.

Redondo, Augustin. "Le discours d'exclusion des 'deviants' tenu par l'Inquisition à l'époque de Charles V." In *Les problèmes de l'exclusion en Espagne (XVIe–XVIIe siècles)*, edited by Augustin Redondo, 23–49. Paris: Publications de la Sorbonne, 1983.

———. *Revisitando las culturas del Siglo de Oro*. Salamanca: Universidad de Salamanca, 2007.

Roca Barea, María Elvira. *Imperiofobia y leyenda negra: Roma, Rusia, Estados Unidos y el Imperio español*. 14th ed. Madrid: Siruela, 2017.

Rodríguez, Alberto. "Del episodio del rebuzno al gobierno de Sancho: la evolución simbólica de la imagen del burro." In *Peregrinamente peregrinos: Actas del V Congreso Internacional de la Asociación de Cervantistas*, edited by Alicia Villar Lecumberri, 2:1675–1686. Palma de Mallorca: Asociación de Cervantistas, 2004.

Rodríguez Cacho, Lina. *Pecados sociales y literatura satírica en el siglo XVI*. Madrid: Universidad Autónoma de Madrid, 1989.

Rodríguez de Escavias, Gabriel. *Exhortación al herege que puso en la ciudad de Granada jueves santo en la noche cinco de abril del año de mil y seiscientos y quarenta un papel contra nuestra Santa Fe Católica*. Granada: Francisco García de Velasco, 1640.

Rodríguez Pérez, Yolanda, Antonio Sánchez Jiménez, and Harm den Boer, eds. *España ante sus críticos: las claves de la Leyenda Negra.* Madrid: Iberoamericana, 2015.

Rojas, Fernando de. *La Celestina.* Edited by Dorothy S. Severin. Madrid: Cátedra, 1993.

Roncero López, Victoriano. "El humor y la risa en las preceptivas de los siglos de oro." In *Demócrito áureo: los códigos de la risa en el Siglo de Oro,* edited by Ignacio Arellano and Victoriano Roncero López, 285–328. Seville: Renacimiento, 2006.

Rozenblat, William. "Cervantes y los conversos (algunas reflexiones acerca del *Retablo de las maravillas*)." *Anales Cervantinos* 17 (1978): 99–110.

Rudders, Robert S. "Lazarillo de Tormes y los peces: la continuación homónima de 1555." *Explicación de textos literarios* 2 (1974): 257–266.

———. "Nueva luz sobre Juan de Luna." In *La picaresca: Orígenes, textos y estructuras,* edited by Manuel Criado del Val, 485–491. Madrid: Fundación Universitaria Española, 1979.

Ruiz Astiz, Javier. "Libelos y pasquines en la vida comunitaria: conflictividad social en Navarra (1512–1808)." In *Opinión pública y espacio urbano en la Edad Moderna,* edited by Antonio Castillo Gómez and James S. Amelang, 399–422. Gijón: Trea, 2010.

Ruwet, Nicolas. *Grammaire des insultes et autres études.* Paris: Éditions du Seuil, 1982.

Sabat de Rivers, Georgina. "La moral que Lázaro nos propone." *MLN* 95, no. 2 (1980): 233–251.

Salamanca Ballesteros, Alberto. *Monstruos, ostentos y hermafroditas.* Granada: Universidad de Granada, 2007.

Salazar Rincón, Javier. "Insulto y exclusión social: Algo más sobre la polémica entre Cervantes y Lope de Vega." *Bulletin Hispanique* 113, no. 2 (2011): 701–724.

Salomon, Noël. *Lo villano en el teatro del Siglo de Oro.* Translated by Beatriz Chenot. Madrid: Castalia, 1985.

Salucio, Agustín. *Discurso sobre los estatutos de limpieza de sangre.* Ed. facsimile Antonio Pérez y Gómez. Cieza: ". . . la fonte que mana y corre. . . ." 1975.

Sánchez Jiménez, Antonio. *Leyenda negra: la batalla sobre la imagen de España en tiempos de Lope de Vega.* Madrid: Cátedra, 2016.

Sánchez Portero, Antonio. *Cervantes y Liñán de Riaza: el autor del otro* Quijote *atribuido a Avellaneda.* Calatayud: Centro de Estudios Bilbilitanos de la Institución "Fernando el Católico," 2011.

Santa Cruz, Melchor de. *Floresta española.* Edited by María Pilar Cuartero and Maxime Chevalier. Barcelona: Crítica, 1997.

Santa María, Cipriano de. *Sermón predicado en el primer día del Octavario que celebró la nobleza de la ciudad de Xerez de la Frontera, en desagravio de nuestra santa Fe.* Jerez de la Frontera, 1640.

Santana Molina, Manuel. *El delito de blasfemia en el tribunal inquisitorial de Cuenca.* Alicante: Universidad de Alicante, 2004.

Scholberg, Kenneth R. *Sátira e invectiva en la España medieval.* Madrid: Gredos, 1971.

Sears, Theresa Ann. *A Marriage of Convenience: Ideal and Ideology in the* Novelas ejemplares. New York: Peter Lang, 1993.

Segura Urra, Félix. "*Verba vituperosa*: El papel de la injuria en la sociedad bajomedieval." In *Aportaciones a la historia social del lenguaje: España siglos XIV–XVIII,* edited by Rocío García Bourrellier and Jesús María Usunáriz, 149–195. Madrid: Iberoamericana, 2006.

Selig, Karl-Ludwig. "*Don Quijote*, II, XXIV-XXVIII: La aventura del rebuzno." *Teaching Language through Literature* 22 (1983): 24-29.

Serra Ruiz, Rafael. *Honor, honra e injuria en el derecho medieval español.* Murcia: Universidad de Murcia, 1969.

Shipley, George A. "The Critic as Witness for the Prosecution: Making the Case against Lázaro de Tormes." *PMLA* 97, no. 2 (1982): 179-194.

Sicroff, Albert A. *Los estatutos de limpieza de sangre: Controversias entre los siglos XV y XVII.* Translated by Mauro Armiño. Madrid: Taurus, 1985.

Soria Mesa, Enrique. "Los linajudos: Honor y conflicto social en la Granada del Siglo de Oro." In *Violencia y conflictividad en el universo barroco*, edited by Julián J. Lozano Navarro and Juan Luis Castellano, 401-427. Granada: Comares, 2010.

———. *Los últimos moriscos: Pervivencias de la población de origen islámico en el reino de Granada (siglos XVII-XVIII).* Valencia: Universitat de València, 2014.

Soto, Domingo de. *Relecciones y opúsculos. II-1, El abuso de los juramentos: Ocultación y revelación de secretos.* Edited by Antonio Osuna Fernández-Largo. Salamanca: San Esteban, 2000.

Souviron López, Begoña. *La mujer en la ficción arcádica: aproximación a la novela pastoril española.* Frankfurt: Vervuert, 1997.

Stallaert, Christiane. *Ni una gota de sangre impura: La España inquisitorial y la Alemania nazi cara a cara.* Barcelona: Galaxia Gutenberg, 2006.

Stewart, Frank Henderson. *Honor.* Chicago: University of Chicago Press, 1994.

Suárez Figaredo, Enrique. *Cervantes, Figueroa, y el crimen de Avellaneda.* Barcelona: Carena, 2004.

Surtz, Ronald. "Cardinal Juan Martínez Silíceo in an Allegorical *entremés* of 1556." In *Essays on Hispanic Literature in Honor of Edmund L. King*, edited by Silvia Molloy and Luis Fernández Cifuentes, 225-232. London: Tamesis, 1983.

———. "Pastores judíos y reyes magos gentiles: Teatro franciscano y milenarismo en Nueva España." *Nueva Revista de Filología Hispánica* 36, no. 1 (1998): 333-344.

Tabernero Sala, Cristina. "Injurias, maldiciones y juramentos en la lengua española del siglo XVII." *Revista de Lexicografía* 16 (2010): 101-122.

Tabernero, Cristina, and Jesús María Usunáriz. *Diccionario de injurias de los siglos XVI y XVII.* Kassel: Reichenberger, 2019.

Talavera, Hernando de. *Breue y muy prouechosa doctrina de lo que deue saber todo Christiano.* Granada: Meinardo Ungut and Juan Pegnitzer, 1496.

Taylor, Scott K. *Honor and Violence in Golden Age Spain.* New Haven: Yale University Press, 2008.

Teijeiro Fuentes, Miguel Ángel. "Galicia y los gallegos en la literatura española del Siglo de Oro." *Scriptura* 11 (1996): 203-246.

Tijerina Revilla, Anita, and José Manuel Santillana. "Jotería Identity and Consciousness." *Aztlán* 39, no. 1 (2014): 167-179.

Torrecilla, Jesús. *España exótica: La formación de la imagen española moderna.* Boulder: Society of Spanish and Spanish-American Studies, 2004.

Torres, Luis de. *Veintiquatro discursos sobre los peccados de la lengua.* Burgos: Felipe de Junta, 1590.

Tratado de los dos caminos, por un morisco refugiado en Túnez. Edited by Álvaro Galmés de Fuentes and Juan Carlos Villaverde Amieva. Madrid: Instituto Universitario Seminario Menéndez Pidal, 2005.

Trujillo, Tomás de. *Libro llamado reprobación de trajes, y abuso de juramentos.* Estella: Adrián de Anvers, 1563.

Tueller, James B. *Good and Faithful Christians: Moriscos and Catholicism in Early Modern Spain.* New Orleans: University Press of the South, 2002.

Unamuno, Miguel de. *Del sentimiento trágico de la vida.* Madrid: Espasa-Calpe, 1980.

Urrea, Jerónimo de. *Diálogo de la verdadera honra militar.* Venice: Joan Griso, 1566.

Usunáriz, Jesús María. "Un análisis de los insultos en el *Quijote* desde la historia social del lenguaje." *Anales Cervantinos* 49 (2017): 59–73.

———. "*Verbum maledictionis.* La blasfemia y el blasfemo de los siglos XVI y XVII." In *Aportaciones a la historia social del lenguaje: España, siglos XIV–XVIII,* edited by Rocío García Bourrellier and Jesús María Usunáriz, 197–221. Madrid: Iberoamericana, 2006.

Vaca de Osma, José Antonio. *El imperio y la leyenda negra.* Madrid: Rialp, 2004.

Valencia, Pedro de. *Tratado acerca de los moriscos de España.* Edited by Joaquín Gil Sanjuán. Málaga: Algazara, 1997.

Van Beysterveldt, Antonie Adrianus. *Répercussions du souci de la pureté de sang sur la conception de l'honneur dans la "comedia nueva" espagnole.* Leiden: Brill, 1966.

Van Limborch, Philip. *Historia Inquisitionis.* Amsterdam: Henriciem Westenimi, 1692.

Velasco, Sherry. *Lesbians in Early Modern Spain.* Nashville: Vanderbilt University Press, 2011.

Vélez, Iván. *Sobre la leyenda negra.* Madrid: Encuentro, 2014.

Vélez-Quiñones, Harry. *Monstrous Displays: Representation and Perversion in Spanish Literature.* New Orleans: University Press of the South, 1999.

Vila, Juan Diego. "El *Quijote* y la sugestión conversa: silencios, elisiones y desvíos para una predicación inefable." In *Cervantes y las religiones,* edited by Ruth Fine and Santiago López Navia, 521–546. Pamplona: Universidad de Navarra, 2008.

Villacañas, José Luis. *Imperiofilia y el populismo nacional-católico.* Madrid: Lengua de Trapo, 2019.

Villa-Flores, Javier. *Dangerous Speech: A Social History of Blasphemy in Colonial Mexico.* Tucson: University of Arizona Press, 2006.

Villalba Pérez, Enrique. *La administración de la justicia penal en Castilla y en la corte a comienzos del siglo XVII.* Madrid: Actas, 1993.

Villanueva, Jesús. *Leyenda negra: Una polémica nacionalista en la España del siglo XX.* Madrid: Catarata, 2011.

Villaseñor Black, Charlene, and Mari-Tere Álvarez, eds. *Renaissance Futurities: Science, Art, Invention.* Oakland: University of California Press, 2000.

Villegas, Alonso de. *Fructus Sanctorum y quinta parte del Flos Sanctorum.* Cuenca: Juan Masselin, 1594.

Vollendorf, Lisa. *The Lives of Women: A New History of Inquisitorial Spain.* Nashville: Vanderbilt University Press, 2005.

Wagschal, Steven. *Minding Animals in the Old and New Worlds: A Cognitive Historical Analysis.* Toronto: University of Toronto Press, 2018.

Wardropper, Bruce W. "The Butt of the Satire in *El retablo de las maravillas.*" *Cervantes* 4, no. 1 (1984): 25–33.

Wertheimer, Elaine C. *Honor, Love, and Religion in the Theater before Lope de Vega.* Newark: Juan de la Cuesta, 2003.

White, Hayden. *Tropics of Discourse: Essays in Cultural Criticism.* Baltimore: Johns Hopkins University Press, 1990.

Whitenack, Judith A. "'Cronista y no autor': Juan de Luna's *Lazarillo.*" *Hispanic Journal* 15, no. 1 (1994): 45–62.

———. "Juan de Luna's *Lazarillo*: Continuation or Subversion?" *Philological Quarterly* 67, no. 2 (1988): 177–194.

Williamson, Edwin. "Challenging the Hierarchies: The Interplay of Romance and the Picaresque in *La ilustre fregona.*" *Bulletin of Spanish Studies* 81, no. 4–5 (2004): 655–674.

Yarbro-Bejarano, Yvonne. "Juan del Encina and Lucas Fernández: Conflicting Attitudes towards the Passion." *Bulletin of the Comediantes* 36, no. 1 (1984): 5–21.

Zapata, Luis. *Miscelánea o varia historia.* Edited by Antonio Carrasco González. Llerena: Editores Extremeños, 1999.

Ziga, Itziar. *Devenir perra.* Santa Cruz de Tenerife: Melusina, 2009.

Zimic, Stanislav. *Los cuentos y las novelas del* Quijote. Pamplona: Universidad de Navarra, 2003.

Index

Note: Page numbers in italics indicate figures.

affronters, communities of, 14–38
Aldrete, Bernardo, *Del origen y principio de la lengua castellana*, 25
Alejandro, Francisco, 104–105
Alemán, Mateo, *Guzmán de Alfarache*, 165–166n48
almadrabas, 50, 151n16
Alpujarras, uprising of the, 89
alternate communities, 8–9, 12, 135
Althusser, Louis, 5–6
ambition, 85
Andalusia, 106
Andersen, Hans Christian, "The Emperor's New Clothes," 73–74
Anderson, Benedict, 37
animality, 31, 55, 117, 165–166n48
anti-Morisco authors, 91–92
anti-Semitism, 14–16, 60, 76–77, 103, 106, 107, 162n13, 163n21
Arabic, 22–23
Aragon, 89
Aristotle, 18–19
asinine semantic space, 118, 165–166n48
ass symbology, 18, 165–166n48
autos de fe, 4, 55, 61, 68, 91, 104; in Cervantes, 93–96, 99; representations of, 122, *123*, *126*, *127*; *sambenitos* and, 12, 27, 36, 80–82
Ávila, Nicolás de, *Suma de mandamientos*, 20
Aznar Cardona, Pedro, *Expulsión justificada de los Moriscos Españoles*, 70–71

Azpilcueta, Martín de, 47; *Commento sobre el capitulo Interverba XI q. III*, 19–20; *Tratado de alabanza y murmuración*, 19–20, 39

Baena, Julio, 46, 54, 76–77
Barrientos, Lope de, 103, 148n44
Barrionuevo y Moya, Juan de, *Primera parte de la soledad entretenida*, 103–104
behetrías, 27–28, 31–32, 149n57
"berenjeneros," 111, 114
Berruguete, Pedro de, 122
Bethencourt, Francisco, 120, 123
Beusterien, John, 68
Black Death, 60
"black legend," 13, 122, 128–135, 167–168n28, 167n22, 167n24, 168n41
Blacks, 4
"blasones populares," 111, 114
blasphemy, 11, 20–21, 147n33; Catholic identity and, 21; Christian identity and, 21–22; defiance and, 21; definitions and context of, 20; gambling and, 21; punishment of, 55; social purpose of, 20–22
Bleda, Jaime, *Corónica de los moros de España*, 91–92
blood purity, 16, 24–26, 60–79; in Cervantes, 74–79, 107, 164n34; in del Rosal, 27–28; obsession with, 121; Old Christians and, 102–103; paradoxical effects of laws, 66–67, 72; reputation and, 121; statutes of, 12, 66–67, 102–103, 120

Booker, M. Keith, 9

Bouttats, Frederik, 97, *98*, *112*, 123–124, 127

Braun, Georg, *Civitates Orbis Terrarum*, 51, *52*

Brown, Katherine L., 152n17

Brown, Wendy, 133

Butler, Judith, 5–6, 7, 65, 107

çafio, 24, 32. *See also zafio*

"canalla," 41–42

cancionero poetry, 3

Caro, Rodrigo, *Días geniales y lúdricos*, 34

Carranza, Bartolomé, 19

Carranza de Miranda, Bartolomé, *Comentarios sobre el catecismo christiano*, 20

Carrasco, Rafael, 92

Carrillo, Luis, 92

Castile, 73, 89–91, 114

Castillo Lluch, Mónica, 34, 149n61

Castillo Solórzano, Alonso de: *El obstinado arrepentido*, 86–88; *Jornadas alegres*, 86–88

Castro, Américo, 157–158n3

Catalonia, independence referendum of, 131

Catalonian nationalism, 168n30, 168n38

Cathedral of Toledo, 63–64, 120

Catholic hierarchy, symbols of, 127

Catholic identity: blasphemy and, 21; search for insult of Other to strengthen, 104

Catholicism, 134

Celestina comedy, 3

Cervantes, Miguel de, 107; ability to cope with insults, 151n11; Cervantine fantasies about insults, 11–13; *Don Quixote*, 9–16, 33–37, 40–46, 76, 93–101, *98*, 107–118, *112*, 123–124, 135, 161n43, 165–166n48, 165n43; *La gitanilla*, 17–18; *La ilustre fregona*, 47–50, 54; *El licenciado vidriera*, 37–38, 41; *Novelas ejemplares*, 17–18, 37–38, 41–45, 47–50, 54, 72–79; reaction to Fernández de Avellaneda's description of him, 44–45; *El retablo de las maravillas*, 12, 72–79, 91, 100, 101, 107, 164n34; self-portrait of, 42–46; self-satirization and, 42–43; *Los trabajos de Persiles y Sigismunda*, 107, 151n8, 151n14; *Viaje del Parnaso*, 42

Cetina, Gutierre de, 153n40

Charles V, 89, 120

Chauchadis, Claude, 20, 29–30, 32

Chaunu, Pierre, 128–129

Childers, William, 34, 100, 147n33

Christian identity, 21–22, 104

class, 16–17, 27–28, 34–36

Close, Anthony, 11, 34–35, 53

Colindres, Pedro de, 102; *Triumpho de Christo y María*, 106–107

collective identity, 115–116; articulated through infamy, 11, 135; articulated through insults, 5, 8, 11, 13, 102–103, 107, 118; history and, 102–118; insult and, 102–118; of Spain, 121

community: alternate communities, 8–9, 12, 135; articulated through insults, 37–38; cemented through scapegoats, 5; reputation of, 119–120. *See also* collective identity

confeso, 26

Confraternity of the Name of God, 20

conversos, 4, 12, 14, 23–24, 26, 75, 148n44, 160n30; as "berenjeneros," 114; calls for expulsion of, 154n4; in Cervantes, 74–79; in del Rosal, 26; genealogical lists of, 61–62, 68, 154n4; Inquisition and, 60–68; interpellation and, 75; in "libros verdes," 61–62, 68; practical application of rationale for infamy and, 60–61; in Salucio, 60–68; shepherds as symbols of, 103

Cordoba, 81

cornudo, 50–51, 58–59

corozas, 27, 94–97, 100, 118, 123, 127, 161n42

Correas, Gonzalo, 164–165n36

Corteguera, Luis, 95

Council of State, 69

Covarrubias, Sebastián de, *Tesoro de la lengua castellana o española*, 22, 25

Covarrubias y Horozco, Sebastián de, 34, 38, 41–42, 43, 85, 149n57; on *coroza* vs. *mitra*, 97, 161n42; on cuckoldry, 50–51; *Emblemas morales*, 31; on *sambenitos*, 157–158n3; terms for insulting and defaming in, 148n51; *Tesoro de la lengua castellana o española*, 28–32, 97

cristianos nuevos, 60–68, 148n44, 155n9. *See also conversos*; New Christians

cristianos viejos, 60, 61, 155n9. *See also* Old Christians

crusader, 15

crypto-Jews, 68, 104. *See also conversos*; Jews; New Christians

Cubillo de Aragón, Álvaro, *El hereje*, 105–106

cuckoldry, 2, 3, 12, 153n40; as individual infamy, 50–59; interpellation and, 51,

Spanish-American War, 128–129, 133–134
Spanish Empire, 128–129, 132, 133–134
Spanish history, as *sambenito*, 119–135
Spanish nationalism, 129–135, 168n31, 168n38, 168n39
Stallaert, Christiane, 68, 69
"stubborn attachment," 6
subjectivity, 46, 152n20
subjectivization, 4–8, 11, 12, 54–56, 59, 101, 135
sumptuary laws, 4, 61, 80–101. *See also* sambenitos
Supreme Council of the Inquisition, 68
swear words, 20–21. *See also* blasphemy

taboo, 115, 117–118
Talavera, Hernando de, 145n18; *Breve y muy provechosa doctrina de lo que debe saber todo Christiano*, 19
Tecamachalco, Mexico, 81, 95, 96
timelines, 9, 10–11
"tizones," 61–62
Toledo, 114
Torres, Luis de, *Veintiquatro discursos sobre los peccados de la lengua*, 18–19, 20
Trujillo, Tomás de, *Libro llamado reprobación de trajes, y abuso de juramentos*, 20
Tui, 81, 83, 158n5

Unamuno, Miguel de, 168n32; *Del sentimiento trágico de la vida*, 132
United States, 129, 167n24

Urrea, Jerónimo de, *Diálogo de la verdadera honra militar*, 18
utopia, 9

Vaca de Osma, José Antonio, 132–133, 167–168n28
Valencia, Pedro de, 39, 158n4; *Tratado acerca de los Moriscos de España*, 69–70, 71, 90–91, 121
Valladolid, Juan de, 103
Van Limborch, Philip, *Historia Inquisitionis*, 123, 125
"vejamen," 34–35
Vélez, Iván, 130
Vélez-Quiñones, Harry, 57–58
Vida de Lazarillo de Tormes, 51–55, 57–58
Vila, Juan Diego, 14–16
Villa-Flores, Javier, 147n33
Villanueva, Jesús, 129–130, 167n22, 168n32
Villegas, Alonso, *Fructus Sanctorum y quinta parte del Flos Sanctorum*, 80, 84
Villegas, Alonso de, 97
violence, insults and, 36

wittiness, 34–35
women, insults against, 30–31

xenophobia, 15
"xuetas," 68

zafio, 24
zahareño(s), 24
Zapata, Luis, *Miscelánea*, 34–35

About the Author

JAVIER IRIGOYEN-GARCÍA is a professor of Spanish studies at the University of Illinois at Urbana-Champaign. His research focuses on the representation of race and ethnicity in early modern Spain. He has published *The Spanish Arcadia: Sheep Herding, Pastoral Discourse, and Ethnicity in Early Modern Spain* (2013) and *"Moors Dressed as Moors": Clothing, Social Distinction, and Ethnicity in Early Modern Iberia* (2017).